This

UMI
BOOKS ON DEMAND™

UMI
A Bell & Howell Company

300 North Zeeb Road
P.O. Box 1346
Ann Arbor, Michigan 48106-1346

1-800-521-0600   734-761-4700
http://www.bellhowell.infolearning.com

Printed in 2001 by xerographic process on acid-free paper

MONITORING
GROWTH CYCLES IN
MARKET-ORIENTED COUNTRIES

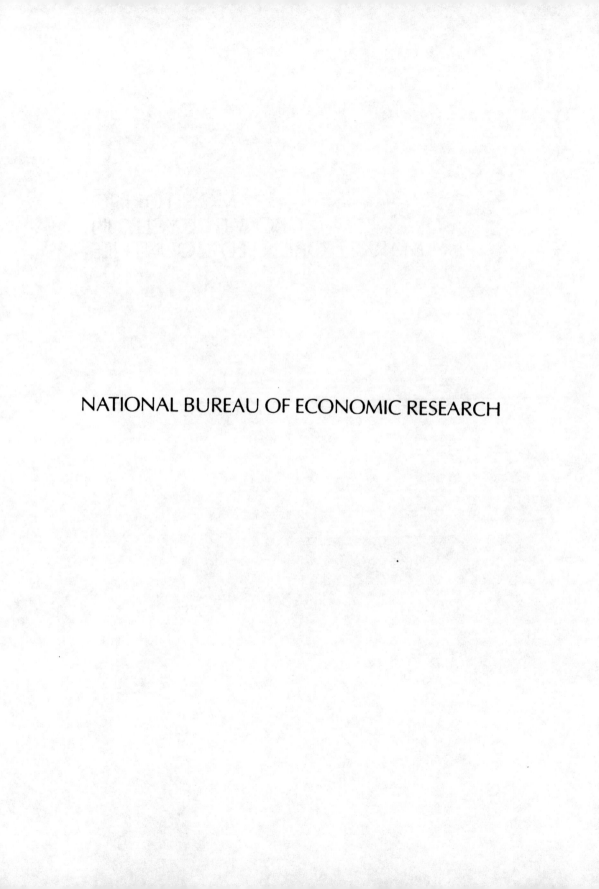

NATIONAL BUREAU OF ECONOMIC RESEARCH

Philip A. Klein

The Pennsylvania State University and Center for International Business Cycle Research Columbia University

and

Geoffrey H. Moore

Center for International Business Cycle Research Columbia University

Monitoring Growth Cycles In Market-Oriented Countries: Developing and Using International Economic Indicators

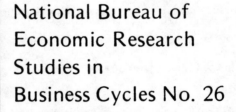

National Bureau of Economic Research Studies in Business Cycles No. 26

Published for the
NATIONAL BUREAU OF
ECONOMIC RESEARCH, INC.
by
BALLINGER PUBLISHING COMPANY
A Subsidiary of Harper & Row, Publishers, Inc.
Cambridge, Mass.
1985

International Standard Book Number: 0-88730-041-3

Library of Congress Catalog Card Number: 85-1297

Printed in the United States of America

Library of Congress Cataloging in Publication Data

Klein, Philip A.
  Monitoring growth cycles in market-oriented countries.

  Bibliography: p.
  Includes index. .
  1. Business cycles. 2. Economic indicators.
I. Moore, Geoffrey Hoyt. II. Title. III. Title:
Growth cycles in market-oriented countries.
HB3711.K58 1985   338.5'42   85-1297
ISBN 0-88730-041-3

To the memory of
Ilse Mintz, who pioneered the development of growth cycle analysis
and
Beatrice N. Vaccara, who strove always to make economic indicators
a more useful tool.

Their professional standards were surpassed only by their warmth
and worth as human beings.

Relation of the Directors to the
Work and Publications of the
National Bureau of Economic Research

1. The object of the National Bureau of Economic Research is to ascertain and to present to the public important economic facts and their interpretation in a scientific and impartial manner. The Board of Directors is charged with the responsibility of ensuring that the work of the National Bureau is carried on in strict conformity with this object.

2. The President of the National Bureau shall submit to the Board of Directors, or to its Executive Committee, for their formal adoption all specific proposals for research to be instituted.

3. No research report shall be published by the National Bureau until the President has sent each member of the Board a notice that a manuscript is recommended for publication and that in the President's opinion it is suitable for publication in accordance with the principles of the National Bureau. Such notification will include an abstract or summary of the manuscript's content and a response form for use by those Directors who desire a copy of the manuscript for review. Each manuscript shall contain a summary drawing attention to the nature and treatment of the problem studied, the character of the data and their utilization in the report, and the main conclusions reached.

4. For each manuscript so submitted, a special committee of the Directors (including Directors Emeriti) shall be appointed by majority agreement of the President and Vice Presidents (or by the Executive Committee in case of inability to decide on the part of the President and Vice Presidents), consisting of three Directors selected as nearly as may be one from each general division of the Board. The names of the special manuscript committee shall be stated to each Director when notice of the proposed publication is submitted to him. It shall be the duty of each member of the special manuscript committee to read the manuscript. If each member of the manuscript committee signifies his approval within thirty days of the transmittal of the manuscript, the report may be published. If at the end of that period any member of the manuscript committee withholds his approval, the President shall then notify each member of the Board, requesting approval or disapproval of publication, and thirty days additional shall be granted for this purpose. The manuscript shall then not be published unless at least a majority of the entire Board who shall have voted on the proposal within the time fixed for the receipt of votes shall have approved.

5. No manuscript may be published, though approved by each member of the special manuscript committee, until forty-five days have elapsed from the transmittal of the report in manuscript form. The interval is allowed for the receipt of any memorandum of dissent or reservation, together with a brief statement of his reasons, that any member may wish to express; and such memorandum of dissent or reservation shall be published with the manuscript if he so desires. Publication does not, however, imply that each member of the Board has read the manuscript, or that either members of the Board in general or the special committee have passed on its validity in every detail.

6. Publications of the National Bureau issued for informational purposes concerning the work of the Bureau and its staff, or issued to inform the public of activities of Bureau staff, and volumes issued as a result of various conferences involving the National Bureau shall contain a specific disclaimer noting that such publication has not passed through the normal review procedures required in this resolution. The Executive Committee of the Board is charged with review of all such publications from time to time to ensure that they do not take on the character of formal research reports of the National Bureau, requiring formal Board approval.

7. Unless otherwise determined by the Board or exempted by the terms of paragraph 6, a copy of this resolution shall be printed in each National Bureau publication.

(Resolution adopted October 25, 1926, as revised through September 30, 1974)

CONTENTS

LIST OF FIGURES

xiii

LIST OF TABLES

PREFACE

The primary objective of this volume is to show that the system of economic indicators developed over the past fifty years and based on Wesley Mitchell's and Arthur Burns' early work can be successfully applied to the study of growth cycles as well as classical cycles in various world markets. Growth cycles are fluctuations in growth about a long-run trend; classical cycles are up and down movements in the level of activity. We believe that our use of Mitchell and Burns' original methodology in meeting these new objectives is clearly demonstrated in the historical analysis of the ten countries presented here.

We have traced the performance of these indicators through 1980 wherever possible, but readers will inevitably wonder how the indicators have been used most recently and how they might contribute to our understanding of the recession and recovery patterns in various countries during the early 1980s. The temptation of including such an up-to-date assessment has been resisted, however, for, in the perceptive phrasing of Burns and Mitchell, business cycles are phenomena in which "one phase merges into the next." At whatever point one chooses to publish one's findings, therefore, another cycle phase will be in the process of making itself manifest.

The events of 1973–75 and since have suggested in all the countries included in this volume, as well as in many more, that along with attention to the growth cycle, we must continue to pay attention to classical or conventional cycles. It is no doubt somewhat confusing and partly redundant to monitor instability in both growth cycle and classical cycle form. For the immediate future, however, we see no alternative. Were classical cycles to be really in the process of disappearing, as many experts appeared to be convinced was the case in the 1960s, it would be possible to switch entirely to the growth cycle approach, and be thankful that the indicators developed over the long years of research on classical cycles proved to be sufficiently sensitive to enable us to apply them to growth cycles. Many countries do concentrate attention now on growth cycles. Unfortunately, the classical cycle has not disappeared. Whether the years immediately ahead will bring more classical recessions, more growth recessions, more of both, or neither, no one can say for certain. The historical record strongly suggests, though, that instability in one or the other of these forms will be a characteristic of all market-oriented economies in the future as it has in the past. We must be prepared in the future, as we have tried to be in the past, to study emergent instability with appropriate techniques. We hope and believe this volume will play a useful part in that preparation.

The obligations we have incurred in researching this book are heavy indeed. Without the cooperation of many individuals in each of the countries under study the task of obtaining basic data would have been far greater. Much of the requisite material is simply not available in the United States. In 1973-74 the London School of Economics generously made space and facilities available to Klein as an Academic Visitor, thereby helping us to obtain European data. The computer facilities of the Central Statistical Office in London were indispensable in early experimentation leading to the methodology we ultimately adopted. For this, as well as making data available and much helpful advice on appropriate British turning points and idiosyncrasies of recent British economic experience, we are grateful to Owen Nankivell, Peter Kenney, John S. Dryden, Michael Murphy, and more recently, John Richardson, Michael Lockyer, and Sir Claus A. Moser, all of whom are or were associated with the Central Statistical Office. We also thank Desmond J. O'Dea, whose counsel, based on his early work on British indicators at the National Institute of Economic and Social Research, was of great help. The Director of the NIESR, Mr. G. D. N. Worswick, was generous in giving counsel and making the facilities of the institute available in the initial stages of our work. We acknowledge, too, the assistance of Michael Ryan of the London *Financial Times.*

In the Federal Republic of Germany we obtained much advice, as well as data, from the IFO-Institute of Munich. We are grateful to its members, and in particular we thank Dr. Werner F. Strigel and Charles C. Roberts. Other data for West Germany came from the Statistisches Bundesamt in Wiesbaden. We are happy to acknowledge the assistance of this office and of the officials who cooperated with us: Dr. Hamer, Wolfgang Gloeckler, Ulrich Mauer, and Dr. Vermouth. We also acknowledge the assistance of the German Department of Labor in Nürnberg in providing data for the project.

In France we have incurred obligations to a number of individuals. Early in our work we received invaluable assistance from M. G. Vangrevelinghe, who was then head of the Business Cycle Unit at the Institut National de la Statistique et des Etudes Economiques (INSEE). Others who have provided advice and counsel or data include M. Jacques Plassard, who is head of the Société d'Etudes et de Documentation Economiques, Industrielles, et Sociales (SEDEIS) in Paris, M. S. Wickham, vice-president of the Centre d'Observation Economique (COE) of the Paris Chamber of Commerce and Industry, and M. B. Hugonnier, an economic consultant at the Chamber of Commerce.

In Italy our principal obligation is to Sig. Eugenio De Nicola and his associates at the Istituto Nazionale per lo Studio della Congiuntura (ISCO). ISCO is the premier agency studying business cycles in Italy, and it has been most helpful and generous in providing both advice and data germane to our efforts to develop Italian economic indicators. We also received invaluable assistance from Sig. Luigi Pinto and his associates at the Istituto Centrale di Statistica (ISTAT). We are also grateful to Dott. Franco Cotula of the Servisio Studi della Banca D'Italia and Sig. Luciano Lugli of the Administrazione Centrale of the Bank of Italy for providing initial data for us.

In Stockholm we would like to thank Mr. Ola Virin of the Swedish Federation of Employers and Mr. Akě Lonnqvist of the Central Statistical Bureau for helping with data collection and analysis. We also appreciate the help of Mr. Sune Davidsson of the Ministry of Finance. In Belgium we had the assistance of Dr. Federico Prades and Professor Paul Lowenthal of the Institute for Economic and Social Research of the Catholic University of Louvain. We also acknowledge the help provided by M. R. Dereymaecker while he was Directeur Generale of the Institut Nationale de la Statistique in Brussels, H. J. Stokx of the Kredietbank, and E. Coenen and R. Elgem of the Banque Nationale de Belgique. In the Netherlands we appreciated the assistance of Mr. C. A. Oomens and his colleagues at the Netherlands Central Bureau of Statistics and Prof. P. S. Verdoorn of the Central Planning Bureau.

In Canada the following individuals were most helpful in consultation and in acquiring essential data: Peter G. Kirkham and P.N. Triandafillou of Statistics Canada; Robert de Cotret of the Conference Board; Ross Wilson of the Bank of Canada; David W. Slater of the Department of Finance; Charles Schwartz of the Department of Industry, Trade, and Commerce; R.A. Jenness of the Economic Council of Canada; and Roman Senkiw of the Royal Bank of Canada.

The excellent Japanese studies of business cycle indicators made our task of assembling appropriate data far easier than it otherwise would have been. For assistance in acquiring and interpreting the figures, we express our appreciation to Ryuji Mikita and Masaru Yanagisawa of the Japanese Economic Planning Agency and Yoshuaki Tsuroka of the Japan Trade Center in New York.

In the United States we, of course, utilized the National Bureau of Economic Research (NBER) Data Bank, under the direction of Charlotte Boschan and Josephine Su. We also acknowledge our indebtedness to the Bureau of Economic Analysis of the Department of Commerce, especially the late Beatrice Vaccara, and Feliks Tamm, Betty Tunstall, and Barry Beckman, for enabling us to utilize some of the material as well as the results of computer programs available from *Business Conditions Digest*. A number of others offered help of various kinds in this country. Among them we express particularly our obligation to Elmer S. Biles of the Bureau of the Census, Joseph W. Duncan of the Office of Management and Budget, Lester Tepper and Donald Niewiaroski of the Office of Competitive Assessment of the Commerce Department, and Sidney Zabludoff of the Council on International Economic Policy.

A number of individuals in international agencies have been of assistance to us, and we acknowledge particularly our gratitude to René Bertrand, Bernoit Reynaud, Randolf Granzer, John Dryden, Beatrice du Bois, and Jill Leyland of the OECD in Paris; Simon Goldberg of the UN Statistical Office in New York; Barrie N. Davies of the Statistical Division of the European Economic Community in Geneva; and Bernard Molitor and Tomas de Hora of the EEC in Brussels.

The research underlying the present volume was funded by grants from the U.S. Department of Commerce, the American Enterprise Institute, the Scherman Foundation, and the general funds of the National Bureau. In an age when research projects find funding an increasingly acute problem, our gratitude to these agencies is at once apparent. In this connection we also wish to acknowledge the support of those who have since joined the contributors to the larger project on International Economic Indicators—the Departments of

State, Treasury, Labor, Commerce, and Agriculture, the Federal Reserve Board and Reserve Banks, as well as several American enterprises—AT&T, Exxon, Eastman Kodak, International Paper, Ford Motor, and International Business Machines.

The work was begun at the National Bureau and completed at the Center for International Business Cycle Research now at Columbia University. As always, we have relied on the help of a number of people. The early computer analysis was conducted by Walter Ebanks, Elizabeth Wehle, and Susan Tebbetts, and subsequent work was done by Jean Maltz, Chantal Dubrin, Young Kwon, Theodore Joyce, Angela Femino, and Harvey Kaish. Joyce Geiger performed this work during the last year of our research and did far more than we had any right to expect. She has our special thanks.

Most of the manuscript was typed by DonnaMae Weber at The Pennsylvania State University and she has our appreciation. It is a pleasure to acknowledge also our debt to Mildred Courtney who in the first years of our work not only did a great deal of typing on various drafts, but also kept track of all the correspondence and other necessary materials that accumulated along the way. More recently this work was in the care of Lynn Hodges, Bertha Daniels and Stuart D'ver, and to them we express our thanks. Finally, we are grateful to Michael J. Halm, of Graphic Services at the Pennsylvania State University who was in charge of the drawing of all figures.

PART I

INTERNATIONAL ECONOMIC INDICATORS
A Tracking and Early Warning System

Chapter 1

INTRODUCTION

For many years a system of leading, coincident, and lagging economic indicators, first developed in the 1930s by the National Bureau of Economic Research (NBER), has been widely used in the United States to appraise the state of the business cycle. Since 1961 the current monthly figures for these indicators have been published by the U.S. Department of Commerce in *Business Conditions Digest*. Similar systems have been developed by government or private agencies in Canada, Japan, the United Kingdom, and more recently in many other countries. A few years ago the Organization for Economic Cooperation and Development (OECD) set up a working party to develop this type of analysis and most of the member countries participated. The Center for International Business Cycle Research (CIBCR) has given guidance in this field to some fifteen countries in recent years in Europe, Asia, the Middle East, Africa, and South America.

Our purpose in this chapter is to explain briefly the theory and rationale underlying this approach to economic forecasting. We will also provide a brief summary of our study, detailing how the indicators have performed in practice, in the United States and nine other countries. The book will conclude with some suggestions for future research and development, including the application of the approach to the analysis of inflation.

MITCHELL'S VIEW OF BUSINESS
CYCLE ANALYSIS

Wesley Clair Mitchell's first major work on business cycles was published in 1913.[1] Many of his contemporaries thought business cycles were essentially short-run, self-correcting phenomena scarcely in need of special policy, let alone study. From the very beginning Mitchell seems to have understood the necessity of acquiring factual information about economic instability before attempting to develop theoretical explanations for the phenomena so many others of that time chose to ignore. As long ago as 1927, for example, Mitchell wrote: "For theoretical uses, there is needed a systematic record of cyclical alternations of prosperity and depression, covering all countries in which the phenomena have appeared, and designed to make clear the recurrent features of the alternations."[2] Thus, the approach to the analysis of instability was international virtually from the outset. What Mitchell proposed to do was to examine the "cycles of reality" in a fairly large numbr of countries by amassing as many of the statistical records of these fluctuations as could be found. This was one of the reasons why in 1920 he launched the National Bureau of Economic Research. It is critical to bear in mind that this statistical collection and analysis was but a part of his overall plan that was basically directed toward explaining these cycles of reality. We should, therefore, underscore that in the 1927 comment quoted above it was for theoretical uses that the systematic statistical record was needed. The methodology to be summarized in Chapter 2 was many years in the making, and involved a lengthy process of collection and detailed analysis of many time series that together were and continue to be reflections of the fluctuations market-oriented economies have experienced at least since the Industrial Revolution.

This methodology was essentially completed in the late 1930s and was presented in a 1946 volume by Arthur F. Burns and W.C. Mitchell entitled *Measuring Business Cycles.*[3] When Burns and Mitchell published this pioneering work, it represented the culmination of a quarter century's thought about the nature of cyclical disturbances in industrialized market-oriented economies and how such disturbances might be studied. The book set off arguments about whether or not one could productively measure anything without a "proper" theory or hypothesis, and there were arguments at a more technical level surrounding the methodology itself. Thus, debate in the 1940s frequently revolved around the relationship of the National Bureau methodology to earlier theories of business fluctuations, as well as to the relationships between the Mitchellian approach to cyclical analysis, the Keynesian policies of the day, and the emergent econometric revolution.

Today instability manifests itself primarily by widespread and more or less unremitting difficulties in controlling inflation and unemployment in most of the industrialized market-oriented economies of the developed world. Economists of whatever methodological persuasion, and of whatever policy school, are increasingly being asked to account for the continued presence of phenomena that have proved remarkably resistant to both understanding and control. Why do we continue to experience business cycles? Is another recession as severe as 1973–75, let alone 1929–32, likely to occur? How do cycles spread from one country to another? How can they best be ameliorated? These are among the most pressing economic questions of our time. Mitchell's methodology and the business cycle indicators he launched have a contribution to make to the international search for answers.

A Mitchellian Perspective:
Measurement with Theory

It is widely held that Burns and Mitchell's *Measuring Business Cycles* was nontheoretical, if not antitheoretical. They considered the relation of their work to extant theories of business fluctuations and stated their view of the relationship of what they were doing to that body of theory in the following way:

> Our aim is to determine as thoroughly as we can what business cycles are.
> . . . This objective is always before us in later monographs, where we prepare materials as well as we can in advance for a systematic attack in a theoretical volume. But we believe that an intelligible notion of what business cycles are can best be reached from available statistical records by a process of successive approximation. The primary objective of our monograph on cyclical behavior is to describe in a preliminary way the typical features of business cycles.[4]

Mitchell died before the theoretical volume could be written, but as this and many other passages make clear, he regarded his work as a necessary stage in the development of a viable and reasonably realistic theory of business fluctuations.

The approach Burns and Mitchell took largely eschewed many previous theoretical explanations, and we shall return to those explanations and their relationship to the Bureau's methodology. Here we note only that Burns and Mitchell both regarded the methodology and their book detailing that methodology as contributing to a theoretical understanding of cyclical instability. Having developed the methodology, for example, and having developed ultimately a set of indicators that typically lead or lag behind business cycle turning points emerging from the application of that methodology, Mitchell commented, "No attempt is made [here] to explain why the series behave as they do, but anyone who goes over the entries thoughtfully will find his mind seething with rationalizations, and with conjectures regarding the effects produced by the recorded movements."[5] That this was Burns's view as well is clear from many of his statements. In his introduction to *What Happens During Business Cycles*, for example, Burns no doubt expressed his own as well as Mitchell's wish when he noted,

> The wish to contribute to economic policy was strong in Mitchell. Stronger still was his conviction that intelligent control of business cycles depends upon sound theoretical understanding, which requires tolerably full and accurate knowledge of what the business cycles of experience have been like.[6]

It is true that *Measuring Business Cycles* made more references to statisticians and others concerned with measuring cycles than to the multitude of economists who have tried to develop theories of the cycles. There are references to Jevons, Juglar, Keynes, Schumpeter, and the like. But there are more references to Leonard Ayres, Roger Babson, Frederick Macaulay, Geoffrey Moore, Frederick Mills, Warren Persons, Willard Thorp, and others whose work is even now rarely connected with any particular theory of instability. There are also references to investigators like Abramowitz who defy such neat categorization.

Economic theory in general has scarcely been immune to the charge of oversimplification. In this regard it is worth recalling that at the end of his summary of extant business cycle theories, R.A. Gordon felt compelled to comment, "None of these models should be taken too seriously as an explanation of what happens during the cycles of reality. They are too simple."[7] Whatever else one says of the methodology developed at the National Bureau, it did not regard the cycle as a simple phenomenon.

Rejecting the simplistic, therefore, Mitchell and his co-workers at the National Bureau determined to begin with a review of the statistical record. Burns and Mitchell wrote, "The way we have chosen is to observe the business cycles of history as closely and systematically as we can before making a fresh attempt to explain them."[8] The material set out in *Measuring Business Cycles*, initially criticized as "measurement without theory,"[9] has long since been accepted and forms the basis of much current cyclical analysis in the United States.

The Role of Reference Dates

One of the crucial steps in the Burns–Mitchell approach to the analysis of cyclical disturbances lies in the choice of reference dates. "Reference dates" is the National Bureau's term for the peaks and troughs, selected after study of many time series and chosen to represent the turning points in a country's business cycles. The considerations that enter into their selection, originally quite judgmental, have now been codified to be programmed for the computer.[10] Computer-selected turning points are still corroborated by visual inspection, however, because of known inadequacies in the programmed criteria.

Reference dates are important because they ultimately form the basis for subsequent analysis of all time series, including the classification into leading, roughly coincident, or lagging indicators. These indicators, discussed in the next section of this chapter, represent kinds of economic activity, culled from long years of experimentation with literally hundreds of series, which, in the experience of National Bureau analysis, have historically been most reliable in forecasting, recording, and confirming U.S. business cycles. It is important, therefore, that reference dates reflect as accurately as possible the shift from expansion to contraction in "the aggregate economic activity" of the business enterprise economies to which Burns and Mitchell applied their technique.

The choice of reference dates begins with the selection of appropriate turning points in a number of individual time series, primarily those series that in themselves constitute measures of aggregate economic activity—that is, income, output, employment, and trade. The considerations involved in such selections are, of course, akin to those used for choosing turning points in any time series. The conversion of such information into reference dates involves judicious determination of what constitutes the "preponderence" of evidence with respect to cyclical fluctuations in aggregate economic activity. Ultimately, one can judge the appropriateness of the reference dates by the behavior of a variety of measures of economic activity around these points of reference. Thus, while the reference dates are required to differentiate leading, roughly coincident, and lagging indicators, the appropriateness of the dates can also be judged, when there is a considerable historical record on which to base timing classifications, by the consistency with which leaders lead, coinciders coincide, and laggers lag. In a sense, the analysis of timing becomes an interactive process.

Since the original formulation by Burns and Mitchell, such a historical record has, of course, been built up, most particularly for the United States. But *Measuring Business Cycles*, despite its understandable emphasis on the United States, included an effort to develop reference cycle chronologies for other countries as well.

THE INDICATOR SYSTEM

The leading, coincident, and lagging indicators cover a wide variety of economic processes that have been found to be important in business cycles. The leading indicators are, for the most part, measures of anticipations or new commitments. They have a "look-ahead" quality and are highly sensitive to changes in the economic climate as perceived in the marketplace. The coincident indicators are comprehensive measures of economic performance, pertaining to output, employment, income, and trade. They are the measures to which everyone looks to determine whether a nation is prosperous or depressed. The lagging indicators are more sluggish in their reactions to the economic climate, but they serve two useful functions. First, since lagging indicators are usually very smooth, they help to confirm changes in trend that are initially reflected in the more erratic leading and coincident indicators. Second, their very sluggishness can be an asset in cyclical analysis, because when they do begin to move, or when they move more rapidly, they may show that excesses or imbalances in the economy are developing or subsiding. Hence, the lagging indicators frequently provide the earliest warnings of all, as when rapid increases in costs of production outstrip price increases and threaten profit margins, thus inhibiting new commitments to invest, which are among the leading indicators.

The list of the "most reliable indicators" has been revised a number of times (1938 was the first such publication, and subsequent revisions were made in 1950, 1960, 1966, and 1975). Our study of international economic indicators is based heavily on the 1966 U.S. list.[11] This list was the current one at the time the international work was begun. As we shall illustrate below, however, many of these indicators have survived one of the longest continuous testing programs of empirical findings against subsequent data in the field of economics—from 1938 to 1976. These indicators are at the heart of the international analysis presented here.

The procedure in selecting and classifying indicators is one in which economic theory and empirical observation closely interact. The indicator that has a near-perfect record of performance during a business cycle, but whose behavior cannot be explained, will not command or warrant much attention, since faith depends on understanding. On the other hand, the indicator that is suggested by theoretical considerations but has not been tested or does not perform as theory predicts will not command much attention either, since faith depends on performance. With these precepts in mind let us look at the classification of U.S. indicators that we have been using in developing an international system of business cycle indicators (Table 1-1).

The first column on the left lists six broad types of economic process that figure in most theories of the business cycle. Most of the variables that are today employed in econometric models can be found under one or another of these categories. There are, however, some important exceptions. Foreign trade is not shown explicitly, although it is implicit in the second group (production, income, consumption, and trade). Taxes and government expenditures do not appear explicitly either, although they are conspicuous in most models. Here the reason is not that government has no impact on the business cycle, but rather that most measures of its activity have not performed very consistently as indicators. The same comment could be made about agricultural production.

The indicators in the body of the table were selected from the six types of economic process, again with a view both to their contribution to theory and empirical performance. Performance has been judged primarily with respect to the consistency with which the measure has conformed to business cycles and led, coincided, or lagged behind the cycles' turning points. An indicator can have too many cycles or too few; one-to-one correspondence is preferable. An indicator can lead on some occasions and lag at other times; uniformity in timing is preferable. Other criteria play a role too. Comprehensive coverage of the economy is preferable to narrow coverage. Prompt availability of current figures is important, and, coupled with that, monthly figures are preferred to quarterly.

Within each of the economic process groups, reading across the table, are indicators that lead as well as those that coincide or lag. This is one reason for thinking of them as processes. The activities represented normally follow a sequence. The average workweek, for example, is one of the first variables pertaining to employment that manufacturing enterprises change, either by increasing or reducing the amount of overtime work or by changing the number of persons working short hours or fewer days per week. Changes in the number of persons employed usually occur a few months later, because such changes are less easily reversed and are more expensive to accomplish.

Every entry in Table 1-1 has been supported by detailed studies showing that the indicators not only behave in the manner specified by the classification but also that there are cogent economic reasons for this behavior. In addition, these studies have considered not only

Table 1-1. Cross-Classification of U.S. Indicators by Economic Process and Cyclical Timing.[a]

Economic Process	Cyclical Timing		
	Leading	Roughly Coincident	Lagging
Employment and unemployment	Average work week, manufacturing New unemployment insurance claims, inverted	Nonfarm employment Unemployment, inverted	Long-duration unemployment, inverted
Production, income, consumption, and trade	New orders, consumer goods and materials[b]	Gross national product[b] Industrial production Personal income[b] Manufacturing and trade sales[b]	
Fixed capital investment	Formation of business enterprises Contracts and orders, plant and equipment[b] Building permits, housing		Investment expenditures, plant and equipment[b]
Inventories and inventory investment	Change in business inventories[b]		Business inventories[b]
Prices, costs, and profits	Industrial materials price index Stock price index Profits[b] Ratio, price to unit labor cost, nonfarm		Change in output per man-hour, manufacturing, inverted
Money, credit and interest rates	Change, consumer installment debt[b]		Commercial and industrial loans outstanding[b] Bank interest rates, business loans

Notes to Table 1-1

a. The list and classification is substantially the same as that prepared in 1966 and published in Geoffrey H. Moore and Julius Shiskin, *Indicators of Business Expansions and Contractions* (New York: National Bureau of Economic Research, 1967). The chief modification is that those series marked with note (b) are converted to constant prices. The timing classification for each series is the same as shown in *Business Conditions Digest* for all turns (see Table 1, column 1, in any recent issue), except as follows: Unemployment is unclassified (*U*) at all turns in *BCD* because it leads at peaks and lags at troughs, but here it is classified roughly coincident, as in the 1966 list. Four series that here are in constant prices are shown in *BCD* only in current prices: change in consumer installment debt, investment expenditures for plant and equipment, commercial and industrial loans outstanding, and change in output per man-hour, manufacturing, inverted, which is the constant price equivalent of labor cost per unit of output. The constant price series are assigned the same classification as the current price series.

Although the indicators listed here share a common ancestry and rationale with those currently used in the composite indexes published in *Business Conditions Digest*, only about half the series are identical. A number of series in the two lists are closely related but some are quite different. Despite these differences, the movements in the U.S. indexes shown below are broadly similar to those in *BCD*.

b. In constant prices.

the sequences across columns but also the more or less simultaneous relationships among the indicators within each column: how stock prices are related to profits, materials prices to inventory investment, production to employment, sales to income, and so on. Finally, these studies have developed the reasons for and evidence underlying a relationship not explicitly shown in the table—a relationship that helps to explain why one business cycle tends to generate the next one.

This relationship has to do with the influence of the lagging indicators upon the subsequent movements of the leading indicators. An increase in the level of inventories, especially in relation to sales, if it proceeds far enough, is likely to cause buyers to cut back their orders. Here a lagging indicator, inventories, has an inverse effect upon a leading indicator, new orders. Similarly, a rapid increase in expenditures for new plant and equipment may, as output and capital utilization rates build up, result in a cutback in contracts for new plant construction. Likewise, an increase in interest rates on business loans may at some stage trigger decisions to reduce orders for machinery and equipment and to reduce the rate at which inventories of materials are accumulated. In short, there are feedback relationships running from the lagging indicators to the subsequent, opposite turns in the leading indicators. These relationships, too, have been documented empirically, as we shall see.

The hardest test for a theory or system of indicators to meet, as with any other economic theory or system, is one that requires it to perform on data that were not available when it was formulated. The U.S. indicators have experienced many such tests. One, covering twenty-five years and based on data not available when, in 1950, a set of indicators was selected and classified, is contained in Table 1-2.

The empirical evidence used to select and classify indicators in the 1950 study covered periods of varying length but ended in 1938. Twenty-one indicators were selected as the end-product of a study covering some 800 series. Eight of the twenty-one were classified as leading, eight coincident, and five lagging. Fifteen of the twenty-one are still shown currently in *Business Conditions Digest*, and close equivalents of the other six are also in that publication. From these twenty-one series in *BCD* we have constructed composite indexes, using a method developed in the late 1950s, and covering the period 1948 to 1975. The indexes have been adjusted for long-run trend, using a method developed in the 1970s. The turning points in the trend-adjusted series are compared in Table 1-2 with the peaks and troughs in a chronology of growth cycles, a concept of the business cycle that has come into use in many countries only in recent years, which we shall discuss more fully below.

The test in Table 1-2, therefore, not only confronts the twenty-one indicators with data not available when they were chosen, but also with methods of analysis unavailable then. The results, recorded in the left-hand section of the table, show that the expected sequence among the three groups of indicators occurred at almost every turn throughout the period. The lagging indicators not only lag the growth cycle as expected but also lead the opposite turns in the leaders, which is also as expected and as demonstrated in 1950.

Even though the indicators selected in 1950 turned in a good record during the next twenty-five years, research on indicators and business cycles did not stand still. (Chapter 2 will discuss some of these changes in methodology.) In addition, the indicators themselves have improved. More of them are available in deflated form, more are published in seasonally adjusted form, some are available more promptly, there is better coverage of inventories and of price/cost relationships, and so on. In 1975 the Department of Commerce established a new list of indicators, and its record during the preceding twenty-five years is shown on the right-hand side of Table 1-2. The results are similar, on the whole, to those achieved by the 1950 list, partly because the content overlaps to a considerable extent. The user of indicators would, however, not hesitate a moment in opting for the 1975 list in view of its improved coverage of significant variables.

From this brief review of U.S. experience we contend that the conceptual framework underlying the indicator approach to business cycle forecasting has stood up well under repeated tests on subsequent data. Much room for error and uncertainty remains, as witness the uncertainty in 1982 over the prospects for recovery from the then current U.S. recession. But we know much more about the merits and limitations of the system than we did thirty years ago.

The study of foreign countries constitutes a further test of the Burns-Mitchell approach. If the results of our study reveal that the series that prove reliable both as leading and confirming indicators in the United States exhibit similar behavior in relation to cyclical turning points in other countries, this would confirm a fundamental theorem of Burns and Mitchell: namely, that their method of analysis is applicable to cycles in countries that organize their work mainly in business enterprises—not just the U.S. economy.

Table 1-2.   Leads and Lags at Growth Cycle Peaks and Troughs: Two Sets of Trend-Adjusted Composite Indexes, 1948-75.

A. Lead (−) or Lag (+), in Months, at Growth Cycle Peaks

Growth Cycle Peak	Indexes Based on 1950 List of Indicators				Indexes Based on 1975 List of Indicators			
	Lagging, Inverted	Leading	Coincident	Lagging	Lagging, Inverted	Leading	Coincident	Lagging
July 1948	n.c.ª	−6	+1	+1	n.c.	−6	−1	+1
Mar. 1951	−15	−2	−2	−1	−12	−7	−2	n.c.
Mar. 1953	−12	n.c.	+2	+3	n.c.	0	0	+6
Feb. 1957	−28	−17	0	+7	−22	−17	−14	+7
Feb. 1960	−17	−10	−9	+2	−15	−10	−8	+4
May 1962	−13	−5	−3	+5	−5	−3	−8	+4
June 1966	−19	−5	0	+3	n.c.	−3	n.c.	n.c.
Mar. 1969	−17	+2	0	+5	−17	−2	+4	+7
Mar. 1973	−9	−1	+17	+17	−13	−1	+7	+7
							+8	+18
Mean	−16	−6	+1	+5	−14	−5	−1	+7
St. Dev.	6	6	7	5	6	5	7	5
Correlation with Leads in Leading Index	+0.76			+0.11	+0.64			+0.31

Table 1-2. continued

B. Lead (−) or Lag (+), in Months, at Growth Cycle Troughs

Growth Cycle Trough	Indexes Based on 1950 List of Indicators				Indexes Based on 1975 List of Indicators			
	Lagging, Inverted	Leading	Coincident	Lagging	Lagging, Inverted	Leading	Coincident	Lagging
Oct. 1949	−14	−4	0	+2	−14	−4	0	+5
July 1952	−17	n.c.	0	−4	n.c.	−8	0	n.c.
Aug. 1954	−14	−8	0	+2	−11	−7	0	+8
Apr. 1958	−7	0	0	+5	−7	−3	+1	+7
Feb. 1961	−10	−2	0	+2	−8	−2	0	+10
Oct. 1964	−24	−24	0	+1	n.c.	−28	n.c.	n.c.
Oct. 1967	−13	−10	0	0	−9	−8	−3	0
Nov. 1970	−15	−2	0	+19	−13	0	0	+15
Mar. 1975	−7	0	0	+20	−6	−1	0	+21
Mean	−13	−6	0	+5	−10	−7	0	+9
St. Dev.	5	8	0	8	3	8	1	7
Correlation with Leads in Leading Index	+0.89			+0.49	+0.09			+0.79

Note:

a. n.c. = no timing comparison.

Source: Geoffrey H. Moore, "The Forty-Second Anniversary of the Leading Indicators," in William Fellner, ed., *Contemporary Economic Problems, 1979*, American Enterprise Institute, 1980, pp. 428−29.

FROM CLASSICAL CYCLES
TO GROWTH CYCLES

It is clearly a coincidence that the Great Depression occurred just before *Measuring Business Cycles* was completed (its publication was delayed by World War II) and that there has not been a depression of such severity since. While most postwar cycles have been milder and of a somewhat different character than the prewar cycles, even relatively severe ones have not disappeared. If the long expansion of the 1960s in the United States and favorable experience abroad led some to declare that the business cycle was obsolete, this was a euphoric view that was far from universally held, and it was all too soon refuted by the widespread contraction of 1973-75.[12]

While such contractions may be rare in the future, we now realize that to the NBER's previous emphasis on expansion and contraction in the absolute level of economic activity must be added efforts to account for changes in the rate of growth. Concern about growth rates has increased as our willingness to tolerate either high inflation or high unemployment has declined. Fortunately, growth cycles, as we shall see, give considerable evidence of being simply a variant within the same species of business fluctuations.

Ilse Mintz noted the significance of growth cycles in her study of postwar cycles in Germany.[13] She also focused attention at the National Bureau on applying the basic methodology for cyclical analysis to countries outside the United States. Her study therefore represented a major effort to date turning points in business cycles when the latter were defined and measured as upswings and downswings in the rate of growth ("growth cycles") rather than as expansions and contractions in levels of aggregate activity ("classical cycles"), the type of turning point typically found in the pre-World War II period. This distinction has come to the fore especially since World War II. Prior to that time there were, of course, many cyclical episodes in the United States, some severe, and some not so severe. But, in general, cyclical episodes were of sufficient severity that viewing a business cycle as a period of absolute expansion and absolute contraction in the level of aggregate economic activity made sense. Such a view of business cycles concentrates on what we now refer to as "classical cycles." For many years after World War II real growth tended to be fairly rapid in the United States, and even more rapid in many other industrialized market-oriented economies. More recently, the upsurge in inflation has produced even more spectacular growth rates in aggregate economic activity expressed in current prices.[14]

The result was that for long periods, by historical standards, there were no classical cycles. The decade of the 1960s was such a period in the United States, and the postwar period (through 1965) was such a period in West Germany. But Mintz found that if cycles were viewed not as periods of absolute expansion and decline in the level of activity, but rather as cyclical changes in the rate of growth, one could discern a good many more cycles, and they could be found during long periods characterized by the absence of classical cycles. These "growth cycles" are represented by deviations from a long-run trend that generally depicts long-term growth. Growth cycle turning points are related to, but are not the same as, turning points in classical cycles. One can, therefore, produce two business cycle chronologies for a given country, one depicting classical cycles and the other growth cycles. Classical cycles will generally show up in a growth cycle chronology, but all growth cycles will not appear in classical cycle chronologies.

The historical experience with dating business fluctuations at the National Bureau has been confined largely to classical cycles, although Burns and Mitchell's *Measuring Business Cycles* contained a chapter devoted to the effect of trend adjustment upon cyclical measures, thus anticipating the distinction between growth and classical cycles. The Mintz study of West German fluctuations in the postwar period and her subsequent study developing a growth cycle chronology for the United States represent significant efforts to apply the techniques developed previously for dating classical cycles to the kind of growth cycles typical of enterprise-oriented economies since World War II. In the next chapter we shall describe the technique as we have applied it to growth cycle analysis.

By concentrating on the dating of these "growth cycles," rather than on what we now call "classical cycles," the emphasis in this book is, therefore, placed on the kind of instability most typical of the market-oriented economies of the contemporary world. In this approach classical recessions (periods of negative growth) are regarded as part of the low-growth phases. While there are good reasons for concentrating here on growth cycles, the worldwide recessions in 1973–75 and 1979–81 showed clearly that classical cycles are by no means a thing of the past, regardless of whether or not growth cycles are the wave of the future.

PREVIOUS WORK ON INTERNATIONAL INDICATORS

Twenty years ago Julius Shiskin, writing on the possible uses of monthly reporting on the status of the indicators (an idea that came to fruition in the United States with the publication, beginning in 1961, of *Business Conditions Digest*), concluded:

> The indicator series and summary measures provide a sensitive and revealing picture of the ebb and flow of economic tides, which a skillful analyst of the economic, political, and international scene can use to improve his chances of making a good forecast of short-run economic trends. In summary, if one is aware of their limitations and alert to events in the world around him, the indicators do provide useful guideposts for taking stock of the economy and its needs.[15]

Indicators had always been viewed merely as one useful addition to the forecasting and diagnostic tools of business cycle specialists. Today the U.S. indicators are widely watched and followed, but we would still claim no more for them than Shiskin did. The possibility of developing them for a number of industrialized market-oriented economies, and reporting their status monthly, however, opens many new and potentially valuable avenues for further research and progress toward prompt diagnosis of international economic instability and inflationary pressures.

Before turning to an analysis of the indicator data provided by our work on the International Economic Indicator project, let us summarize what has been done in the years since Shiskin's judicious assessment of the prospect of improving our understanding of cyclical developments and forecasting ability by use of indicators (see Bibliography). We shall focus on work done for countries other than the United States.

One of the difficulties arising from such a review is the ambiguous nature of the term "indicator." Most countries now produce some publication concerning recent developments with regard to indicators. Almost invariably, however, the word simply refers to measures of aggregate economic activity or related economic data, which the publication reports on a current basis. This usage, of course, follows the long-standing practice of agencies such as the OECD, which for many years has published the principal series from the national accounts of member countries along with a group of other important time series (balance of payments, interest rates, exchange rates, price indexes, etc.) under the title *Main Economic Indicators*. Even where the word "indicator" is not used, as in the United Nations' *Monthly Bulletin of Statistics*, the meaning is similar. Our usage is more restricted and refers to economic variables that are classified according to their cyclical behavior.

We have already noted Mintz's pioneering study of postwar German cycles.[16] This study was not only the first to focus on growth cycles rather than classical cycles, but was devoted particularly to developing roughly coincident indicators from which postwar Germany's growth cycle turning points could be selected. Mintz, however, did not deal with leading or lagging indicators. This gap is now being filled by the work reported here and by that of the IFO-Institute in Munich.[17]

Another early effort to compare internationally the behavior of cyclical indicators was Kathleen H. Moore's study of indicators in the United States, Canada, and Japan.[18] This work was aided enormously by the publication in the early 1970s (through the Japanese Economic Planning Agency) of a bi-monthly report called *Japanese Economic Indicators*. Also, the Canadian Department of Trade and Commerce has issued a similar monthly publication entitled *Current Economic Indicators*. These two reports were the only official ones at all comparable to the work with NBER-type indicators developed in the United States, until the Central Statistical Office in London began in 1975 to devote a section of their *Economic Trends* to British indicators of growth cycles.

Working with twenty-four U.S. leading, roughly coincident, and lagging indicators, and with twenty-eight Japanese and twenty-two Canadian equivalents to the U.S. list, Moore examined the timing relationships to discover whether the classifications found appropriate in the United States were also appropriate in the two foreign countries. This analysis enabled her to conclude, with some qualifications, that " . . . comparable series exhibit similar timing relationships in all three countries."[19] Utilizing summary indexes for each of the three groups of indicators in each country, she considered how regularly the leaders led the roughly coincident indicators, and how regularly the latter led the lagging indicators. Moreover, she considered whether the lagging index in each country was a reliable leader of the opposite turn in the leading index, a particularly valuable property associated with lagging indicators in the United States. For all three countries and considering the reference dates available at that time (roughly during the period 1948–61), she discovered that the expected sequences prevailed at fifty-eight out of sixty-five turning points (or close to 90% of the time). She found a perfect record for the United States, four exceptions out of twenty-three for Japan, and three out of nineteen for Canada.[20]

In the early 1970s Desmond J. O'Dea concerned himself with the application of the indicator technique to the United Kingdom. Working at the National Institute of Economic and Social Research in London, O'Dea discussed with the authors the NBER approach to the study of indicators. (London was the base from which the essential underlying historical data for the international economic indicators project was collected during the year 1973-74.) While O'Dea was, therefore, aware of our basic approach, he chose to apply it to the recent U.K. experience only in a somewhat amended form. His first study was restricted to labor market indicators and compared their cyclical behavior in the United States and in Great Britain.[21] This study reflected his decision to view indicators more narrowly by examining specific kinds of series that might be expected to be reliable indicators for what he called target variables, in this instance unemployment. Thus, he used each target variable to provide a different set of reference dates, rather than develop a generalized set of reference dates as the NBER has customarily employed. O'Dea went on to expand his labor market indicators approach in this direction, and presented indicators of investment and production as well.[22]

O'Dea noted in the introduction to this work the extensive discussions he had had with the authors and with officials of the Central Statistical Office in London with a view to selecting a generalized reference chronology for the United Kingdom, but decided that the quest was futile. Recognizing the utility of a general reference chronology, he was nonetheless forced to conclude that " . . . it is not possible to construct a general cycle by detailed consideration of a selection of major economic variables, as in the National Bureau's approach. . . ."[23] O'Dea argued, as indeed have others, that there were too many irregularities and special circumstances pertinent to the British experience since World War II to make a general method like that of the NBER feasible. The other participants in these discussions, nevertheless, have now produced growth cycle chronologies for postwar Britain. O'Dea indeed produced one in his 1975 book, only to reject it. Thus, instead of no chronologies for the United Kingdom, we now have several (see Chapter 2, especially Table 2-3).

Mention should also be made of the earliest experiments conducted by OECD with NBER-type indicators. Randolf Granzer's article, "Cyclical Indicators for Manufacturing Industries," utilized trend deviations for the Index of Industrial Production as the "reference cycle" in each country.[24] He then compared a small group of leading indicators and a small group of lagging indicators to this growth cycle referrent. In general, his leading indicators, including results of surveys concerning orders or the ratio of orders to stocks, reflect the European emphasis since the 1950s on "qualitative indicators"—that is, on surveys of entrepreneurial judgment with respect to present and future conditions. (Our own work in this area is the subject of Chapter 5.) Granzer regarded his leaders as primarily "demand-oriented," while his lagging indicators were, in his view, "supply-oriented" (primarily investment and employment). The countries examined, for the decade 1963–1973, included Canada, the United States, Japan, Belgium, Denmark, France, Germany, Italy, Spain, Sweden, and the United Kingdom. The article reflected growing awareness in the OECD that leading, coincident, and lagging indicators can play a useful role both in cyclical analysis and in forecasting. Unfortunately, the findings were presented almost entirely in graphic form, with no summary measures of leading and lagging indicator behavior. Granzer's study represented, nonetheless, a highly useful step, and provided a welcome indication of the heightened interest in dating growth cycles and developing reliable indicators, both leading and lagging, in countries outside the United States.

From this modest first step, interest in monitoring growth cycles has increased greatly at the OECD. Almost from the outset of our efforts to construct a test of the feasibility of an international indicator system we have been in contact with officials at the OECD. Because they represent a well-established agency collecting and analyzing economic time series for many countries, they were an obvious focus of our attention. Accordingly, we initiated discussions that resulted in a continuing collaborative effort.

In 1978 the OECD established a working party on Cyclical Analysis and Leading Indicators, which held meetings at least once a year during the period 1978–1981, in which the authors participated. This effort resulted in the establishment of growth cycle chronologies for all of the twenty-four member countries. These chronologies were not all established on the same basis—some were primarily the work of national experts, others were developed by the secretariat. We have already noted that the working party decided early on that growth cycles should attempt to measure and track cycles in "output—broadly defined." Thus, the efforts at the OECD have diverged somewhat from those reported here. For example, they do not attempt a common set of indicators for the roughly coincident, much less for the leaders. Lagging indicators are planned but have not yet been developed in most cases. There is more or less common treatment of time series, as all countries have or can get access to the basic computer programs developed at the National Bureau and utilized today at the Center for International Business Cycle Research.

The OECD working party no longer meets, but the work it commenced continues as part of the operation of the secretariat, which in turn is authorized to maintain contact with national experts. A recent report summarizes the activities of both the OECD and the member countries in this field.[25] A section in *Main Economic Indicators* also presents preliminary work on growth cycle indicators for member countries.

Outside the OECD interest in growth cycle indicators is increasing as well. At the European Economic Community a decision has been made to monitor growth cycle developments in those OECD countries that belong to the Common Market. No formal publications have emerged from the EEC, but several papers dealing with the analysis of growth cycles in member countries have been prepared for use by the EEC staff, and continuing contacts with the CIBCR are maintained as well.

PLAN OF THE BOOK

The findings reported in this book emerged from our work on international economic indicators launched at the National Bureau in August 1973 and continued at the Center for International Business Cycle Research.[26]

The initial questions prompting the present study can be summarized as follows: (1) Can business cycles be dated in other countries by means of the technique developed at the NBER for the United States? (2) Could the NBER approach as developed for classical cycles in the United States be adapted to the measurement and forecasting of growth cycles both in the United States and in other countries? That is, is the notion of a growth cycle a useful approach t the study of cyclical instability in a number of market-oriented economies, as Mintz's original work on postwar German cycles led one to expect? (3) Could the system of leading, roughly coincident, and lagging indicators developed at the NBER for classical cycles be effectively employed in the study of growth cycles both in the U.S. and elsewhere? These questions, in turn, lead to several related problems that must be explored. Could indicators of classical cycles behave with sufficient sensitivity to act as reliable indicators of growth cycles? Could the U.S. set of indicators be replicated for other countries? If so, do these indicators (or rough equivalents thereof) exhibit comparable tendencies to lead or lag growth cycle turning points abroad? Assuming that growth cycle chronologies can indeed be developed for a number of countries, do they shed light on current problems such as: the way in which instability is transmitted internationally; the consilience among growth cycles in industrial economies and its relationship to the generation of inflationary booms or severe recessions; the comparative study of particular indicators— such as those related to the labor market—in different countries; and the study of the competitiveness of a particular country vis-à-vis its trading partners?

The chapters that follow provide the evidence we have uncovered in an attempt to deal with these questions. Overall, our findings support the validity of the indicator approach and encourage us to move forward in developing and improving this system both in the United States and in other industrialized economies.

Chapter 2 summarizes the methodology underlying the selection of growth cycle turning points and presents the growth cycle chronologies we have developed for the ten countries included in this study. These chronologies are based on substantially the same measures of economic activity for each country, covering output, employment, unemployment, real income, and real volume of trade. The growth cycle peak and trough dates represent the consensus among the turning points of these indicators after adjustment is made for long-run trend.

Chapter 3 provides an overview of the indicator system for each country by examining the summary measures of leading, roughly coincident, and lagging indicators. We then consider the composite indexes in each country, constructed from indicators classified according to U.S. experience, as well as the median timing of the groups of indicators.

The behavior of the individual indicators at growth cycle turning points for all ten countries is analyzed in Chapter 4. The result is a detailed test of the system, which has both scientific value and practical advantages. If individual indicators that have proved to lead or lag consistently in U.S. experience can be shown to have similar temporal relationships in other countries, the case for indicators— both in theory and in application to forecasting efforts—would be strengthened.

One possibility for improving the ability to forecast growth cycles with leading indicators, which is explored in Chapter 5, has involved the use of so-called qualitative indicators. Survey results dealing with what entrepreneurs think, for example, about their sales possibilities are now regularly collected in many countries. Because of the popularity of these surveys abroad, their inclusion here is of considerable potential usefulness.

Chapter 6 considers the possibility of utilizing composite indexes for more than one country to study fluctuations in areas of the world such as Europe, or North America, or even the entire industrialized world. We find that this approach is useful in examining the degree to which business cycles in market-oriented economies have exhibited consilience in the years since World War II. Examining the evidence of a world cycle is also useful in studying the spread of general economic instability. The multicountry composite indexes used were constructed by weighting each country's index according to its 1970 GNP.

In Chapter 7 we consider the possibilities for forecasting trade flows by utilizing composite leading indexes that reflect economic conditions as they develop for any country's trading partners.

Chapter 8 examines another possible application of the indicator systems presented in this study: forecasting inflation-rate changes for market-oriented economies. The development of leading, coincident, and lagging indicators of inflation is an open field, and we need to sharpen our awareness of new inflationary trends, or disinflationary trends. What are the most reliable indicators for detecting these trends? Can available measures be improved? The preliminary results reported here have barely scratched the surface of this area of research.

Finally, Chapter 9 suggests some ideas for future studies that will be needed if the monitoring of international economic indicators is to play a useful role in helping us understand, predict, and ameliorate cyclical fluctuations.

NOTES TO CHAPTER 1

1. W. C. Mitchell, *Business Cycles* (Berkeley: University of California Press, 1913).

2. W. C. Mitchell, *Business Cycles, The Problem and Its Setting* (New York: NBER, 1927), p. 361.

3. A. F. Burns and W. C. Mitchell, *Measuring Business Cycles* (New York: NBER, 1946).

4. Ibid., p. 383.

5. W. C. Mitchell, *What Happens During Business Cycles* (New York: NBER, 1951), pp. 69 and 72.

6. Ibid., p. x.

7. R. A. Gordon, *Business Fluctuations* (New York: Harper & Row, 1961), 1st ed., p. 340.

8. Burns and Mitchell, *Measuring Business Cycles*, p. 4.

9. Tjalling Koopmans, "Measurement Without Theory," *Review of Economics and Statistics* (August 1947); Rutledge Vining, "Koopmans on the Choice of Variables to be Studied and of Methods of Measurement," *Review of Economics and Statistics* (May 1949); Reply by Koopmans and Rejoinder by Vining, *Review of Economics and Statistics* (May 1949). The entire exchange has been reprinted in American Economics Association *Readings in Business Cycles*, R. A. Gordon and L. R. Klein, eds., along with a significant Additional Comment by Koopmans. The Comment states that in the intervening years— that is, between 1949 (the year of the original review of the Burns–Mitchell book and the debate with Vining over the methodology it employed) and 1965 when the A.E.A. readings appeared—Koopmans had decided that the use of indicators and their development along the lines the NBER had pursued might produce "reasonably efficient summaries" of relevant information contained in time series. The change was, in a sense, a recognition of the degree to which National Bureau methods, at least for the United States, had become widely accepted and ceased to be controversial. The whole debate about whether or not the NBER was attempting "measurement without theory," carried on in the exchange between Koopmans and Vining, could have been avoided, or at least shortened, had it begun with a proper understanding of where Mitchell began. As we have noted, only after having considered all the extant theories, as well as attempting an analysis of the essential character of modern industrial economies, and a review of the history of business cycles in the United States, England, France, and Germany in the years up to 1913 did Mitchell conclude that to advance our knowledge of the subject "we must know the facts." With a firm grounding in theories previously expounded, Mitchell launched both his own inquiry (and ultimately that of the NBER) by declaring, "For an investigation upon any line we must provide such statistical data as these theories show to be required." (*Business Cycles* (Berkeley: University of California Press, 1913), p. 91. Part Three was reprinted in 1941 as *Business Cycles and Their Causes.*)

10. Gerhard Bry and Charlotte Boschan, *Cyclical Analysis of Time Series: Selected Procedures and Computer Programs* (New York: NBER, Technical Paper No. 20, 1971).

11. Since we began the study, the 1966 U.S. list has been revised once again. See U.S. Department of Commerce, *Business Conditions Digest* (May 1975 and November 1975). While our discussion in Chapter 2 includes comparison with the 1975 list, the emphasis is on the continuity between the 1966 list and the earlier lists. The differences between the 1966 and 1975 lists take one of two general forms. The first group consists of substitutes for series in the 1966 list that have been found to behave somewhat better for the United States than the older series. Some series with mixed behavior (i.e., behavior that is different at peaks than it is at troughs) have been excluded. Many of the substitutes from the 1966 list to the 1975 list reflect the improvement in data, and this has been a major reason for substitutions on successive revisions of indicators since the beginning. Thus, for example, the substitution of net change in inventories-on-hand and on-order for the change in book value, manufacturing, and trade inventories is made partly because the new series includes a sensitive component,

the change in unfilled orders. Other changes are for similar reasons. All this suggests, of course, that the generalizations reached in the earlier discussion concerning changes in the series continue more or less as valid for the most recent list. The fact that it is still related to classical rather than growth cycles should be borne in mind.

The other major kind of change reflects the impact of inflation, and so parallels a change, previously considered, that we have made in this analysis of growth cycles in the wake of the 1973–75 classical recession, even though at the outset we did not adjust for inflation. In the 1975 revision, following our own practice, all series in nominal terms have been deflated so that all indicators are in physical volume or in real terms. This enables us to differentiate inflationary from real factors in assessing ongoing economic developments. Earlier this might not have mattered so much, but increasingly, as inflationary rates have leaped upward, price effects must be explicitly accounted for.

12. See Geoffrey H. Moore's comment at a London conference organized in 1967 to discuss the question, "Is the Business Cycle Obsolete?" Said Moore, "The question posed by this conference may be obsolete, the problem of booms and recessions is not." (Cf. Martin Bronfenbrenner, ed., *Is the Business Cycle Obsolete?* (New York: Wiley-Interscience, Division of John Wiley and Sons, 1969), p. 40.

13. Ilse Mintz, *Dating Postwar Business Cycles: Methods and their Application to Western Germany, 1950–67* (New York: NBER, Occasional Paper No. 107, 1969).

14. One of the results of this upsurge is that we have altered our technique for measuring both classical and growth cycles to include deflating almost all the indicators expressed in price units. Thus, the Department of Commerce has deflated all indicators (with a couple of exceptions) on the 1975 short list, and we have instituted comparable deflation procedures since beginning our original study of international growth cycles in 1973. The impact of this deflation is discussed methodologically in Chapter 2 and in terms of its economic impact later in the book.

15. Julius Shiskin, *Signals of Recession and Recovery* (New York: NBER, Occasional Paper No. 77, 1961), pp. 113–14.

16. Ilse Mintz, *Dating Postwar Business Cycles.*

17. Cf. Werner H. Strigel, *Trade Cycle Indicators Derived from Qualitative Data* (CIRET Study 19, 1972, and references cited therein).

18. Kathleen H. Moore, "The Comparative Performance of Economic Indicators in the United States, Canada, and Japan," *Western Economic Journal* IX, no. 4 (December 1971).

19. Ibid., p. 420.

20. Ibid., p. 425.

21. Desmond J. O'Dea, "The Cyclical Timing of Labor Market Indicators in Great Britain and the United States," *Explorations in Economic Research* 2, no. 1 (Winter 1975): pp. 18–53.

22. Desmond J. O'Dea, *Cyclical Indicators for the Postwar British Economy*, National Institute of Economic and Social Research (Cambridge: Cambridge University Press, 1975). NBER researchers have also used reference cycle frame-

works derived from specific series. For example, Hultgren used railway ton-miles (*American Transportation in Prosperity and Depression*, NBER, 1948); Mintz used world imports (*Cyclical Fluctuations in the Exports of the United States since 1879*, NBER, 1967), and Michaely used the balance of payments (*Balance of Payments Adjustment Policies: Japan, Germany and the Netherlands*, NBER, 1968) for this purpose.

23. O'Dea, *Cyclical Indicators for the Postwar British Economy*, p. 21.

24. OECD Economic Outlook, *Occasional Studies* (December 1973): 23–55.

25. Cf. John Dryden, "The OECD System of Leading Indicators" (Paper delivered at the International Atlantic Economic Conference, Paris, March 11–19, 1983).

26. That an international economic indicator system could be useful was clear at least from 1977 when the Department of Commerce published in mimeographed form the first version of the present study—a monograph entitled *Monitoring Business Cycles at Home and Abroad*, which concentrated on developing leading, roughly coincident, and lagging indicators for the United States, Canada, Japan, the United Kingdom, and West Germany.

Chapter 2

DEVELOPING GROWTH CYCLE CHRONOLOGIES FOR MARKET-ORIENTED COUNTRIES

METHODOLOGY

Before considering how we have adapted the traditional Burns–Mitchell methodology for measuring classical cycles to the demands of growth cycle analysis, it is well to review briefly the original Burns–Mitchell view of trend. Unlike older ways of undertaking cyclical analysis (the Harvard Method of Cyclical Analysis, for example), in which a rigid differentiation of trend, seasonal, cyclical, and irregular variation is postulated, the Burns–Mitchell method was to establish the cycle, including the trend, as the unit of experience under study. Burns and Mitchell, consequently, began by distinguishing "intercycle trend" from "intracycle trend." Only the former, which usually pushes the average level of one cycle to a higher level than that of the previous cycle, was to be eliminated via their averaging procedure. The impact of trend *within* a cycle, which usually prevents recessions from taking the economy down as far as the preceding or following expansion carries it up, was to be retained. As has recently been said of the result, " . . . the only trend forces measured in the traditional Burns–Mitchell business cycle analysis are the intercyclical ones, that is, a step function of changes in levels from cycle to cycle, not a continuous trend line."[1]

Clearly, the differentiation of trend from cycle would be easier to encompass were one's view restricted to linear trend. But this was never the Burns–Mitchell approach, and thus our adaptation of traditional techniques for measuring classical cycles to growth cycles has not required as radical a shift in the basic view of trend as might be thought. In this connection Haberler once commented that "the statistical decomposition of time series cycles and trend is an insoluble problem."[2] Rather than being an insoluble problem, we should perhaps say that there is no ideal solution. The solution chosen must, therefore, depend upon the objective being sought. In the case of growth cycle analysis the objective sought is a statistical one: to measure those long-run movements in economic time series that are statistically independent of the short-run movements and analyze the latter separately. Even Hicks, in his well-known trade cycle model, ultimately took a view of trend consistent with Haberler's. His model basically revolves around a long-run average rate of growth for the system. But, of course, *any* rate of change, no matter how irregular, could be smoothed out into some long-run average. Hicks, therefore, comments, "The actual course of autonomous investment cannot possibly be so very regular—it must experience autonomous fluctuations on its own."[3] He accordingly redraws his long-run trend in nonlinear fashion, not unlike the flexible trends we produced in our growth cycle analysis.

In dating growth cycles we have continued, as in the case of classical cycles, to base the selection of reference turns on computer-selected turns in a number of series, rather than on a single aggregate measure or index. We believe, moreover, that a growth cycle, like its classical predecessor, should have a duration of more than one year from peak to peak or from trough to trough. Cycle phases, in general, must be at least six months (or two quarters) in length. In terms of amplitude, we have followed the general rule that cycles should never be divisible into shorter periods with amplitude as large as that of the selected cycle.

When we began our present work on growth cycle analysis in 1973, we took advantage of the earlier work on postwar West Germany done by Ilse Mintz.[4] Mintz relied exclusively on the computer for processing her series and ultimately for determining the turning points. Similarly, an essential part of our study has been to subject all the data to computer analysis. However, we have reviewed all the computer-selected turns visually and occasionally eliminated, altered, or added turns to those selected by the computer.[5] Throughout this study we have used an asterisk in our charts to identify computer-selected turns. When we have rejected the computer turn we circle the asterisk, and when we have selected a different turning point we place the asterisk inside a square. As will be noted, the percentage of alterations is, however, small.

Our work in growth cycle analysis involved both turning point selection and trend adjustment. The turning point selection program was developed by Gerhard Bry and Charlotte Boschan[6] to select turning points in classical cycles according to the specifications inherent in the Burns-Mitchell approach. This program is capable of selecting turns in either original, seasonally adjusted time series or in trend-adjusted time series, applying the same criteria to both.

The Bry-Boschan program identified turning points in a preliminary fashion from time series smoothed by a twelve-month moving average in which only extreme observations have been replaced. Employing Spencer curves as a further aid in eliminating erratic movements in the data, the program also utilizes the months for cyclical dominance technique to smooth the data and thus identify the highest (and lowest) value within plus or minus five months of the turns in the Spencer curve. With this as a basis, the actual turns are then selected from the original, unsmoothed monthly or quarterly data. Turns are then eliminated which occur within six months of the beginning or end of the time series, which identify cycles of less than fifteen months, or which identify phases lasting less than five months. Unfortunately, the program does not use an explicit measure of the amplitude of change as a turning point determinant—the smoothing procedures do this only indirectly. This explains a large number of the judgmental divergences from the turns selected by the computer.

In adapting the computer program for dating classical cycles to the task of producing a growth cycle chronology, we have built on the technique of trend adjustment developed by Mintz.[7] Trend-adjusted or growth cycles are sometimes referred to as "deviation cycles" because they are measured by calculating the deviations of the monthly observations from the trend. Our technique for measuring the long-run trend involves a two-stage procedure. The first stage is to subject the data to a seventy-five-month moving average, as Mintz did. This seventy-five-month period is long enough to smooth away virtually all of the irregular variation and most of the cyclical variation, since growth cycles rarely exceed six years in duration. Nevertheless, we found that there was still some tendency for the seventy-five-month moving average to exhibit undue flexibility in the resulting trend rate of growth. That is, we found the trend rate to be noticeably affected by the shorter cycles in the data.

We therefore have refined the results by adding a step to the determination of the trend from which the deviations producing the growth cycle turning points are measured. The basic requirement was to devise a trend-fitting technique that would work on series of varying lengths containing shorter cyclical movements of varying duration, and that could be brought up to date without extensive revision of earlier results.

We found that the "Phase-Average Trend" technique (PAT) provided the best results. After smoothing the seasonally adjusted data with a seventy-five-month moving average, we calculate the deviations of the seasonally adjusted, individual observations from the trend.[8] This computation produces a rough "deviation cycle" from which it is possible to pick tentative peaks and troughs according to the procedures already specified and so arrive at a first approximation of a growth cycle chronology for the series. The initial cycle phases so measured are often of widely varying lengths. We then break this chronology into phases—that is, expansion, contraction, expansion and so forth—and compute a three-phase moving average of the original, seasonally adjusted data, interpolating monthly between the centered values of these averages. This procedure produces a final estimate of trend that is more satisfactory than the original, because the three-phase moving average does a more complete job of separating cyclical influences from the underlying trend.[9] We then use this refined and flexible trend estimate to calculate the deviations of the original, seasonally adjusted data from this final trend.

The deviation cycles so calculated represent periods when the rate of growth in the series was above the long-run trend rate, alternating with periods when it was below the trend rate. The trend-fitting method yields relatively stable trend rates of growth, unassociated with the shorter cycles, which are our primary concern. This is often not the case when the trend is represented by a moving average of any fixed length, including the seventy-five-month period used for the initial determination of phases. Since trend rates of growth are useful data for other purposes, such as studies of long-run growth, this is a considerable advantage. Finally, unlike most trend-fitting procedures using regression techniques, the method provides for updating the trend without extensive revision of past observations, other than those occasioned by revisions of the recent cycle dates. For an example of the fitted trend, the trend-adjusted data, and the turning points in U.S. industrial production, together with the U.S. growth cycle reference chronology, see Figures 2–1 and 2–2.

These graphs make several important aspects of our method visually apparent. Figure 2–1 suggests that cycles in the original data, when the economy under examination has been experiencing rapid growth, may well be difficult to observe clearly. How much sharper and clearer the underlying cycles are when viewed from a growth

How to Read Figure 2-1 and Figure 2-2.

Peak (P) and trough (T) of growth cycle
for the country, as designated by NBER.

Month in which peak or trough of growth
cycle occurs. For year, see scale at
bottom.

Vertical short-dash lines are peaks (P)
of growth cycle.

Vertical long-dash or solid lines are
troughs (T) of growth cycle.

Computer-selected turning point that
has been eliminated judgmentally.

Judgmentally selected turning point.

Ratio to trend of seasonally adjusted
data. Trend level equals 100. For data
with plus and minus values scale shows
deviations from trend in original units.

Monthly or quarterly seasonally adjusted,
trend-adjusted data.

Computer-selected turning point.

All scales are arithmetic.

Figure 2-1. U.S. Index of Industrial Production: Original Data and Trend.

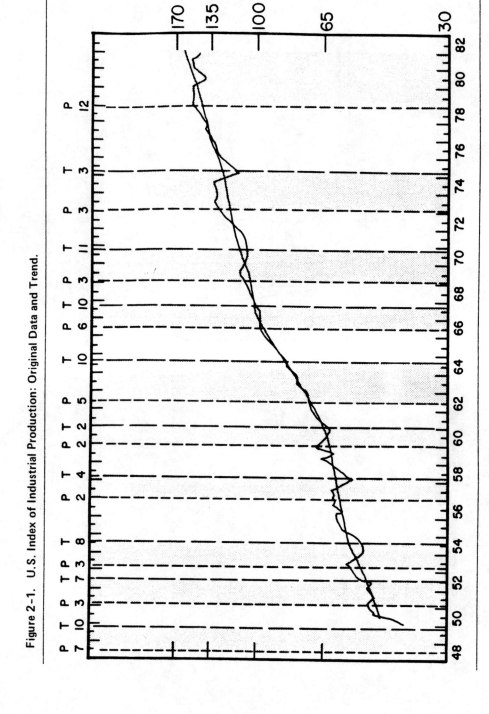

Figure 2-2. U.S. Index of Industrial Production: Deviations from Trend.

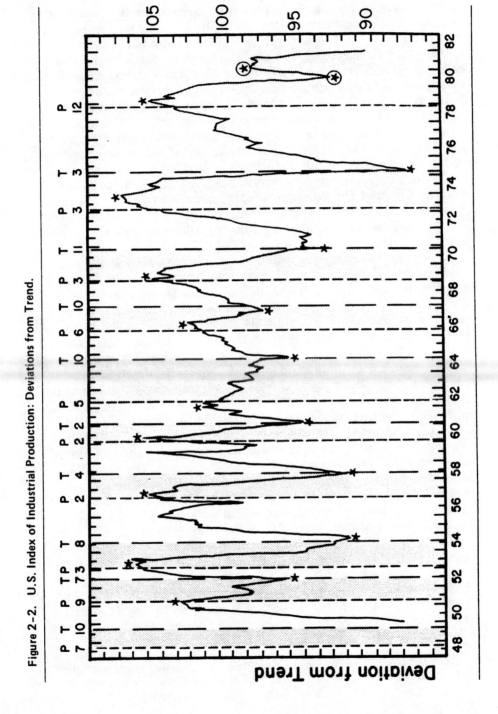

cycle perspective (i.e., as deviations from a rising trend) is made evident by comparing Figure 2-2 with Figure 2-1. We may note, too, that the selection of growth cycle turning points is carried out, as stated earlier, under rules that conform to those for selecting classical cycle turning points, and so all possible peaks and troughs are not always selected. Sometimes the amplitude and duration are both inappropriately small, as, for example, is the case in the small upturn visible in Figure 2-2 during the contraction from 1950 to 1952. Sometimes the amplitude is acceptable but the duration is too short to justify including the turns in a chronology of cycles, as is the case in the same chart for the disturbance in 1959, where a steel strike accounted for most of the short, sharp contraction. In general, though, the rules for choosing turning points of growth cycles (i.e., from detrended series) reflect the original rules developed by Burns and Mitchell as incorporated into the Bry-Boschan program previously described.

It should perhaps be added that the basic data underlying this study have in most instances been obtained from official government agencies (usually the central statistical office in each country). In certain cases data were obtained from private or semiofficial agencies. Where data were not available in seasonally adjusted form,[10] these adjustments were made. Summary information on data sources is given in Appendix 2A.[11]

The technical difficulties involved in adapting the classical cycle computer program at the NBER to the requirements of the growth cycle were complex, but we feel were ultimately adequately dealt with. The resulting turning points in individual series were, as noted previously, reviewed visually and in certain cases amended. These turning points in the roughly coincident series were then employed to select reference chronologies for each country. These chronologies, therefore, represent periods when aggregate economic activity was rising more rapidly or less rapidly than its long-run trend. The classical and growth cycles correspond in many respects, but not entirely. For example, since 1948 there were three growth cycle downswings in the United States that do not show up as classical recessions. They were periods of reduced, but not negative, growth. In 1980-81 there was a classical cycle expansion but no growth cycle expansion. In addition, as we have considered in some detail in Chapter 1, where classical cycles and growth cycles overlap, growth cycle phases will often be dated somewhat differently. As Mintz has stated:

> ... In those instances in which an absolute decline in activity has occurred, [growth cycle dates] will tend to differ from dates selected on the basis of

the classical business cycle concept. Downturns will come earlier, upturns later in trend-adjusted series with upward trends than in unadjusted series. Therefore upswings will be shorter and downswings longer than in classical cycles.[12]

This systematic difference in the choice of turning points in individual time series will, of course, show up as well in the reference turns based on them. An example is provided in Table 2-1.

In selecting final reference dates, we utilize three summary measures as aids in the selection process. The first is the composite index developed originally by Julius Shiskin and now widely used to summarize the behavior of a number of series that are homogeneous with respect to some specific, cyclical characteristic. In this case, of course, the relevant characteristic is rough coincidence with the business cycle, and composite indexes of roughly coincident indicators were constructed for each country. In order to construct a composite index, month-to-month percent changes are calculated for each individual time series to be included. These rates of change for each series are then standardized so that their average, without regard to sign, over a specified period (e.g., 1955–70) is unity. The standardized month-to-month changes for all the series to be included in a composite index are averaged for each month, the resulting averages are again standardized, and then cumulated to form an index with a certain base period (say 1967) set equal to 100.[13]

These indexes have been constructed from seasonally adjusted data without adjustment for trend; the trend-adjustment procedure is applied to the index as a final step. This method has the advantage of yielding indexes with and without trend, as well as the trend line for the index itself, all of which may be useful in identifying classical turning points, as for the period 1973–75. Also, as has already been noted, the trend for the most recent period is based on extrapolation, and so it is useful to know exactly what that trend is.[14]

When we began our work in 1973, we did not attempt to allow systematically for the effect of inflation on series expressed in current prices. In some cases deflated data were not readily available, and we believed that the trend-adjustment procedure would remove much of the impact of inflation. But inflation soon accelerated sharply in the countries with which we were concerned, and we therefore adopted the practice of deflating series expressed in current prices. As was noted in Chapter 1, there are but two exceptions to this rule among the leading indicators: we have not attempted to deflate stock price or raw materials price indexes. Also, among the lagging indicators, we have not attempted to adjust interest rates for inflation.

Table 2-1. United States, Comparison of Growth Cycle and Classical Cycle Turning Points, 1948–1982.

	Peaks			Troughs		
	Growth Cycles[a]	Classical Cycles	Lead (–) or Lag (+), in Months	Growth Cycles[a]	Classical Cycles	Lead (–) or Lag (+), in Months
	7/48	11/48	–4	10/49	10/49	0
	3/51	—	—	7/52	—	—
	3/53	7/53	–4	8/54	5/54	+3
	2/57	8/57	–6	4/58	4/58	0
	2/60	4/60	–2	2/61	2/61	0
	5/62	—	—	10/64	—	—
	6/66	—	—	10/67	—	—
	3/69	12/69	–9	11/70	11/70	0
	3/73	11/73	–8	3/75	3/75	0
	12/78	1/80	–13	—	7/80	—
	—	7/81	—	12/82	11/82	+1
Mean Timing at Peaks						
at Troughs						
at Peaks and Troughs			–7	–3		0
Median Timing at Peaks			–6			
at Troughs						
at Peaks and Troughs				–1		0

Note:

a. The growth cycle concept used here and elsewhere in this volume corresponds to what Mintz termed "deflated," namely, all series used in determining the dates were expressed either in physical units or in constant prices.

Source: Growth Cycles: Ilse Mintz, "Dating United States Growth Cycles," in NBER, *Explorations in Economic Research 1*, no. 1: 60, as revised and updated at the Center for International Business Cycle Research. Classical Cycles: National Bureau of Economic Research.

Finally, we apply a *reverse* trend-adjustment procedure to each of the indexes. Since trend rates of growth vary from one series to another, and since the particular series available vary to some extent from one country to another, the trend rates of growth in the composite indexes also vary to some extent. This could conceivably reduce the comparability of the results from one country to another. It also means that the trend rate of growth in the leading, coincident, and lagging indexes might differ. Julius Shiskin devised a method of allowing for this possibility by adjusting the original trend in each index so that it conforms to some target trend, for example, that in the coincident index.

We have utilized this basic approach by setting the trends in our indexes equal to the long-run rate of growth in real GNP during a specified period.[15] These real growth rates of course vary from country to country.

We also use a second summary measure—cumulative diffusion indexes—in selecting reference dates. Diffusion indexes represent a somewhat different method of summarizing the cyclical behavior of a group of time series. Essentially, as its name suggests, a diffusion index shows how widely diffused among its components a movement may be at any one time. A diffusion index of roughly coincident indicators, for example, shows what percentage of these indicators are rising in each month covered.

The basic notion of diffusion has been a part of the Burns–Mitchell view of economic fluctuations from the start. Along with duration and amplitude of fluctuations in any particular sector of the economy, the question of how widely diffused any particular cyclical manifestation may be has always constituted a major consideration in identifying business cycles. In *Measuring Business Cycles* Burns and Mitchell summarized a section on the "Diffusion of Specific Cycles" by noting: "Our hypothesis . . . is that a period in which expansions are concentrated is succeeded by another in which cyclical peaks are concentrated, by another in which contractions are concentrated, by another in which cyclical troughs are concentrated; and this round of events is repeated again and again."[16] This basic notion of diffusion implies that turning points will cluster in what Burns and Mitchell called turning zones. Diffusion can also be applied to any group of time series, and so aids in identifying turning points in industries, sectors, or an entire economy.

Historical diffusion indexes are based on cyclical turning points in time series determined by the methods outlined above. A particularly valuable characteristic of diffusion indexes is that their turning points typically lead the turning points in the aggregate of the series whose behavior they are designed to summarize. On the other hand, when diffusion indexes are cumulated through time (i.e., the net percent expanding in each month is added to the sum of all preceding months), the turning points in the cumulated index represent a type of summary of the turning points in the individual component series. Such indexes have been used in determining the growth cycle chronologies reported below.

We also use a third summary statistic, which consists of computing for each turning point the median date of each cluster of peaks (or of troughs) in all the roughly coincident indicators. Together, the median dates, the turns in cumulated diffusion indexes, and the turns in composite indexes have all been used in determining the growth cycle reference dates, along with a careful study of the individual indicators of aggregate activity, including gross national product, industrial production, nonfarm employment, unemployment, personal income, and volume of trade.

It should be underscored that this methodology reflects a number of long-standing convictions resulting from the many years of research on cyclical activity begun by Burns and Mitchell. One of these convictions is that the type of fluctuation being analyzed is best viewed as a pattern of instability reflecting the interaction of a number of significant economic activities. No single measure, no matter how broad, can be relied upon to represent accurately the most balanced judgment concerning when a given economy has moved from expansion to contraction, or contraction to expansion. When turning points in the several measures of aggregate economic activity are closely concentrated in a short span of time, of course, the turning point selection process is relatively easy. In spite of the well-known tendency of these turning points to cluster, it is precisely *because* there will be times when the "turning zones" are extended that reliance on any single measure is inadvisable. Some countries have utilized the index of industrial production as a proxy for all the measures of aggregate economic activity our methods are designed to encompass. The reader will note a number of instances in the growth cycle chronologies discussed below when the turn in the chronology diverges from the turn in the production index, which means that other evidence did not support the latter. In many advanced market-oriented economies the service industries are the fastest-growing sector and industrial production (mining and manufacturing) is consequently a decreasing percentage of aggregate economic activity.

As we shall see, the Organization for Economic Cooperation and Development, which has recently taken an interest in developing reference chronologies for its twenty-four member countries, has chosen "output—broadly defined" as the appropriate measure to use. This presumably encompasses GNP as well as industrial production, but ignores other dimensions such as employment, income, and volume of trade. We shall return to this question in a later discussion.

TEN GROWTH CYCLE CHRONOLOGIES

For many years following World War II real growth rates were high in many of the major industrialized market-oriented economies. Increasingly, too, inflation appeared to have become an endemic economic problem. As a result of both tendencies, a system for monitoring instability from the perspective implicit in the growth cycle concept became more and more appealing. The period 1973–1975 reveals that the classical cycle is by no means dead. Accordingly, there is much to be said for maintaining the kind of classical cycle monitoring system that Burns and Mitchell inaugurated in the United States. The National Bureau of Economic Research has continued its periodic review of economic activity with a view to updating the classical chronology. This chronology is used in the monthly publication of the Department of Commerce, *Business Conditions Digest*. The Commerce Department has also considered carefully the question of growth cycles, and at some future time they may begin monitoring these cycles, along with classical cycles. The primary drawback to this procedure, of course, is that the use of two different business chronologies might be confusing to the public and considerably more cumbersome to work with.

In other countries cyclical indicator systems patterned after the Burns–Mitchell approach have been developed in recent years. Canada and Japan have had such systems since the 1950s, and the United Kingdom inaugurated its system in 1974. Britain was the first to utilize the growth cycle approach reported in this study. Similarly, the international organizations now interested in monitoring cycles—principally the OECD and the EEC—have chosen to concentrate on growth cycles. A major advantage in growth cycle analysis, of course, if one is to opt for only one system, is that all classical recessions will show up in a growth cycle chronology as periods of negative growth, whereas growth cycle slowdowns may not show up at all in a classical cycle chronology. In any case, the kind of comparison of growth cycle turns with classical cycle turns presented for the United States in Table 2-1 cannot at this time be repeated for most other countries.[17] We therefore present only growth cycle chronologies for these countries. On the other hand, the cycle chronologies for the pre-World War II era growing out of the work of Burns and Mitchell are for classical cycles, and we have not yet ventured to produce growth cycle chronologies for this period, either in the United States or elsewhere.

Table 2-2 shows how pervasive growth cycles have been in ten major market-oriented economies. There is also a good deal of evidence to suggest that growth cycles are typical now in many other economies. The chronologies of Table 2-2 can perhaps be more easily reviewed by examining them in the schematic form of Figure 2-3. A major question raised by any analysis of growth cycles, of course, is whether they represent simply a new manifestation of the interrelationships typically reflected in the pre–World War II period by classical cycles, or whether they describe a significantly different phenomenon.[18] Ideally, this question could best be approached by careful comparison of growth cycle and classical cycle chronologies for a large number of countries, but, as noted above, this has not been attempted. Approximations could be achieved by comparing growth cycle and classical cycle turning points in important aggregate indicators. Comparisons of this nature were made by Burns and Mitchell in their 1946 volume, *Measuring Business Cycles*, and they revealed differences similar to those shown in Table 2-1.

Growth cycles and classical cycles are, of course, merely different ways of looking at the overall phenomenon of instability. Sometimes the interactive forces making for business cycles are severe enough to produce fluctuations in the level of activity and sometimes they are less severe, producing only fluctuations in the rate of change. Analyzing both growth cycles and classical cycles is, therefore, a way to organize the record of economic instability so as to learn more about how instability affects the economy. The introduction of trend-adjustment procedures in the examination of growth cycles is an integral part of this process.

A larger number of cycles usually emerges when growth cycle techniques are employed than when classical cycle techniques are used, because the former represent a more sensitive measure of instability.[19] Classical cycles and growth cycles usually occur at approximately the same time, allowing for the systematic differences in turning points previously commented on. All this suggests, of course, that it is probably safe to conclude that growth cycles are simply the most commonly encountered form currently taken by the instability long visible in market-oriented economies. But the growth cycle notion itself—the more or less cyclical variations in growth rates—has been discussed in NBER work and elsewhere for many years.[20] More rapid real growth, various changes in economic institutions that mitigate recessions, and greater attention to countercyclical policy

Table 2-2. Growth Cycle Chronologies for Ten Market-Oriented Economies.

Date of Turn and Interval, in Months, from Preceding Turn

United States		Belgium		Canada		France	
Peak	Trough	Peak	Trough	Peak	Trough	Peak	Trough
7/48							
	10/49 (15)						
3/51 (17)				4/51			
	7/52 (16)				12/51 (8)		
3/53 (8)				3/53 (15)			
	8/54 (17)				10/54 (19)		
				11/56 (25)			
2/57 (30)						8/57	
	4/58 (14)				8/58 (21)		
							8/59 (24)
				10/59 (14)			
2/60 (22)							
	2/61 (12)				3/61 (17)		
				3/62 (12)			
5/62 (15)							
					5/63 (14)		
						2/64 (54)	
	10/64 (29)	10/64					
							6/65 (16)
				3/66 (34)			
6/66 (20)						6/66 (12)	
	10/67 (16)						
					2/68 (23)		
							5/68 (23)
			7/68 (45)				
				2/69 (12)			
3/69 (17)							
						11/69 (18)	
		9/70 (26)					
	11/70 (20)				12/70 (22)		
			7/71 (10)				
							11/71 (24)
3/73 (28)							
				2/74 (40)			
						5/74 (30)	
		7/74 (36)					
	3/75 (12)						
							6/75 (13)
			10/75 (15)		10/75 (20)		
				5/76 (7)			
					7/77 (14)		
12/78 (45)							
		6/79 (44)					
						8/79 (50)	
				9/79 (26)			
					6/80 (9)		

Average Durations, in Months

	United States		Belgium		Canada		France	
Expansions	22		35		21		33	
Contractions		17		23		17		20
Cycles (P to P)	40		59		42		53	
Cycles (T to T)	38		44		38		48	

(*Table 2-2. continued overleaf*)

Table 2-2. continued

	United States		Italy		Japan		Netherlands	
	Peak	Trough	Peak	Trough	Peak	Trough	Peak	Trough
	7/48							
	3/51 (17)	10/49 (15)					7/50	
	3/53 (8)	7/52 (16)			12/53			6/52 (23)
	2/57 (30)	8/54 (17)	10/56		5/57 (23)	6/55 (18)	10/56 (52)	
	2/60 (22)	4/58 (14)		7/59 (33)		1/59 (20)		5/58 (19)
	5/62 (15)	2/61 (12)	9/63 (50)		1/62 (36)	1/63 (12)	3/61 (34)	
	6/66 (20)	10/64 (29)		3/65 (18)	7/64 (18)	2/66 (19)	11/65 (33)	2/63 (23)
	3/69 (17)	10/67 (16)	8/69 (53)		6/70 (52)	1/72 (19)	11/70 (39)	8/67 (21)
	3/73 (28)	11/70 (20)	4/74 (19)	9/72 (37)	11/73 (22)	3/75 (16)	8/74 (24)	8/72 (21)
		3/75 (12)	12/76 (19)	5/75 (13)			9/76 (14)	7/75 (11)
	12/78 (45)		2/80 (28)	10/77 (10)	2/80[a] (59)		12/79 (25)	11/77 (14)

Average Durations, in Months

	United States	Italy	Japan	Netherlands
Expansions	22	34	25	32
Contractions	17	22	17	19
Cycles (P to P)	40	56	43	52
Cycles (T to T)	38	49	47	51

Table 2-2. continued

United States Peak	United States Trough	Sweden Peak	Sweden Trough	United Kingdom Peak	United Kingdom Trough	West Germany Peak	West Germany Trough
7/48	10/49 (15)						
3/51 (17)	7/52 (16)			3/51	8/52 (17)	2/51	2/54 (36)
3/53 (8)	8/54 (17)						
2/57 (30)	4/58 (14)			12/55 (40)	11/58 (35)	10/55 (20)	4/59 (42)
2/60 (22)	2/61 (12)			3/61 (28)	2/63 (23)	2/61 (22)	2/63 (24)
5/62 (15)	10/64 (29)						
6/66 (20)	10/67 (16)	2/65	7/67 (29)	2/66 (36)	8/67 (18)	5/65 (27)	8/67 (27)
3/69 (17)	11/70 (20)	7/70 (36)	7/72 (24)	6/69 (22)	2/72 (32)	5/70 (33)	12/71 (19)
3/73 (28)	3/75 (12)	6/74 (23)	7/78 (49)	6/73 (16)	8/75 (26)	8/73 (20)	5/75 (21)
12/78 (45)				6/79 (46)		2/80 (57)	

Average Durations, in Months

	United States	Sweden	United Kingdom	West Germany
Expansions	22	30	31	30
Contractions	17	34	25	28
Cycles (P to P)	40	56	57	58
Cycles (T to T)	38	66	55	51

Note:

a. Based on composite index.

Source: Center for International Business Cycle Research.

Figure 2-3.   Growth Cycle Chronologies for Ten Countries, and Leads (-) and Lags (+) vis-à-vis the U.S. Chronology.

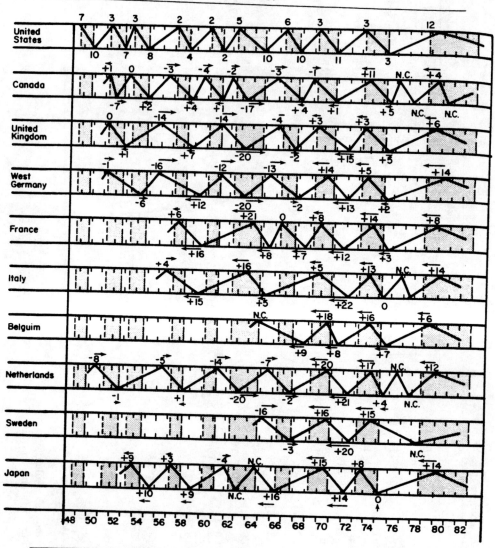

Notes:

An arrow pointing right (→) indicates a lead relative to the U.S. turn equal to the number of months shown. An arrow pointing to the left (←) indicates a lag relative to the U.S. turn equal to the number of months shown.

Figure 2–4. Coincident Composite Indexes, Deviations from Trend for Ten Countries.

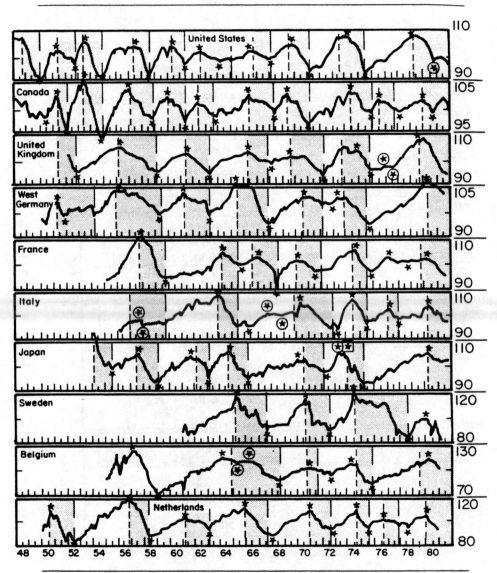

Figure 2–5.   Coincident Composite Indexes, Six-month Smoothed Rates of Change for Ten Countries.

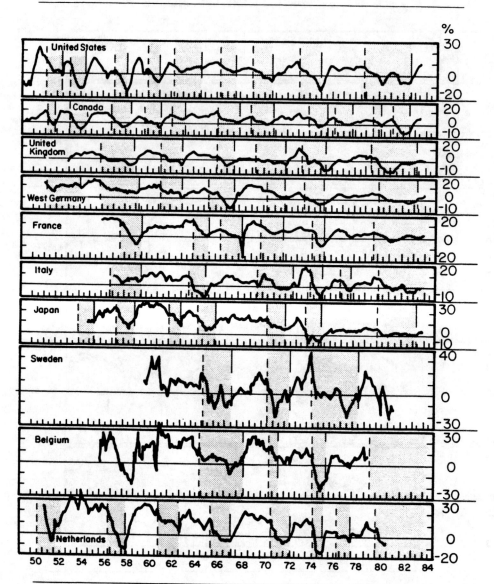

can reduce declines that might earlier have been severe absolute declines compared to the milder disturbances we now call growth recessions. The 1973–75 experience, on the other hand, proved that classical recessions are still a real, if less frequent, threat as well.

The growth cycle chronologies may be visualized in another way in Figure 2–4, which shows the trend-adjusted coincident composite indexes for the ten major countries we have analyzed. Figure 2–5 displays the rate of change in these indexes. We shall return to a consideration of the evidence revealed in these figures in Chapter 6, which is concerned with the existence of a "world cycle." At this point, however, we simply conclude that the growth cycle chronologies give an encouraging, affirmative answer to at least the opening questions our project posed: Is the notion of the growth cycle a useful approach to the study of cyclical instability in a number of market-oriented economies, and can growth cycle chronologies be established in a comparable manner for a number of market-oriented economies? Clearly it is and they can.[21]

OTHER GROWTH CYCLE CHRONOLOGIES

In the period since 1973, when we began the International Economic Indicators project, a number of other chronologies have appeared. While there are disadvantages to having more than one chronology for a single country, one of the by-products that we hoped would result from the project was a general upsurge of interest in growth cycle analysis in other countries. At the time the project was launched there were few chronologies for classical business cycles in the postwar period outside the United States and only one for growth cycles (Mintz's German chronology). Classical chronologies had been produced for Austria, Canada, Japan, Italy, and the United Kingdom,[22] but these studies did not employ a common methodology. In the United Kingdom the decision of the Central Statistical Office to develop a growth cycle chronology of its own was a direct result of its involvement in the early stages of the IEI project.[23]

Some of the characteristics of emergent growth cycle chronologies may be seen by using the United Kingdom experience as an illustration. Table 2–3 shows the current CSO chronology, as well as its earlier chronology. We have also included the OECD chronology, which is based on "output—broadly defined." In principle this chronology ought to resemble the official national chronology. Except for the latest peak it does not. Included in the table as well is the original chronology produced for the present work on growth cycles (labeled Klein) and the chronology devised by Desmond O'Dea.

Table 2-3.   United Kingdom, Six Alternative Growth Cycle Chronologies.

Dates of Peaks (P) and Trough (T), and Lead (–) or Lag (+), in Months, from CIBCR Chronology

CIBCR 1981		CSO[a] 1981		OECD[b] 1981	
P	T	P	T	P	T
3/51					
	3/52				
12/55					
	11/58		12/58 (+1)		12/58 (+1)
3/61		4/60 (–11)		4/60 (–11)	
	2/63		1/63 (–1)		1/63 (–1)
2/66		12/64 (–14)		12/64 (–14)	
	8/67		3/67 (–5)		3/67 (–5)
6/69		5/69 (–1)		5/69 (–1)	
	2/72		2/72 (0)		2/72 (0)
6/73		5/73 (–1)		5/73 (–1)	
	11/75		8/75 (–3)		8/75 (–3)
6/79		5/79 (–1)		8/78 (–10)	

Average Timing at:

	P	T	P + T
CSO	–6	–2	–4
OECD	–7	–2	–4

Sources:

a. Central Statistical Office, 1981. Report on Reference Cycle Chronologies and Composite.

b. OECD, Paris, Unpublished Cyclical Indicators, Working Party on Cyclical Analysis and Leading Indicators, Paris (March 1981).

c. Central Statistical Office, "Cyclical Indicators for the United Kingdom," *Economic Trends*, no. 257 (March 1975): 98.

d. Philip A. Klein, "Postwar Growth Cycles in the United Kingdom, An Interim Report," NBER, *Explorations in Economic Research* 3, no. 1 (Winter 1976): 110.

e. D. J. O'Dea, *Cyclical Indicators for the Postwar British Economy*, National Institute of Economic and Social Research (Cambridge: Cambridge University Press, Occasional Paper XXVIII, 1975), Table 7.2, p. 39.

The table suggests broad agreement concerning the number of growth cycles experienced by the British economy and relatively high correspondence in the dating of growth cycle peaks and troughs. This correspondence is notable because while all the more recent chronologies were produced by subjecting the underlying data to some variant of the Bry–Boschan turning point program as adapted to growth cycles, they do not all include the same time series. Moreover, we make it a practice to review the turns judgmentally, and this practice may not be followed consistently elsewhere. Nevertheless,

Table 2-3. continued

Dates of Peaks (P) and Trough (T), and Lead (−) or Lag (+),
in Months, from CIBCR Chronology (continued)

CSO[c] 1974		Klein[d] 1976		O'Dea[e] 1975	
P	T	P	T	P	T
		2/51 (−1)		2/51 (−1)	
			10/52 (+2)		7/52 (−11)
		12/55 (0)		12/55 (0)	
	10/58 (−1)		11/58 (0)		9/58 (−2)
3/60 (−12)		11/60 (−4)		7/60 (−8)	
	10/62 (−4)		2/63 (0)		1/63 (−1)
12/64 (−14)		8/65 (−6)		1/65 (−13)	
	12/66 (−8)		8/62 (0)		8/67 (0)
5/69 (−1)		12/68 (−6)		3/69 (−3)	
	3/71 (−11)		2/72 (0)		2/72 (0)
7/73 (+1)					

−6		−3		−5	
	−6		0		−1
−6		−2		−3	

the consilience among the lists of growth cycles and their dating suggests that the subjective element is minimal. It is noteworthy, however, that all of the chronologies exhibit a tendency for the peaks and troughs to precede those established by the CIBCR. A partial explanation may be that our chronology places more weight on employment and unemployment statistics, which display some tendency to lag (see Chapters 4 and 5).

Virtually all the chronologies produced in recent years have been based on the growth cycle concept. Major exceptions include the classical chronologies currently used in the United States, Canada, and Japan. In order to establish empirical regularities, it is necessary to compare the evidence contained within these two approaches to describing business cycles. According to theory, growth peaks were expected to lead classical peaks, and the growth troughs were expected either to coincide with or follow the classical troughs (in economies with rising trends). Our review of the U.S. evidence (Table 2-1) corroborated these expectations. Table 2-4 suggests that the evidence for Canada and Japan is in line with these theoretical expectations as well. Growth peaks precede classical peaks quite con-

Table 2-4. Japan and Canada, Comparison of Growth Cycles and Classical Cycles, 1954-1971.

	Japan						Canada					
	Classical Cycles[a] (1)		Growth Cycles[b] (2)		Lead (−) or Lag (+) in Months (2) vs. (1) (3)		Classical Cycles[c] (4)		Growth Cycles[d] (5)		Lead (−) or Lag (+) in Months (5) vs. (4) (6)	
	P	T	P	T	P	T	P	T	P	T	P	T
	6/51	10/51					5/51	12/51	4/51	12/51	−1	0
	1/54	11/54	12/53	6/55	−1	+7	5/53	6/54	3/53	10/54	−2	+4
	6/57	6/58	5/57	1/59	−1	+7	1/57	1/58	11/56	8/58	−2	+7
	12/61	10/62	1/62	1/63	+1	+3	3/60	1/61	10/59	3/61	−5	+2
	10/64	10/65	7/64	2/66	−3	+4			3/62	5/63		
	7/70	12/71	6/70	1/72	−1	+1			3/66	2/68		
	11/73	3/75	11/73	3/75	0	0			2/69	12/70		
			2/80				5/74	3/75	2/74	10/75	−3	+7
									5/76	7/77		
							10/79	6/80	9/79		−1	0
							6/81					

Average Timing at:

P	-1	-2
T	+4	+3
P + T	+1	0

Sources:

a. Japanese Economic Planning Agency. Based upon a number of roughly coincident indicators selected and analyzed by the EPA. The data are not adjusted for long-run trend.

b. Center for International Business Cycle Research, Columbia University.

c. Philip Cross, "The Business Cycle in Canada 1950–1981," *Current Economic Analysis* (March 1982), Statistics Canada Catalogue 13–004E.

d. CIBCR, Columbia University.

sistently but not by very long intervals. At troughs the growth turns follow the classical turns quite regularly in both countries.[24]

It is interesting to note that the placement of turning points for growth cycles in the alternative chronologies exhibits larger deviations from the peaks emerging through our method than is the case at troughs. This suggests that dating of growth cycle peaks may be more difficult—that is, more uncertain—than dating growth cycle troughs.

Different methods may obviously produce different turning points, but a most important factor in rendering useful the comparison of growth cycles in a number of countries is that turning points be selected by means of a common methodology. There is ground for the view that economic experts in a particular country are in the best position to select cyclical turning points because they are most intimately acquainted with economic developments in that country, and can pinpoint genuine cyclical changes. It is, of course, precisely for this reason that we have urged that basic data should be acquired from official government agencies wherever possible, and that our analysis should be carried out with the closest possible cooperation from experts in each country. This is surely the most promising path to accurate results and productive work in this field.

From the outset of the discussions at the OECD, we have also urged the adoption of a standard method so that results would make international comparisons meaningful. This point has generally been accepted, and most of the chronologies have been based on some variant of the Bry-Boschan method. There is, however, no uniformity in the decision to review evidence judgmentally or not. Some countries do and others apparently do not.

Even more contentious has been the question of what measure of economic activity the chronology should pertain to. We have taken the position—initiated by Burns and Mitchell for classical cycle analysis—that a number of measures of aggregate economic activity—including output, employment, income and trade—should be used. The OECD working party, on the other hand, concluded that growth cycle chronologies ought to pertain to "output—broadly defined." Because each country has been left to define this term for itself, the number and types of indicators included in the evidence used to derive growth cycle chronologies have varied.

One of the avenues of greatest productive potential emerging from the development of growth cycle chronologies for a number of countries is the possibility of furthering our understanding of the transmission mechanisms involved in the international spread of economic instability and inflation. Progress in this area will continue to be hindered if experts in different countries do not utilize comparable methodologies, if no consideration is given to basing chronologies on comparable time series, or if different experts in a given country utilize different chronologies. We maintain the hope, however, that, as work on growth cycles proceeds, common understandings will be possible concerning the measurement of growth cycles and a consensus will emerge on the dating of turning points. The long history of business cycle chronologies in the United States, which in recent years has converged on the one established by the National Bureau, shows that these are not unreasonable objectives. Progress can be furthered through the cooperative endeavors of the CIBCR, the OECD, the EEC, and the national statistical agencies in the countries here under review.

ASSESSING THE IEI GROWTH CHRONOLOGIES

The Burns–Mitchell definition of business cycles pointed to measures of aggregate economic activity but did not specify what measures. One of the major pieces of U.S. legislation bearing on macro-economic policy was the Employment Act of 1946, which specifically mentioned employment, output, and purchasing power as the appropriate dimensions of activity to be considered. The Humphrey-Hawkins Act of 1979 called for a similar perspective on economic activity.

The coincident indicators that we have used for the United States include three measures in constant dollars (gross national product, personal income, and manufacturing and trade sales), and three expressed in physical units (industrial production, employees on nonfarm payrolls, and the total unemployment rate). Thus, the major dimensions of aggregate economic activity are covered. As will be clear in the next chapter, we were able to find reasonable equivalents to most of these measures for each of the foreign economies involved. (See Appendix 2C for the list of indicators utilized for each country.)

We have already alluded to some of the difficulties encountered in settling on a common list of indicators. In many countries employment, for example, is regarded as a lagging indicator, and during 1982 the U.S. unemployment rate became the country's best known lagging indicator.[25] We have also already noted that the OECD decided not only to use "output—broadly defined" as the appropriate aggregate to measure, but to leave the precise definition of this term to each country. Equivalent measures of aggregate activity are, of course, not always available. In our own work we have aimed for comparability in the series chosen in order to facilitate the international comparative analyses considered later in this book. In the end, much is to be said for developing two sets of cyclical indicators: one designed to maximize international comparability by stressing commonality in the series included and the analytical techniques employed; the other designed to develop the most cyclically sensitive set of indicators country by country. The discussion in this volume, particularly in Chapter 1, leads to the expectation that these two approaches would nonetheless produce a large area of agreement.

How accurate or valid are the reference dates we have selected for each of the ten countries? This is, of course, always the crucial question in connection with any reference chronology. The simplest way to consider the degree to which turning points represent the central movement of coincident indicators is to examine the composite indexes derived from these indicators and consider how well they reflect the turns (see Figure 2–4). At the same time, one should bear in mind that while turning point selection is based solely upon the behavior of the measures of aggregate activity represented in the coincident indicators, a full evaluation of their appropriateness involves a further examination of the consistency with which leading activities lead and lagging activities lag the reference turns selected. This we shall be doing in the next chapter.

In a large proportion of cases the median lead or lag of the composite indexes of the coincident indicators at growth cycle peaks and troughs was zero. This simply means that the growth cycle chronologies fit the coincident indexes closely, and vice versa.[26] The following chapters contain figures and tables describing the behavior of individual time series at growth cycle turning points in each country. From the coincident indicators in these illustrations the reader will be able to verify that the composite indexes of Figure 2–4 do indeed accurately summarize the economic history of those countries under study. As we develop the evidence further, deal with the behavior of other indicators, and utilize the chronologies in particular economic investigations, the choice of turning points may, however, require some revision.

NOTES TO CHAPTER 2

1. Charlotte Boschan and Walter W. Ebanks, "The Phase-Average Trend: A New Way of Measuring Economic Growth," Proceedings of the Business and Economics Statistics Section, American Statistical Association (1978): 332.

2. Gottfried Haberler, *Prosperity and Depression*, New and Revised Edition (Cambridge, Mass.: Harvard University Press, 1958), p. 458. To the above comment Haberler appended the following interesting footnote:

It is perhaps more correct to say that the problem is meaningless, at least in the sense in which it is—or rather was, for it is no longer a very live issue—usually formulated. The question is usually framed as a causal one: How to separate the effects of the causes responsible for the cycle from the effects of the causes responsible for the trend. The further assumption is made that the two sets of effects are additive. This assumption is surely unwarranted. The causes making for cyclical fluctuations, when impinging on a growing system, will produce very different results than they would produce in a stationary system. And similarly the growth factors would produce different results in an economic system that, unlike the one we live in, is not subject to cyclical fluctuations. As a consequence, if we could make the experiment of abstracting from the actual system which is subject to the joint operation of both sets of causes, first those that make for cycles, and second those that make for trend, the sum of the two effects would change.

3. J.R. Hicks, *The Trade Cycle* (Oxford: Clarendon Press, 1950), p. 120.

4. Ilse Mintz, *Dating Postwar Business Cycles: Methods and their Application to Western Germany, 1950–67* (New York: NBER, Occasional Paper No. 107, 1969).

5. In cases where there are "double" peaks or troughs, for example, the choice of a single peak or trough sometimes hinges on factors of judgment in which the computer program makes one choice that, on balance, is less appropriate than can be justified by all the evidence. There are also occasional turns selected by the computer that are too near the beginning or the end of a series for us to be ready to accept them. Occasionally, too, the computer selects a peak and a trough that identify a cycle of much smaller amplitude than those that are characteristic of the series. The program does not explicitly include an amplitude criterion. Our judgment, therefore, is that the computer program is extremely useful in preselecting turning points, but that the computer choices are best reviewed visually for judgmental corroboration.

6. Gerhard Bry and Charlotte Boschan, *Cyclical Analysis of Times Series: Selected Procedures and Computer Programs* (New York: NBER, Technical Paper No. 20, 1971).

7. Mintz experimented with several methods of dating growth cycle turning points. She adapted one technique, based on what are called step cycles, from earlier work by Milton Friedman and Anna Schwartz. Cf. Milton Friedman and Anna Schwartz, *A Monetary History of the United States* (New York: NBER, 1963). Cf. also their more recent study *Monetary Trends in the United States and the United Kingdom, 1870–1975*, esp. Chapter 3 (New York: NBER, 1982). The technical details involved in step cycles need not concern us here for the reasons explained below. The other major technique Mintz used was based on taking deviations from a seventy-five-month moving average. Mintz concluded that in 96 out of 147 cases both techniques produced exactly the same turning point for her West German data. In another 48 cases she found "matching" turns, even though there was some discrepancy in the exact month selected by the two methods. She found only 3 turns in 147 deviation cycles and 19 of 163 turns in step cycles were not matched at least roughly by turns in the cycles measured by the other technique. Because in the final analysis both techniques give such similar results, and deviation cycles are considerably simpler to explain,

we use the deviation technique. Our adaptation of it is, therefore, the one explained in the text.

8. The trend at the beginning (and end) of the series is extrapolated by using the rate of change between the average of the first (last) seventy-five months and that of the seventy-five months starting two years later (earlier). The final steps in the procedure modify these results.

9. Pursuant to the point raised in Note 8 concerning the treatment of trend estimates at the beginning and end of the series, we assume the first phase starts with the first observation and ends with the first turn, the last phase starts with the last turn and ends with the last observation, and we then extrapolate by computing the slope from the first (last) midpoint in the three-phase triplets so that the trend values of terminal segments in both directions equal the sum of the original observations. That this can be a source of forecasting error is evident.

10. Trading-day adjustments (adjustment for the variation from month to month in the number of working days) were included routinely in seasonal adjustments whenever appropriate, and when necessary, information for such adjustments was obtained from officials in each country.

11. More complete information on data sources are available in *International Economic Indicators: A Sourcebook*, by Geoffrey H. Moore and Melita H. Moore (Westport, Conn.: Greenwood Press, 1985). This book describes in some detail the source and construction of the basic indicator series employed in seven of the ten countries included in this study. (The countries not included in the source book but included here are Sweden, the Netherlands, and Belgium.)

12. Mintz, *Dating Postwar Business Cycles*, p. 9.

13. Details of composite index construction may be found in Julius Shiskin, *Signals of Recession and Recovery: An Experiment with Monthly Reporting* (New York: NBER, Occasional Paper No. 77, 1961), Appendix A; and Victor Zarnowitz and Charlotte Boschan, "Cyclical Indicators: An Evaluation and New Leading Indexes," *Business Conditions Digest* (May 1975): pp. v–xix (reprinted in *Handbook of Cyclical Indicators*, Department of Commerce [1976]).

14. Of course the same objectives could be reached by computing two indexes, one based on trend-adjusted data and the other on raw data, but this would clearly be more cumbersome. Moreover, the implicit trend in the indexes is a more complex estimate, but not necessarily better. We should add that in calculating composite indexes for our work on international indicators we have modified one of the final steps in the Shiskin procedure. We have adjusted the composite indexes to the average rate of change without regard to sign in the cyclical component ($\bar{c}$) of the index of industrial production for each country.

15. The Department of Commerce adjusts its current indexes in similar fashion by making the composite index trend equal to the average trend of the four roughly coincident indicators on the 1975 list. This is approximately the same as the trend rate for real GNP. Our international version of the same process involves setting the composite index equal to the average trend in real GNP in each country for the period 1969–79. This is done by computing the average per month change in both the composite index and the GNP for the period 1969–79, calculating the difference, and multiplying the index each month by the differential trend.

16. Burns and Mitchell, p. 70. For a fuller discussion of diffusion indexes, see Arthur F. Burns, "New Facts on Business Cycles" (NBER, 1950) reprinted in Geoffrey H. Moore, ed., *Business Cycle Indicators* (New York: NBER, 1961), pp. 13-44; Julius Shiskin, *Signals of Recession and Recovery*, pp. 56 ff; Ilse Mintz, "Dating United States Growth Cycles," *Explorations in Economic Research* 1, no. 1 (Summer 1974): 22-23; and Geoffrey H. Moore, "Diffusion Indexes," in D. Greenwald, ed., *Encyclopedia of Economics* (New York: McGraw-Hill, 1982), pp. 240-43.

17. The CIBCR has made such comparisons only for Canada and Australia.

18. The question was discussed in Philip A. Klein, *Business Cycles in the Postwar World: Some Reflections on Recent Research* (Washington, D.C.: American Enterprise Institute, 1976), especially Chapter II ("Growth Cycles: New Wine or New Bottles?").

19. A recent exception occurred in the United States, where in 1980-81 a classical cycle expansion took place but with such a modest growth rate that it could not be classified as a growth cycle expansion. Hence, there were two classical recessions between 1980 and 1982 but only one growth recession in the 1978-1982 period.

20. See, for example, G.H. Moore's foreword to Mintz's *Dating Postwar Business Cycles*, page 107, in which he notes that students of instability have long considered the notion that business cycles might appropriately be viewed as deviations from long-term trend. He cites particularly Henry L. Moore, Warren M. Persons, Frederick R. Macaulay, and Edwin Frickey, all of whom developed this approach during the period 1910-30. Mitchell himself adjusted for trend in a number of cases in *Business Cycles: The Problem and its Setting* (New York: NBER, 1927), especially pages 190-233.

21. In this report we concentrate our attention on ten countries: the United Kingdom, Canada, Japan, West Germany, France, Italy, Belgium, the Netherlands, Sweden, and of course the United States. We have also produced growth cycle chronologies for Australia, South Korea, and Switzerland, which are presented in Appendix 2B, and additional data have been gathered for several other countries. The Center for International Business Cycle Research has instituted a series of training seminars to afford interested economists the opportunity to familiarize themselves with our computer programs and methods and to experiment with data from their own countries. One of the results has been evidence of the feasibility of developing growth cycle chronologies in several smaller economies—Austria, Denmark, Israel, Malaysia, South Africa, Taiwan, and Venezuela. Consultations have been held with officials in Ireland and Finland. Other countries, of course, are working in this area through participation in the OECD experiment with indicators.

22. See for example, R.C. Drakatos, "Leading Indicators for the British Economy," *National Institute Economic Review* (May 1963): 42-49; R.C.O. Matthews, "Postwar Business Cycles in the United Kingdom," in M. Bronfenbrenner, ed., *Is the Business Cycle Obsolete?* (New York: Wiley-Interscience, Division of John Wiley and Sons, 1969), pp. 99-135; Gunther Tichy, *Indikatoren der Österreichischen Konjunktur 1950 bis 1970*, Österreichisches Institut für Wirtschaftsforschung (Vienna, 1972); Angus Maddison, "The Post-War Busi-

ness Cycle in Western Europe," *Banca Nazionale del Lavoro Quarterly Review* (June 1960); Gideon Rosenbluth, "Changes in Canadian Sensitivity to United States Business Fluctuations," *Canadian Journal of Economics and Political Science* 23 (1957): 480–503; "Changes in Structural Factors in Canadian Sensitivity to United States Business Fluctuations," *Canadian Journal of Economics and Political Science* 24 (1958): pp. 21–43. Chronologies had also been produced in Japan by the Japanese Economic Planning Agency, and in Italy by Istituto Nazionale per lo Studio della Congiuntura.

23. The United Kingdom was the first major country for which we collected the basic data. Indeed, even before the IEI project was initiated, Desmond O'Dea had begun work at the National Institute of Economic and Social Research on cyclical indicators for the British economy during the postwar period. O'Dea, however, largely eschewed the idea of a general reference chronology in favor of developing what he called target indicators for particular variables, such as employment, investment, etc. His work culminated in the publication of *Cyclical Indicators for the Postwar British Economy* (Cambridge University Press, 1975). An interim report of interest is D. J. O'Dea, "The Cyclical Timing of Labor Market Indicators in Great Britain and the United States," *Explorations in Economic Research* 2, no. 1 (Winter 1975).

The availability of data and interest in indicators by the NIESR, the Central Statistical Office, and the NBER made early progress in the United Kingdom possible. The CSO cooperated fully with Klein during the 1973-1974 year in collecting and analyzing data on indicators for the United Kingdom. A report on this initial effort in international economic indicators, "Postwar Growth Cycles in the United Kingdom—An Interim Report" by Philip A. Klein appeared in *Explorations in Economic Research* 3, no. 1 (Winter 1976). The study developed a tentative growth cycle chronology for the United Kingdom, which is shown in Table 2-3. The study also analyzed the behavior of the U.K. equivalents to the U.S. leading, coincident, and lagging indicators at postwar U.K. growth cycle turning points. Hence, it was an early test of the feasibility of the kind of analyses reported in this study.

24. The Japanese chronology is a variant on the usual classical type, because it is based upon particularly sensitive coincident indicators rather than aggregates such as GNP. The aggregates showed no cyclical declines in Japan before the 1970s.

25. At recent classical cycle turns the evidence for employment in the United States is mixed. Since 1948, nonfarm employment has lagged by one month at two of the seven troughs and by three months at a third, but has coincided exactly at the other four. At peaks the record is even more variable: leads of -2, -1, -5 months at the earlier peaks, an exact coincidence in 1960, but lags of 3, 11, and 2 months at the most recent peaks. The unemployment rate has usually led at classical peaks and lagged at troughs. But the leads and lags of employment and unemployment are generally short, and this justifies, in our view, their classification as roughly coincident.

26. The full information with respect to these median leads and lags is shown in Table 3-1.

APPENDIX 2A
CURRENT SOURCES OF INTERNATIONAL ECONOMIC INDICATORS

International

Main Economic Indicators, Organization for Economic Cooperation and Development, Paris.

United Nations Monthly Bulletin of Statistics and its *Supplement*, United Nations, New York.

Statistical Indicators of Short Term Economic Changes in ECE Countries, United Nations Economic Commission for Europe, Geneva.

European Economy, Commission of the European Communities, Luxembourg.

International Economic Scoreboard, The Conference Board, New York.

International Financial Statistics, International Monetary Fund, Washington.

International Economic Indicators, Center for International Business Cycle Research, New York.

Canada

Current Economic Analysis, Statistics Canada, Ottawa.

Canadian Statistical Review, Statistics Canada, Ottawa.

Bank of Canada Review, Bank of Canada, Ottawa.

France

Bulletin Mensuel de Statistique, Institut National de la Statistique et des Etudes Economiques, Paris.

Tendances de la Conjoncture, Institut National de la Statistique et des Etudes Economiques, Paris.

Informations Rapides, Institut National de la Statistique et des Etudes Economiques, Paris.

Italy

Congiuntura Italiana, Istituto Nazionale per lo Studio Della Congiuntura, Rome.

Bollettino Mensile di Statistica, Istituto Centrale di Statistica, Rome.

Indicatori Mensile, Istituto Centrale di Statistica, Rome.

Japan

Japanese Economic Indicators, Japanese Economic Planning Agency, Tokyo.

Economic Statistics Monthly, Bank of Japan, Tokyo.

Monthly Statistics of Japan, Statistics Bureau, Prime Minister's Office, Tokyo.

United Kingdom

Monthly Digest of Statistics, Central Statistical Office, London.

British Business, Department of Industry and Trade, London.

Economic Trends, Central Statistical Office, London.

United States

Business Conditions Digest, and *Handbook of Cyclical Indicators*, 1984 U.S. Department of Commerce, Washington, D.C.

Survey of Current Business, U.S. Department of Commerce, Washington, D.C.

Federal Reserve Bulletin, Board of Governors of the Federal Reserve System, Washington, D.C.

Economic Indicators, Joint Economic Committee, Washington, D.C.

West Germany

Wirtschaft und Statistik, Statistisches Bundesamt, Wiesbaden.

Statistiche Beihefte zu den Monatsberichten der Deutschen Bundesbank, Deutsche Bundesbank, Frankfurt am Main.

Monthly Report of the Deutsche Bundesbank, Frankfurt am Main.

Statistischer Wochendienst, Statistisches Bundesamt Wiesbaden, W. Kohlhammer GMBH Stuttgart und Mainz.

Sweden

Konjunktur Institutet, Konjunktur Läget.

Sveriges Industriförbund.

Swedish Bank Association (Svenska Bankföreningen)

Monthly Digest of Swedish Statistics, National Central Bureau of Statistics.

Labor Marketatistics, National Central Bureau of Statistics.

Labor Force Surveys, National Central Bureau of Statistics.

Affarsvärlden.

Justistia, AB Svensk Handelstidning.

The Netherlands

Central Bureau of Statistics:
  Monthly Bulletin of Social Statistics.
  Bankruptcies.
  Business Test.
  Monthly Bulletin of Construction Statistics.
  Monthly Bulletin of the Netherlands Central Bureau of Statistics.
  Monthly Bulletin of Financial Statistics.
  Monthly Statistical Bulletin of Manufacturing.
  Monthly Bulletin of Distribution Statistics.

Belgium

Bulletin de Statistique, Institut Nationale de la Statistique.

Enquete sur la conjoncture, Banque Nationale de Belgique.

Institut de Recherches Economique, Université Catholique de Louvain, Service de Conjoncture.

Bulletin Hebdomadaire de la Kredietbank, Kredietbank.

Bulletin Mensuel de l'Onem.

Cahiers Economiques de Bruxelles.

World Financial Markets, Morgan Guaranty Trust Company of New York.

APPENDIX 2B
GROWTH CYCLE CHRONOLOGIES FOR FOUR COUNTRIES, 1948–83

Peak or Trough	Australia	South Korea	Switzerland	Taiwan
P				
T			2/50	
P	4/51		3/51	
T	11/52		2/53	
P				
T				
P	8/55		6/57	
T	1/58		9/58	
P	8/60			
T	9/61			2/63
P			4/64	
T				
P				
T				
P	4/65			4/65
T	1/68	8/66	5/68	8/67
P	5/70	1/69	5/70	11/68
T	3/72	3/72	1/71	1/71
P	2/74	2/74	4/74	12/73
T		6/75	8/75	2/75
P		7/76		6/76
T	10/77			7/77
P				8/78
T				
P	6/81			
T	5/83			10/82

Source: Center for International Business Cycle Research.

APPENDIX 2C

U.S. CYCLICAL INDICATORS AND ROUGH EQUIVALENTS, NINE OTHER COUNTRIES

United States	*Canada*	*United Kingdom*
Leading Indicators	*Leading Indicators*	*Leading Indicators*
Average workweek, mfg.	Average workweek, mfg.	Average workweek, mfg.
Average initial claims, unemployment insurance (inverted)	Initial claims, unemployment insurance (inverted)	
Net business formation		
New orders, consumer goods and materials*	New orders, durable goods*	New companies registered
Contracts & orders, plant and equipment		Business failures (inverted)
New building permits, private housing units	New orders, machinery and equipment*	New orders, engineering industries, volume
Change in business inventories (q)*	Nonresidential building permits	New orders, construction, private industry*
	Residential building permits	Housing starts, thousands
Industrial materials price index	Change in nonfarm business inventories (q)*	Change in stocks and work in progress (q)
Stock price index, 500 S&P common	Industrial materials price index	Basic materials price index
	Stock price index, Toronto Stock Exchange	Common stock price index
Corporate profits after taxes (q)	Corporate profits after taxes (q)*	Companies' profits less U.K. taxes (q)*
Ratio, price/unit labor cost, nonfarm business (q)	Ratio, price to unit labor cost, mfg.	Ratio, price to unit labor cost, mfg.
Change in consumer installment credit*	Change in consumer credit outstanding*	Increase in hire purchase debt*
Roughly Coincident Indicators	*Roughly Coincident Indicators*	*Roughly Coincident Indicators*
Personal income*	Personal income*	Personal disposable income (q)*
Gross national product (q)*	Gross national expenditure (q)*	Gross domestic product (q)*
Industrial production	Industrial production	Industrial production
Mfg. and trade sales*	Retail trade*	Retail sales*
Employees on nonfarm payrolls	Nonfarm employment	Employment in production industries
Unemployment ratio (inverted)	Unemployment rate (inverted)	Unemployed (inverted)

Lagging Indicators	*Lagging Indicators*	*Lagging Indicators*
Unemployment rate, 15 weeks & over, inverted	Long-term unemployment, inverted	Long-term unemployment, inverted
Business expenditure, new plant & equipment, (q)*	Plant and equipment, Canadian dollars*	Investment in plant and equipment*
Mfg. & trade inventories*	Business inventories, Canadian dollars*	Changes in stock & work in progress
Output per manhour, percent change of reciprocal (q)	Change in the inverse of output per manhour	Changes in employment per unit output
Commercial and industrial loans outstanding*	Industrial loans in Canadian dollars*	Loans to industry*
Prime rate on short-term business loans	Canada prime rate	Prime rate

(Appendix 2C. continued overleaf)

Appendix 2C.   continued

West Germany

Leading Indicators

Number working short hours (inverted)
Applications for unemployment compensation (inverted)

Insolvent enterprises (inverted)
New orders, investment goods industry, volume
Housing permits, interior space
Residential construction orders*
Inventory change
Stock price index
Net income from entrepreneurial activity*
Ratio, price to unit labor cost
Change in consumer credit*

Roughly Coincident Indicators

Employment in mining & manufacturing
Unemployment rate
Gross national product*
Industrial production
Disposable income*
Manufacturing sales volume
Retail trade volume

France

Leading Indicators

Average workweek, mfg.

Change in unfilled orders, total

Building permits, residential
Index of stock prices

Ratio, price to unit labor cost, mfg. (q)

Roughly Coincident Indicators

Employment, nonfarm
Registered unemployed (inverted)
Gross domestic product (q)*
Industrial production

Retail sales volume

Italy

Leading Indicators

Hours per month per worker in industry

Change in unfilled orders, total
Declared bankruptcies (inverted)

Building permits, residential

Stock price index

Roughly Coincident Indicators

Nonfarm employment
Unemployment rate (inverted)
Gross domestic product (q)*
Industrial production

Retail sales*

Lagging Indicators

Investment in machinery, equipment
 and construction*
Level of inventories

Bank credits to the economy*
Percent change in the reciprocal of
 output/manhour
Bank rates on large loans

Lagging Indicators

Inventory of finished goods, survey,
 change over four months

Commercial banks, prime rate

Lagging Indicators

Inventory of finished goods, survey,
 change over four months

Commercial banks, prime rate

(Appendix 2C. continued overleaf)

Appendix 2C. continued

Belgium	Netherlands	Sweden	Japan
Leading Indicators	*Leading Indicators*	*Leading Indicators*	*Leading Indicators*
Monthly hours working	Temporary short-time workers	Number of hours worked (in industry)	Index of overtime workers, mfg.
		Number of new job offerings	
Inland orders*	Change in unfilled orders	Value of new orders*	Business failures, number (inverted)
Bankruptcies (inverted)	Bankruptcies (inverted)		New orders, machinery and construction works
Number of nonresidential building permits	Nonresidential building permits (q)		
Number of residential building permits	Dwellings started	Number of housing starts	Dwelling units started
	Change in industrial inventories (q)*		Change in inventories (q)*
	Prices, raw materials and semi-mfred. goods	Raw materials prices	Raw materials price index
Industrial share price	Stock price index	Stock price	Stock price index
	Ratio, price to labor cost (q)	Ratio, price to unit labor cost	Ratio, price to unit labor cost, mfg.
		New loans to households	Change in consumer and housing credit outstanding (q)*
Coincident Indicators	*Coincident Indicators*	*Coincident Indicators*	*Coincident Indicators*
Unemployment rate (inverted)	Employment, mfg. (q)	(Nonfarm) employment	Regular workers' employment, all industries
Real gross domestic product*	Registered unemployed, number (inverted)	Unemployment rate	Unemployment rate (inverted)
		Gross domestic product	Gross national expenditures (q)
Industrial production	Industrial production	Industrial production index	Industrial production
		Disposable income, 1975 prices	Wage and salary income*
Retail sales*	Manufacturing sales (q)*	Retail sales, volume	Retail sales*
	Retail sales*		

Lagging Indicators	*Lagging Indicators*	*Lagging Indicators*	*Lagging Indicators*
Finished goods inventories, change over 4-month span	Long-term unemployed (inverted) (q)	Long-duration unemployment rate (inverted)	Gross fixed capital formation
	New plant equipment expenditures (q)*		Inventory level
	Industrial inventories (end of q)*		
	Output per manhour, 12-month span (inverted)	Output per manhour, 12-month span (inverted)	Output/manhour, percent change of reciprocal, 12-month span
		Personal loans on checking accounts*	Commercial bank loans and discounts*
Bank lending rates to prime borrowers		Discount rate	Contracted rate on loans

* = Deflated series.
q = Quarterly series. All other series are monthly.

Chapter 3

SUMMARY MEASURES OF LEADING, COINCIDENT, AND LAGGING INDICATORS IN TEN COUNTRIES

COMPOSITE INDEXES

By utilizing composite indexes of economic indicators it is possible to observe how rough equivalents to U.S. indicators behave with respect to growth cycle turning points in other countries. Figure 3-1 enlarges the picture presented in Figure 2-4 by including the composite leading index and the composite lagging index for each of the ten countries under study. One further addition is the lagging index on an inverted basis, which we have found usually precedes the leading index. These composite indicators are also related to the national growth cycle chronologies shown in Table 2-2.[1] Each index displays clearly defined cycles, testifying to the pervasiveness and persistence of short-run fluctuations around national growth trends. (See pp. 73-77.)

Figure 3-1 can best be understood in connection with Table 3-1, which summarizes the timing comparisons shown in the figure. The first point to be noted is that the composite indexes confirm that the United States continues to have more business cycles than other countries. Thus, since World War II the United States has exhibited more peaks and troughs than any other country, including Canada, whose economic patterns customarily are most like those of the United States.[2] For much of the 1970s, growth cycles were roughly synchronous in most of the countries under review. This is especially true during the 1973-75 period when a conventional classical recession was experienced in all these economies. Only toward the end of the decade did the United States tend to diverge significantly from this pattern. By the 1980s a continuation of this historical tendency toward synchronism seemed a reasonable, if yet to be tested, assumption.

Overall, the behavior of the composite indexes confirms that the U.S. classification of indicators for classical turning points is appropriate for growth cycle turning points in the United States and in the other nine countries as well. It is, of course, not surprising that the roughly coincident indexes, with few exceptions, exhibit median lead-lag measures of zero months at the peaks and troughs, because these indicators figure so prominently in the selection of growth cycle chronologies in the first place. Far more impressive is the discovery that the timing relationship within each country, among the three composite indexes, is almost invariably what one would expect from the timing classification itself. That classification was based solely on U.S. information. There is also considerable similarity in the length of the median leads or lags, most of them falling within a range of four to six months. In every country a turn in the growth cycle is typically spread over a considerable range of months—usually from eight to thirteen or fourteen months, counting from the turn in the leading index to the subsequent turn in the lagging index. For all ten countries the interval between the average of the medians for the leading and lagging indexes is ten months.

None of the leading composite indexes fails to show median leads. Among the roughly coincident indexes, only in Belgium does the median differ from zero. The lagging indexes turn in a perfect record—median lags in every instance. Moreover, on an inverted basis the median leads in the lagging indexes always exceed those in the leading indexes.

In most of the countries the indexes exhibit few extra or skipped cycles. (See Table 3-2.) In Canada the computer discerned an extra cycle in the lagging index during the 1952-53 period. In the United Kingdom there may be an extra cycle in all three indexes before the reference dates begin (in the late 1940s), but this may simply reflect a paucity of data and an inability to start the reference chronology earlier. An extra cycle in the Japanese leading index in the early 1960s—as well as an extra cycle in the Japanese lagging index in 1968-69—is reflected in a rather high plateau in the leading index (1966-68) but does not show up in the coincident index. There is an extra cycle in the roughly coincident index for West Germany in 1972-73. Our judgmental review eliminated an extra cycle in the West German leading index (1973-74) and in the lagging index (1968-69).

Figure 3-1. Composite Indexes for Ten Countries.

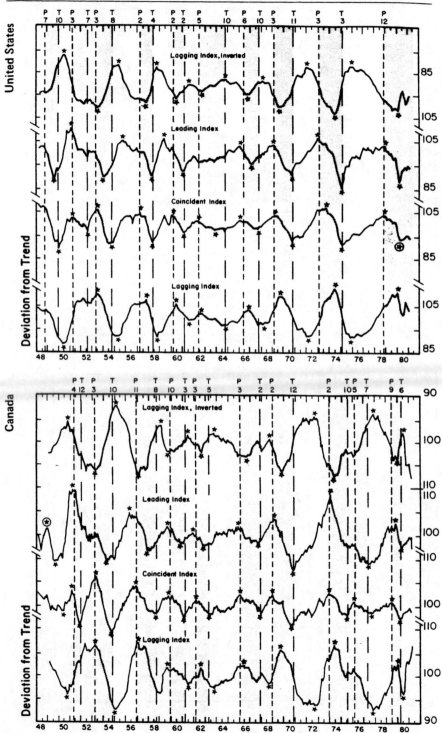

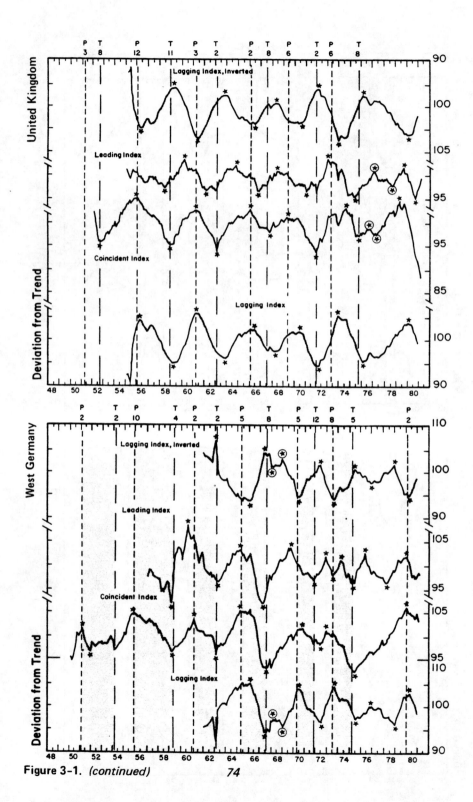

Figure 3-1. *(continued)*

74

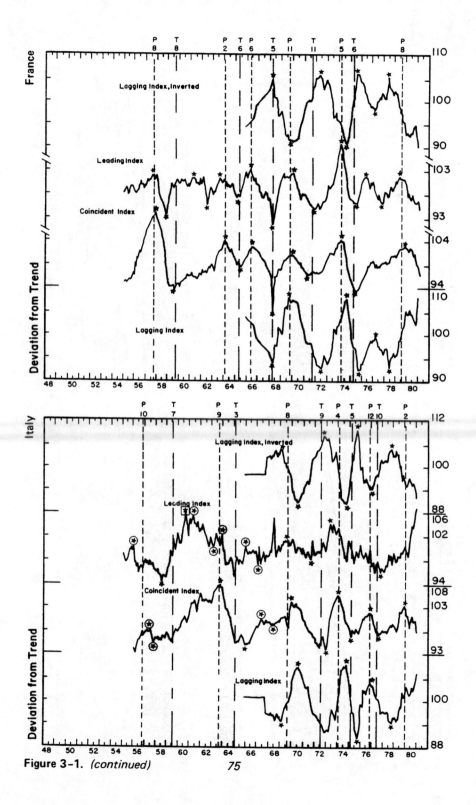

Figure 3-1. *(continued)*

75

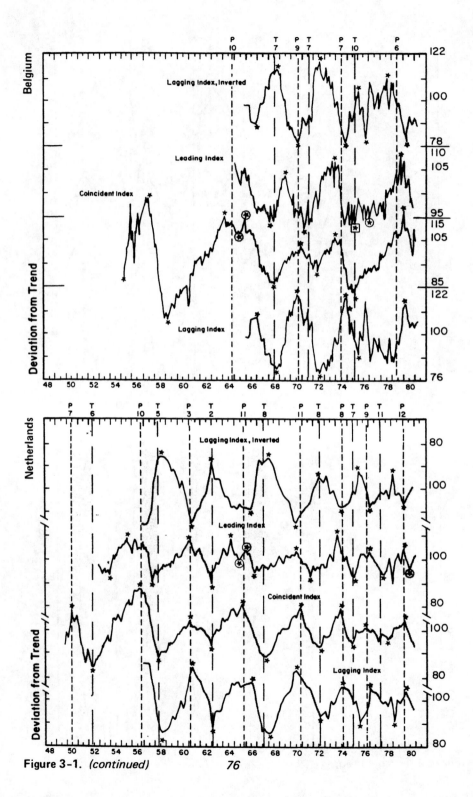

Figure 3-1. *(continued)*   76

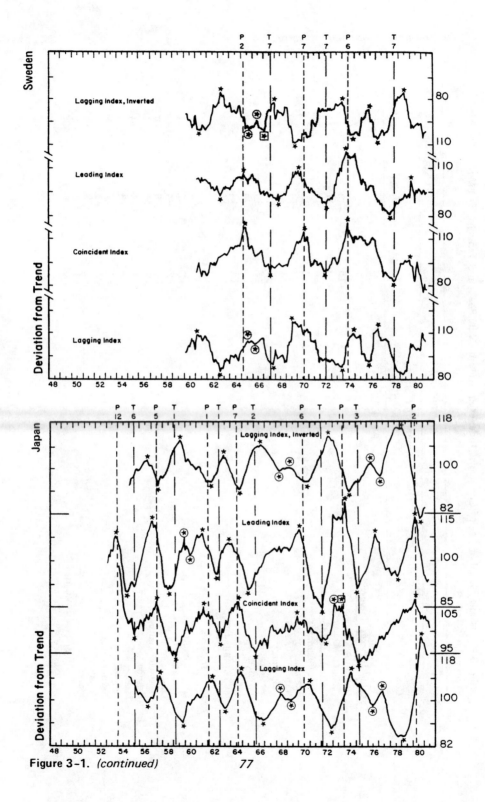

Figure 3-1. *(continued)*

Table 3-1. Median Lead or Lag of Composite Indexes at Growth Cycle Peaks and Troughs, Ten Market-Oriented Economies, 1948-81.

SECTION A

Country	Number of Timing Comparisons	Median Lead (−) or Lag (+), in Months, at		
	P & T	P	T	P & T
Lagging Indexes, Inverted				
United States	17	−15	−11	−12
Canada	20	−15	−16	−15
United Kingdom	11	−24	−19	−22
West Germany	6	−12	−18	−18
France	5	−18	−14	−18
Italy	7	−14	−7	−13
Belgium	5	−26	−14	−20
Netherlands	11	−13	−11	−12
Sweden	6	−18	−24	−22
Japan	11	−14	−14	−14
Mean Timing, Ten Countries	—	−14	−15	−17
Leading Indexes				
United States	18	−2	−2	−2
Canada	20	−2	−4	−2
United Kingdom	10	−10	−9	−10
West Germany	10	−7	−2	−5
France	11	−3	−4	−4
Italy	10	−9	−6	−9
Belgium	7	−2	−2	−2
Netherlands	14	−2	−1	−1
Sweden	6	−3	0	−2
Japan	13	−4	−4	−4
Mean Timing, Ten Countries	—	−4	−3	−4

Roughly Coincident Indexes

United States	18	0	0	0
Canada	20	0	0	0
United Kingdom	12	0	0	0
West Germany	13	0	0	0
France	11	0	0	0
Italy	9	0	+3	0
Belgium	7	-2	-1	-1
Netherlands	15	0	0	0
Sweden	6	0	-1	0
Japan	12	0	0	0
Mean Timing, Ten Countries	—	0	0	0

Lagging Indexes

United States	18	+6	+6	+6
Canada	20	+5	+4	+4
United Kingdom	11	+6	+8	+8
West Germany	7	+3	+4	+3
France	5	+5	+6	+6
Italy	8	+8	+10	+6
Belgium	6	+6	+10	+8
Netherlands	12	+3	+8	+10
Sweden	6	+1	+10	+6
Japan	12	+4	+8	+6
Mean Timing, Ten Countries	—	+5	+7	+7

(*Table 3–1. continued overleaf*)

TABLE 3-1. Continued

SECTION B   Median Lead (−) or Lag (+), in Months

Country		Lagging Index, Inverted	Leading Index	Roughly Coincident Index	Lagging Indexes
United States	P	−15	−2	0	+6
	T	−11	−2	0	+5
	P & T	−12	−2	0	+5
Canada	P	−15	−2	0	+5
	T	−16	−3	0	+4
	P & T	−15	−2	0	+4
United Kingdom	P	−24	−10	0	+6
	T	−19	−9	0	+8
	P & T	−22	−10	0	+8
West Germany	P	−12	−7	0	+3
	T	−18	−2	0	+4
	P & T	−15	−5	0	+3
France	P	−18	−3	0	+5
	T	−14	−4	0	+6
	P & T	−18	−4	0	+6
Italy	P	−13	−9	0	+8
	T	−7	−6	+3	+10
	P & T	−13	−9	0	+8
Belgium	P	−26	−2	−2	+6
	T	−14	−2	−1	+10
	P & T	−20	−2	−1	+8
Netherlands	P	−13	−2	0	+3
	T	−11	−1	0	+8
	P & T	−12	−1	−1	+6
Sweden	P	−18	−3	0	+1
	T	−24	0	−1	+10
	P & T	−22	−2	0	+10
Japan	P	−16	−4	0	+5
	T	−14	−4	0	+6
	P & T	−15	−4	0	+6

Table 3-2. Extra and Skipped Growth Cycles in the Composite Indexes.

	Leading		Coincident		Lagging	
	Extra	Skipped	Extra	Skipped	Extra	Skipped
United States		2				1
Canada		2				1
United Kingdom						
West Germany	2				1	
France	2				1	
Italy		1		1		
Belgium					1	
Netherlands						
Sweden					1	
Japan	1					
Ten Countries	5	5	0	1	4	2

Source: Figure 3-1.

An extra cycle in both the leading and coincident indexes for France showed amplitudes too small to survive our review. This situation provided the basis for eliminating two otherwise extra cycles in the leading index for the Netherlands, and an extra cycle in both the leading and the coincident indexes for Italy. Since these were the only cases of extra cycles, we may say that, after review of the computer-selected turns, no extra cycles existed among the composite indexes for any country except in the German coincident index. One is tempted to conclude that the U.S.-derived indicators on the basis of the summary examination undertaken with this evidence, have behaved somewhat better in a number of foreign countries than in the country where they were developed, at least in recent years!

According to our data, the usual sequence in the growth cycle consists of a turn in the inverted laggers, followed by a turn in the leading index, then in the coincident index, and then the lagging index, which starts another round. Section B of Table 3-1 enables one to see the sequence more clearly. This way of organizing the data reveals the strong tendency for indexes to turn in the order expected at peaks and at troughs. The only exceptions to this expected order involve the Belgian and Swedish leading and coincident indexes at peaks. Hence, in fifty-two out of the fifty-four sequences (six for each of the nine countries) the turns in the composite indexes occurred in the order experienced at U.S. classical turns—a 96 percent success record. The details of the performance, considered in

Table 3-3.   Summary of Sequence of Turns in Composite Indexes at Growth Cycle Turns in Ten Countries.

	Inverted Lagging Index to Leading Index			Leading Index to Coincident Index			Coincident Index to Lagging Index			Total		
	P	T	P&T	P	T	P&T	P	T	P&T	P	T	P&T
United States	100[a]	89	94	90	89	90	100	89	95	97	89	93
Canada	100	100	100	80	80	80	89	78	83	89	86	87
United Kingdom	83	100	92	71	100	85	100	100	100	85	100	92
West Germany	100	100	100	67	80	73	100	100	100	85	92	88
France	100	100	100	100	80	91	100	100	100	100	90	95
Italy	67	100	83	83	67	91	67	100	83	75	100	87
Belgium	100	100	100	75	67	71	100	100	100	90	88	89
Netherlands	100	100	100	50	57	53	71	100	85	71	84	78
Sweden	100	100	100	100	67	83	67	100	83	88	89	88
Japan	100	80	91	86	100	92	83	100	92	90	82	92

Note:
a. In the table 100 means that in all the possible comparisons the inverted lagging index turned before the leading index, excluding cases where both indexes turned in the same month. Fifty would mean that the indexes turned in the expected order half the time. As the text makes clear, the inverted lagging index is expected to turn first, the leading index next, the coincident index third, and the lagging index last. The higher the percentages for a given country the more consistently its indicator system conforms to the expected behavior.
Source: Appendix 3B.

the next section of this chapter, will reveal a number of discrepancies among individual indicators. But the overall pattern of sequential behavior outside the United States (summarized in Table 3-3) is certainly in line with what U.S. experience with the indicators underlying these composites at classical cycles has led us to expect.

Turning again to the evidence in Figure 3-1, three additions to U.S. classical cycle history are revealed in growth cycle analysis—the slowdowns of 1950-51, 1962-64, and 1966-67. Though smaller in terms of amplitude, these slowdowns are clearly reflected in the behavior of the coincident index. Most, though not all, of the reference turns for the United States are confirmed by the appearance of related turns in the composite indexes of the leaders and laggers. There are two skipped cycles in the leading index (1952-53 and 1962-64) and one in the lagging index (1951-52). The skipped cycles are visible but much smaller than the rest. In the other countries there are a few extra or skipped cycles in the leading or lagging indexes (as well as one skipped cycle in the coincident index for France), but for the most part one-to-one correspondence is the rule. The evidence on skipped and extra cycles in the composite index has been summarized in Table 3-2.

The high degree of conformity between the growth cycle chronologies and the behavior of the composite indexes in the countries under study speaks well for the indicator method as adapted to growth cycle measurement and for the objective criteria used for dating turning points. The judgmental screening to which the computer-selected turns were subjected did not affect many of the choices. The results also speak well for the consistent overall behavior of the economic activities embodied in the indicators included in the composite indexes and for the similarity in the timing behavior of each type of indicator. In order to carry the analysis further, however, it is necessary to look at the individual indicators in each timing classification.

MEDIAN TIMING OF INDICATORS

We shall now examine the international record of the twelve leading indicators, six roughly coincident indicators, and six lagging indicators included in the 1966 U.S. list of "most reliable indicators." The median behavior is summarized in Table 3-4. Is the median timing pattern in the nine foreign countries in our study similar to that found in the United States?

Based on Table 3-4 we find that among the leading indicators at peaks the medians fail to lead in nineteen out of seventy-four in-

Table 3-4. Lengths of Median Lead or Lag of Individual Indicators at Growth Cycle Peaks for Ten Countries.

Indicators: U.S. Classification and U.S. Titles[a]	United States	Canada	United Kingdom	West Germany	France
	Lead (-) or Lag (+), in Months				
Leading Indicators					
Average workweek, mfg.	-3	-3	0	-8	-4
New unemployment claims[c]	-1	-1	n.a.	+2	n.a.
New orders, consumer goods[d]	-2	-2	n.a.	n.a.	-11
Formation of bus. enterprises	-11	n.a.	-8	-8	n.a.
Contracts & orders, plant & equipment[d]	+1	+3	-3	-6	n.a.
Building permits, housing	-6	-3	-11	-16	-9
Change in bus. inventories[d]	0	0	-4	-4	n.a.
Industrial materials prices	-1	+2	+5	n.a.	+1
Stock price index	-4	-3	-5	-6	-3
Profits[d]	-4	-5	-4	-8	n.a.
Ratio, price to labor cost	-8	+1	-14	-9	-4
Change in consumer debt[d]	-6	-2	-16	-21	n.a.
Median or Total	-4	-2	-4	-8	-4
Coincident Indicators					
Nonfarm employment	+1	+2	+2	+3	+6
Unemployment rate[c]	0	+1	+2	+3	0
Gross national product[d]	0	0	-13	0	-1
Industrial production	+3	0	0	0	0
Personal income[d]	-1	+1	-4	-6	n.a.
Mfg. & trade sales[d]	-1	-2	-3	-3	-2
Median or Total	0	0	-2	0	0
Lagging Indicators					
Long-duration unemployment[c]	+6	+1	+6	n.a.	n.a.
Plant & equipment investment[d]	+5	+4	+5	-2	n.a.
Business inventories[d]	+6	+9	+10	+15	+8
Productivity change, nonfarm[c]	+11	+15	+8	+11	n.a.
Business loans outstanding[d]	+6	+3	+4	n.a.	n.a.
Interest rates, bus. loans	+7	+5	+5	+2	+6
Median or Total	+6	+4	+6	+6	+7

Notes:

a. The series available for each country are sometimes only roughly equivalent in content to the U.S. series. In some cases two series are used to match the U.S. series and the median includes all observations for both series. The periods covered vary for each indicator and each country, but all are within the years 1948-1981.

b. Matching means that for leading indicators the median is a lead, for lagging indicators the median is a lag, and for coincident indicators the median is a lead or lag of three months or less.

Table 3-4. continued

Italy	Belgium	Netherlands	Sweden	Japan	All Countries	Number of Countries in Which	
						Median Matches U.S.[b]	Median Does Not Match U.S.[b]
Lead (-) or Lag (+), in Months (continued)							
0	-4	-1	0	-4	-3	6	3
n.a.	n.a.	n.a.	+4	n.a.	0	1	2
-8	+1	-5	-4	n.a.	-4	5	1
-4	0	-11	n.a.	-10	-8	5	1
n.a.	-4	-3	n.a.	-5	-4	5	1
-2	-7	-1	n.a.	-12	-6	7	1
n.a.	n.a.	+2	n.a.	-1	0	3	2
n.a.	-11	-4	+1	0	0	2	5
-6	n.a.	-13	-14	-8	-6	8	0
n.a.	n.a.	n.a.	n.a.	-10	-5	4	0
n.a.	n.a.	-2	+7	-2	-2	5	2
n.a.	n.a.	n.a.	+8	-9	-7	4	1
-4	-4	-3	+1	-5	-4	55	19
+6	n.a.	+4	+5	+2	+3	4	4
+1	-1	0	0	0	0	9	0
+1	0	n.a.	0	-5	0	6	2
0	-4	-2	0	0	0	8	1
n.a.	n.a.	n.a.	0	-9	-2	2	3
-1	-17	0	+3	-8	-2	7	2
+1	-2	0	0	-2	0	36	12
n.a.	n.a.	+5	+4	n.a.	+5	4	0
n.a.	n.a.	+2	n.a.	0	+3	3	2
+6	+15	+6	n.a.	+4	+8	8	0
n.a.	n.a.	n.a.	-3	+8	+9	4	1
n.a.	n.a.	n.a.	0	-6	+3	2	2
+3	+5	n.a.	+7	+7	+5	8	0
+4	+10	+5	+2	+4	+5	29	5

c. Inverted.
d. In constant prices.
Source: Appendix Tables 5-1 to 5-10.

Table 3-4. continued.   Lengths of Median Lead or Lag of Individual
Indicators at Growth Cycle Troughs for Ten Countries.

Indicators: U.S. Classification and U.S. Titles[a]	United States	Canada	United Kingdom	West Germany	France
	Lead (−) or Lag (+), in Months				
Leading Indicators					
Average workweek, mfg.	−2	−5	−2	−1	−3
New unemployment claims[c]	−5	−2	n.a.	−3	n.a.
New orders, consumer goods[d]	−2	0	n.a.	n.a.	−12
Formation of bus. enterprises	−1	n.a.	−10	−4	n.a.
Contracts & orders, plant & equipment[d]	−5	0	0	0	n.a.
Building permits, housing	−9	−9	−10	+2	−7
Change in bus. inventories[d]	−2	0	−6	−1	n.a.
Industrial materials prices	−1	−2	+4	n.a.	+4
Stock price index	−4	−6	−8	−8	−9
Profits[d]	−2	−2	−3	−12	n.a.
Ratio, price to labor costs	−7	0	−9	−6	−3
Change in consumer debt[d]	−4	−11	−15	−18	n.a.
Median or Total	−3	−2	−7	−3	−5
Coincident Indicators					
Nonfarm employment	+1	0	+2	+6	+7
Unemployment rate[c]	+1	+2	+1	0	+1
Gross national product[d]	−1	−1	0	0	−4
Industrial production	0	0	0	0	−3
Personal income[d]	0	0	−3	+6	n.a.
Mfg. & trade sales[d]	0	0	−1	0	0
Median or Total	0	0	0	0	0
Lagging Indicators					
Long-duration unemployment[c]	+4	+2	+3	n.a.	n.a.
Plant & equipment investment[d]	+7	+6	+8	0	n.a.
Business inventories[d]	+6	+8	+6	+16	+4
Productivity change, nonfarm[c]	+10	+8	+12	+3	n.a.
Business loans outstanding[d]	+6	+3	+6	n.a.	n.a.
Interest rates, bus. loans	+11	+5	−1	+18	+8
Median or Total	+6	+6	+6	+10	+6

Notes:
a. The series available for each country are sometimes only roughly equivalent in content to the U.S. series. In some cases two series are used to match the U.S. series and the median includes all observations for both series. The periods covered vary for each indicator and each country, but all are within the years 1948–1981.

b. Matching means that for leading indicators the median is a lead, for lagging indicators the median is a lag, and for coincident indicators the median is a lead or lag of three months or less.

Table 3-4. continued.

| | | | | | | Number of Countries in Which | |
| | | | | | | Median Matches U.S.[b] | Median Does Not Match U.S.[b] |
Italy	Belgium	Netherlands	Sweden	Japan	All Countries		
Lead (−) or Lag (+), in Months (continued)							
+4	−1	−2	0	−4	−2	7	2
n.a.	n.a.	n.a.	−5	n.a.	−4	3	0
−9	+5	−13	0	n.a.	−2	3	3
−7	−3	0	n.a.	−14	−4	5	1
n.a.	−2	−3	n.a.	0	0	2	4
−2	−5	−9	n.a.	−6	−7	7	1
n.a.	n.a.	+3	n.a.	−4	−2	3	2
n.a.	−14	−13	+1	+6	+1	3	4
−8	n.a.	−8	−7	−4	−7	8	0
n.a.	n.a.	n.a.	n.a.	−10	−3	4	0
n.a.	n.a.	+6	−2	−2	−2	5	2
n.a.	n.a.	n.a.	−5	−6	−8	5	0
−7	−2	−2	−2	−4	−2	55	19
+8	n.a.	+4	+1	+2	+2	4	4
+7	−1	0	0	+2	+1	8	1
−1	0	n.a.	−8	−2	−1	6	2
0	−6	0	0	0	0	8	1
n.a.	n.a.	n.a.	−4	+1	0	3	2
−7	−11	0	+4	−1	0	6	3
0	−4	0	0	0	0	35	13
n.a.	n.a.	+3	+4	n.a.	+3	4	0
n.a.	n.a.	0	n.a.	+4	+5	3	2
+5	+16	+10	n.a.	+5	+6	8	0
n.a.	n.a.	n.a.	+11	+8	+9	5	0
n.a.	n.a.	n.a.	+6	0	+6	3	1
+9	+4	n.a.	+18	+18	+9	7	1
+7	+10	+3	+8	+5	+6	30	4

c. Inverted.
d. In constant prices.

Table 3-4. continued.   Median Lead or Lag of Individual Indicators at Growth Cycle Peaks and Troughs for Ten Countries.

Indicators: U.S. Classification and U.S. Titles[a]	United States	Canada	United Kingdom	West Germany	France
		Lead (−) or Lag (+), in Months			
Leading Indicators					
Average workweek, mfg.	−2	−4	−2	−2	−3
New unemployment claims[c]	−2	−2	n.a.	−2	n.a.
New orders, consumer goods[d]	−2	−1	n.a.	n.a.	−11
Formation of bus. enterprises	−4	n.a.	−8	−8	n.a.
Contracts & orders, plant & equipment[d]	−2	+2	−3	−4	n.a.
Building permits, housing	−7	−5	−11	+8	−8
Change in bus. inventories[d]	−1	0	−5	−4	n.a.
Industrial materials prices	−1	−2	+5	n.a.	+3
Stock price index	−4	−4	−8	−7	−8
Profits[d]	−2	−3	−3	−9	n.a.
Ratio, price to labor cost	−7	0	−12	−9	−4
Change in consumer debt[d]	−6	−7	−16	−18	n.a.
Median or Total	−2	−2	−6	−5	−6
Coincident Indicators					
Nonfarm employment	+1	0	+2	+3	+7
Unemployment rate[c]	+1	+2	+1	+2	0
Gross national product[d]	−1	−1	−2	0	−4
Industrial production	0	0	0	0	−1
Personal income[d]	0	0	0	0	n.a.
Mfg. & trade sales[d]	0	0	−3	0	0
Median or Total	0	0	−2	+1	0
			−1	0	0
Lagging Indicators					
Long-duration unemployment[c]	+4	+1	+5	n.a.	n.a.
Plant & equipment investment[d]	+6	+5	+6	0	n.a.
Business inventories[d]	+6	+9	+6	+16	+6
Productivity change, nonfarm[c]	+10	+9	+10	+4	n.a.
Business loans outstanding[d]	+4	+3	+4	+4	n.a.
Interest rates, bus. loans	+7	+5	+4	+4	n.a.
Median or Total	+6	+5	+3	+8	+6
			+6	+6	+6

Notes:

a. The series available for each country are sometimes only roughly equivalent in content to the U.S. series. In some cases two series are used to match the U.S. series and the median includes all observations for both series. The periods covered vary for each indicator and each country, but all are within the years 1948–1981.

b. Matching means that for leading indicators the median is a lead, for lagging indicators the median is a lag, and for coincident indicators the median is a lead or lag of three months or less.

Table 3-4. continued.

Italy	Belgium	Netherlands	Sweden	Japan	All Countries	Number of Countries in Which	
						Median Matches U.S.[b]	Median Does Not Match U.S.[b]
Lead (−) or Lag (+), in Months (continued)							
+2	−2	−1	0	−4	−2	7	2
n.a.	n.a.	n.a.	0	n.a.	−2	2	1
−8	+4	−7	−4	n.a.	−4	5	1
−6	−1	−5	n.a.	−13	−6	6	0
n.a.	−2	−4	n.a.	−4	−3	5	1
−2	−5	−9	n.a.	−9	−7	7	1
n.a.	n.a.	+3	n.a.	−2	−2	3	2
n.a.	−14	+7	+1	0	+1	2	5
−8	n.a.	−8	−10	−6	−8	8	0
n.a.	n.a.	n.a.	n.a.	−10	−3	4	0
n.a.	n.a.	+2	−2	−2	−3	5	2
n.a.	n.a.	n.a.	+4	−9	−8	4	1
−7	−2	−4	0	−5	−3	58	16
+6	n.a.	+4	+5	+2	+3	4	4
+4	−2	0	0	+1	+1	8	1
0	0	n.a.	0	−2	−1	7	1
0	−6	0	0	0	0	8	1
n.a.	n.a.	n.a.	0	−5	0	4	1
−2	−11	0	+4	0	0	7	2
0	−4	0	0	0	0	38	10
n.a.	n.a.	+4	+4	n.a.	+4	4	0
n.a.	n.a.	+2	n.a.	0	+4	3	2
+6	+16	+9	n.a.	+4	+6	8	0
n.a.	n.a.	n.a.	+6	+8	+8	5	0
n.a.	n.a.	n.a.	+4	−4	+4	3	1
+9	+4	n.a.	+14	+9	+7	8	0
+8	+10	+4	+5	+4	+5	31	3

c. Inverted.
d. In constant prices.

Table 3-5. Consistency of Timing of Indicators in Ten Countries, 1948-80.

Number of Indicators for which Median Timings were "Right" (R) or "Wrong" (W)[a]

	At Peaks			At Troughs			At Peaks and Troughs		
	Number		Percent	Number		Percent	Number		Percent
	R	W	Wrong	R	W	Wrong	R	W	Wrong
Leading Indicators									
United States	10	2	17%	12	0	0%	12	0	0%
Canada	7	4	57	7	4	36	8	3	27
United Kingdom	8	2	20	9	1	10	9	1	10
West Germany	8	2	20	8	2	20	9	1	10
France	5	1	20	5	1	17	5	1	17
Italy	4	1	20	4	1	20	4	1	20
Belgium	4	2	33	5	1	17	5	1	17
Netherlands	8	1	11	6	3	33	6	3	33
Sweden	2	5	71	4	3	43	3	4	57
Japan	9	1	10	8	2	20	9	1	10
All except U.S.	55	19	26	56	18	24	56	16	22
Roughly Coincident Indicators									
United States	6	0	0	6	0	0	6	0	0
Canada	6	0	0	6	0	0	6	0	0
United Kingdom	4	2	33	6	0	0	6	0	0
West Germany	5	1	17	4	2	33	6	0	0
France	4	1	20	3	2	40	3	2	40
Italy	4	1	20	2	3	60	3	2	40
Belgium	2	2	50	2	2	50	2	2	50
Netherlands	3	1	25	3	1	25	3	1	25
Sweden	5	1	17	3	3	50	4	2	33
Japan	3	3	50	6	0	0	5	1	17
All except U.S.	36	12	25	35	13	27	38	10	21

United States	22	2	0	0
Canada	19	4	0	0
United Kingdom	18	4	1	25
West Germany	16	2	0	0
France	11	2	0	0
Italy	10	4	0	0
Belgium	8	2	0	0
Netherlands	14	7	2	50
Sweden	9	6	2	40
Japan	15	4	0	15
All except U.S.	120	35	5	15

Lagging Indicators

United States	6	0	0	0
Canada	6	0	0	0
United Kingdom	5	1	17	25
West Germany	3	1	25	0
France	2	0	0	0
Italy	2	2	50	0
Belgium	2	0	33	0
Netherlands	4	0	0	0
Sweden	4	1	20	40
Japan	3	1	14	9
All except U.S.	31	5	14	3

All Indicators

United States	24	0	0	0
Canada	20	4	17	13
United Kingdom	21	2	9	5
West Germany	18	4	22	1
France	10	3	23	23
Italy	9	4	33	25
Belgium	9	4	33	25
Netherlands	12	6	27	35
Sweden	11	4	35	19
Japan	17	3	14	19
All except U.S.	127	29	23	23

Note:
a. "Wrong" median timing is defined as follows: leading indicator (exact coincidence or lag); roughly coincident indicator (lead or lag greater than three months); lagging indicator (exact coincidence or lead).
Source: Center for International Business Cycle Research.

stances, or about a quarter of the time. At troughs the medians fail to lead about 24 percent of the time. The best overview, perhaps, is provided by the median timing for peaks and troughs together. Here, the medians fail to lead in sixteen out of seventy-four cases or 22 percent of the time. The exceptions are widely scattered among the nine countries and among the indicators. There is no country without at least one indicator that failed to show a median lead. Only three indicators, the formation of business enterprises, stock prices, and profits, exhibit median leads at peaks and troughs in all countries.

For the roughly coincident indicators, at peaks there are twelve failures out of forty-eight comparisons, a failure rate of 25 percent. There are a number of medians of zero, and the exceptions are widely dispersed. The same situation is found at troughs, where there are thirteen failures out of forty-eight comparisons, a failure rate of 27 percent. Again the exceptions are dispersed. Viewing the peaks and troughs together, among the roughly coincident indicators the medians for the nine countries fail to match the U.S. behavior 21 percent of the time. There are no exceptions in Canada, the United Kingdom, or West Germany, and as noted, the exceptions are widely dispersed among the indicators as well. As for the lagging indicators, at peaks they fail to lag five out of thirty-four times (a failure rate of 15%), and at troughs the medians fail to match five of thirty-five times (a failure rate of 14%). At both peaks and troughs together, for the lagging indicators, only 9 percent of the medians for other countries fail to match the U.S. pattern, and once more there is no particular pattern either by country or by indicator.

Another way of summarizing this information is shown in Table 3-5, where for each country the number of indicators with medians consistent with ("right") or inconsistent with ("wrong") the U.S. classification is shown. For the United States, taking the results for peaks and troughs combined, the indicators behaved as postulated. This is not unexpected, of course, since the original classification, made in 1966, was based on the U.S. record, albeit at classical cycle turns rather than growth cycle turns and for a period that ended with the business cycle trough in 1961. For the other countries combined, 29 of the 156 indicators, or about 1 of 5, failed to behave in the expected manner—that is, in the manner suggested by U.S. experience. The "failure rate" for each country at both peaks and troughs is shown in the extreme left-hand column of the table. This rate varies from a high of 35 percent in Sweden to a low of 5 percent in the United Kingdom. In the rest of the countries the behavior of most of the indicators—between three-fourths and nine-tenths—corresponded to their behavior in the United States.

In general the lagging indicators deviated less often from their U.S. counterparts than the other indicators did. For the leading group, 22 percent of the indicators in the other nine countries (at peaks and troughs combined) deviated from U.S. experience. For the coincident indicators, 21 percent failed to exhibit roughly coincident performance. For the lagging group, only 9 percent failed to lag.

If we consider peak and trough behavior separately, relatively few substantial differences appear. The similarity in results is probably a consequence of the trend adjustment involved in growth cycle analysis. In the United States, we have found that when no trend adjustment is made, differences in the timing behavior of different indicators are more pronounced at peaks than at troughs. While growth cycle analysis may make the distinction between peak and trough behavior less consequential, there is clear confirmation from the foreign record that indicators that lead, coincide, or lag at peaks also tend to perform the same way at troughs.

NOTES TO CHAPTER 3

1. Measures of smoothness and cyclical amplitude are given in Appendix 3A.

2. Where the number of turning point comparisons in Table 3-1 differs from the number of growth cycle turns in Figure 3-1, this is due to turns at which one or more of the composite indicators could not be matched with the reference chronology.

APPENDIX 3A

SUMMARY MEASURES OF SMOOTHNESS AND AMPLITUDE FOR COMPOSITE INDEXES, TEN COUNTRIES

	U.S.	Canada	U.K.	West Germany	France	Italy	Belgium	Netherlands	Sweden	Japan
A. Leading Indexes										
$\overline{CI}$ (one month span)	0.80	0.62	0.46	0.60	0.72	0.76	2.03	0.71	2.19	1.11
$\overline{I}$ (one month span)	0.48	0.45	0.36	0.40	0.56	0.67	1.88	0.53	2.03	0.61
$\overline{C}$ (one month span)	0.60	0.40	0.23	0.38	0.41	0.31	0.70	0.37	0.73	0.87
I/C Ratio (one month span)	0.79	1.14	1.55	1.06	1.36	2.18	2.69	1.41	2.78	0.70
Months for Cyclical Dominance	1	2	2	2	2	3	3	2	3	1
Average Duration of Run (months)										
CI	3.0	2.3	2.2	3.0	2.5	2.0	1.7	2.7	1.8	3.6
I	1.7	1.6	1.7	1.8	1.7	1.7	1.4	1.8	1.5	1.8
C	12.6	13.8	8.8	10.6	9.6	9.9	7.0	7.7	8.0	13.0
MCD	3.0	4.0	3.2	4.0	3.7	3.3	3.7	3.7	3.5	3.6
B. Roughly Coincident Indexes										
$\overline{CI}$ (one month span)	0.75	0.53	0.47	0.62	0.61	0.80	2.08	0.72	1.95	1.05
$\overline{I}$ (one month span)	0.35	0.28	0.29	0.44	0.43	0.57	1.81	0.48	1.43	0.59
$\overline{C}$ (one month span)	0.64	0.45	0.32	0.47	0.44	0.55	0.94	0.52	1.18	0.86
I/C Ratio (one month span)	0.55	0.64	0.90	0.94	0.99	1.03	1.92	0.92	1.22	0.69
Months for Cyclical Dominance	1	1	1	1	1	2	3	1	2	1

Average Duration of Run (months)										
CI	4.6	3.9	3.1	2.8	2.9	3.1	1.9	3.0	2.8	3.6
I	1.7	1.6	1.7	1.6	1.6	1.8	1.5	1.7	1.7	1.6
C	19.1	20.0	11.6	20.9	16.8	14.2	10.5	14.3	12.8	35.4
MCD	4.6	3.9	3.1	2.8	2.9	4.9	3.9	3.0	4.5	3.6
C. *Lagging Indexes*										
$\overline{CI}$ (one month span)	0.70	0.36	0.41	1.09	0.55	0.81	2.45	0.70	1.93	1.05
$\overline{I}$ (one month span)	0.31	0.34	0.14	0.37	0.37	0.52	2.10	0.35	1.82	0.42
$\overline{C}$ (one month span)	0.63	0.46	0.38	0.96	0.33	0.71	1.45	0.56	1.10	0.93
I/C Ratio (one month span)	0.49	0.74	0.36	0.38	1.12	0.72	1.45	0.62	1.65	0.46
Months for Cyclical Dominance	1	1	1	1	2	1	2	1	2	1
Average Duration of Run (months)										
CI	5.5	3.2	8.3	5.2	4.7	6.4	2.8	7.9	1.8	4.6
I	1.8	1.7	2.1	1.9	1.9	2.1	1.8	2.3	1.6	1.7
C	18.0	16.4	16.3	21.1	14.6	9.6	10.8	11.0	10.7	21.0
MCD	5.5	3.2	8.3	5.2	5.5	6.4	3.6	7.9	3.2	4.6

APPENDIX 3B
NUMERICAL ANALYSIS OF SEQUENCE OF TURNS IN COMPOSITE INDEXES, TEN COUNTRIES

Table 3B-1.   United States, Analysis of Sequence of Turns in Composite Indexes, at Growth Cycle Turns.

	Comparison of			
	Inverted Lagging Index to Leading Index	*Leading Index to Coincident Index*	*Coincident Index to Lagging Index*	*Total*
Peaks				
Number of Timings	9	10	10	29
Number of Successes				
Including Ties	9	10	10	29
Excluding Ties	9	9	10	28
Percent of Successes				
Including Ties	100	100	100	100
Excluding Ties	100	90	100	97
Troughs				
Number of Timings	9	9	9	27
Number of Successes				
Including Ties	8	9	8	25
Excluding Ties	8	8	8	24
Percent of Successes				
Including Ties	89	100	89	93
Excluding Ties	89	89	89	89
Total (P + T)				
Number of Timings	18	19	19	56
Number of Successes				
Including Ties	17	19	18	54
Excluding Ties	17	17	18	52
Percent of Successes				
Including Ties	94	100	95	96
Excluding Ties	94	90	95	93

Table 3B-2. Canada, Analysis of Sequence of Turns in Composite Indexes, at Growth Cycle Turns.

	Comparison of			
	Inverted Lagging Index to Leading Index	*Leading Index to Coincident Index*	*Coincident Index to Lagging Index*	*Total*
Peaks				
Number of Timings	8	10	9	27
Number of Successes				
Including Ties	8	8	8	24
Excluding Ties	8	8	8	24
Percent of Successes				
Including Ties	100	80	89	89
Excluding Ties	100	80	89	89
Troughs				
Number of Timings	9	10	9	28
Number of Successes				
Including Ties	9	8	8	25
Excluding Ties	9	8	7	24
Percent of Successes				
Including Ties	100	80	89	89
Excluding Ties	100	80	78	86
Total (P + T)				
Number of Timings	17	20	18	55
Number of Successes				
Including Ties	17	16	16	49
Excluding Ties	17	16	15	48
Percent of Successes				
Including Ties	100	80	89	89
Excluding Ties	100	80	83	87

Table 3B-3.   United Kingdom, Analysis of Sequence of Turns in Composite Indexes, at Growth Cycle Turns.

	Comparison of			
	Inverted Lagging Index to Leading Index	Leading Index to Coincident Index	Coincident Index to Lagging Index	Total
Peaks				
Number of Timings	6	7	7	20
Number of Successes				
Including Ties	5	5	7	17
Excluding Ties	5	5	7	17
Percent of Successes				
Including Ties	83	71	100	85
Excluding Ties	83	71	100	85
Troughs				
Number of Timings	6	6	6	18
Number of Successes				
Including Ties	6	6	6	18
Excluding Ties	6	6	6	18
Percent of Successes				
Including Ties	100	100	100	100
Excluding Ties	100	100	100	100
Total (P + T)				
Number of Timings	12	13	13	38
Number of Successes				
Including Ties	11	11	13	35
Excluding Ties	11	11	13	35
Percent of Successes				
Including Ties	92	85	100	92
Excluding Ties	92	85	100	92

Table 3B–4. West Germany, Analysis of Sequence of Turns in Composite Indexes, at Growth Cycle Turns.

	Comparison of			
	Inverted Lagging Index to Leading Index	*Leading Index to Coincident Index*	*Coincident Index to Lagging Index*	*Total*
Peaks				
Number of Timings	4	6	3	13
Number of Successes				
Including Ties	4	5	3	12
Excluding Ties	4	4	3	11
Percent of Successes				
Including Ties	100	83	100	92
Excluding Ties	100	67	100	85
Troughs				
Number of Timings	3	5	4	12
Number of Successes				
Including Ties	3	4	4	11
Excluding Ties	3	4	4	11
Percent of Successes				
Including Ties	100	80	100	92
Excluding Ties	100	80	100	92
Total (P + T)				
Number of Timings	7	11	7	25
Number of Successes				
Including Ties	7	9	7	23
Excluding Ties	7	8	7	22
Percent of Successes				
Including Ties	100	82	100	92
Excluding Ties	100	73	100	88

Table 3B-5.   France, Analysis of Sequence of Turns in Composite Indexes, at Growth Cycle Turns.

| | Comparison of | | | |
	Inverted Lagging Index to Leading Index	Leading Index to Coincident Index	Coincident Index to Lagging Index	Total
Peaks				
Number of Timings	3	6	2	11
Number of Successes				
Including Ties	3	6	2	11
Excluding Ties	3	6	2	11
Percent of Successes				
Including Ties	100	100	100	100
Excluding Ties	100	100	100	100
Troughs				
Number of Timings	2	5	3	10
Number of Successes				
Including Ties	2	4	3	9
Excluding Ties	2	4	3	9
Percent of Successes				
Including Ties	100	80	100	90
Excluding Ties	100	80	100	90
Total (P + T)				
Number of Timings	5	11	5	21
Number of Successes				
Including Ties	5	10	5	20
Excluding Ties	5	10	5	20
Percent of Successes				
Including Ties	100	91	100	95
Excluding Ties	100	91	100	95

Table 3B-6.   Italy, Analysis of Sequence of Turns in Composite Indexes, at Growth Cycle Turns.

	Comparison of			
	Inverted Lagging Index to Leading Index	*Leading Index to Coincident Index*	*Coincident Index to Lagging Index*	*Total*
Peaks				
Number of Timings	3	6	3	12
Number of Successes				
Including Ties	3	5	3	11
Excluding Ties	2	5	2	9
Percent of Successes				
Including Ties	100	83	100	92
Excluding Ties	67	83	67	75
Troughs				
Number of Timings	3	5	3	11
Number of Successes				
Including Ties	3	5	3	11
Excluding Ties	3	5	3	11
Percent of Successes				
Including Ties	100	100	100	100
Excluding Ties	100	100	100	100
Total (P + T)				
Number of Timings	6	11	6	23
Number of Successes				
Including Ties	6	10	6	22
Excluding Ties	5	10	5	20
Percent of Successes				
Including Ties	100	91	100	96
Excluding Ties	83	91	83	87

Table 3B–7.   Belgium, Analysis of Sequence of Turns in Composite Indexes, at Growth Cycle Turns.

	Comparison of			
	Inverted Lagging Index to Leading Index	*Leading Index to Coincident Index*	*Coincident Index to Lagging Index*	*Total*
Peaks				
Number of Timings	3	4	3	10
Number of Successes				
Including Ties	3	3	3	9
Excluding Ties	3	3	3	9
Percent of Successes				
Including Ties	100	75	100	90
Excluding Ties	100	75	100	90
Troughs				
Number of Timings	2	3	3	8
Number of Successes				
Including Ties	2	3	3	8
Excluding Ties	2	2	3	7
Percent of Successes				
Including Ties	100	100	100	100
Excluding Ties	100	67	100	88
Total (P + T)				
Number of Timings	5	7	6	18
Number of Successes				
Including Ties	5	6	6	17
Excluding Ties	5	5	6	16
Percent of Successes				
Including Ties	100	86	100	94
Excluding Ties	100	71	100	89

Table 3B-8. Netherlands, Analysis of Sequence of Turns in Composite Indexes, at Growth Cycle Turns.

	Comparison of			
	Inverted Lagging Index to Leading Index	*Leading Index to Coincident Index*	*Coincident Index to Lagging Index*	*Total*
Peaks				
Number of Timings	6	8	7	21
Number of Successes				
Including Ties	6	5	7	18
Excluding Ties	6	4	5	15
Percent of Successes				
Including Ties	100	63	100	86
Excluding Ties	100	50	71	71
Troughs				
Number of Timings	6	7	6	19
Number of Successes				
Including Ties	6	5	6	17
Excluding Ties	6	4	6	16
Percent of Successes				
Including Ties	100	71	100	90
Excluding Ties	100	57	100	84
Total (P + T)				
Number of Timings	12	15	13	40
Number of Successes				
Including Ties	12	10	13	35
Excluding Ties	12	8	11	31
Percent of Successes				
Including Ties	100	67	100	88
Excluding Ties	100	53	85	78

Table 3B-9.   Sweden, Analysis of Sequence of Turns in Composite Indexes, at Growth Cycle Turns.

	Comparison of			
	Inverted Lagging Index to Leading Index	*Leading Index to Coincident Index*	*Coincident Index to Lagging Index*	*Total*
Peaks				
Number of Timings	2	3	3	8
Number of Successes				
Including Ties	2	3	2	7
Excluding Ties	2	3	2	7
Percent of Successes				
Including Ties	100	100	67	88
Excluding Ties	100	100	67	88
Troughs				
Number of Timings	3	3	3	9
Number of Successes				
Including Ties	3	2	3	8
Excluding Ties	3	2	3	8
Percent of Successes				
Including Ties	100	67	100	89
Excluding Ties	100	67	100	89
Total (P + T)				
Number of Timings	5	6	6	17
Number of Successes				
Including Ties	5	5	5	15
Excluding Ties	5	5	5	15
Percent of Successes				
Including Ties	100	83	83	88
Excluding Ties	100	83	83	88

Table 3B-10. Japan, Analysis of Sequence of Turns in Composite Indexes, at Growth Cycle Turns.

	Comparison of			
	Inverted Lagging Index to Leading Index	*Leading Index to Coincident Index*	*Coincident Index to Lagging Index*	*Total*
Peaks				
Number of Timings	6	7	6	19
Number of Successes				
Including Ties	6	6	5	17
Excluding Ties	6	5	5	17
Percent of Successes				
Including Ties	100	86	83	90
Excluding Ties	100	86	83	90
Troughs				
Number of Timings	5	6	6	17
Number of Successes				
Including Ties	5	6	6	17
Excluding Ties	4	6	6	14
Percent of Successes				
Including Ties	100	100	100	100
Excluding Ties	80	100	100	82
Total (P + T)				
Number of Timings	11	13	12	36
Number of Successes				
Including Ties	11	12	11	34
Excluding Ties	10	12	11	33
Percent of Successes				
Including Ties	100	92	92	94
Excluding Ties	91	92	92	92

PART II

PERFORMANCE OF INDIVIDUAL INDICATORS IN TEN COUNTRIES

Chapter 4

PERFORMANCE OF INDIVIDUAL INDICATORS
Behavior at Successive
Turning Points

So far we have seen that most of the leading and lagging indicators that display consistent behavior at classical cycle turning points in the United States have a similar record of leading and lagging growth cycle turning points in at least nine additional countries. This finding corroborates our original supposition that if indicators in other market-oriented economies were selected on the same principles as employed for indicators in the U.S. economy, the foreign indicators would perform in a similar manner. The ten countries represent different stages of industrial development, different degrees of reliance on market forces, and a variety of economic policies. But the indicator systems we have developed suggest that the cyclical interrelations among economic processes are quite similar in each of them.

It is perhaps well to recall that by calling the ten economies under study "market-oriented" we mean to convey that they all fit the Burns–Mitchell criterion of economies that organize their work mainly in business enterprises.[1] The fact that the Burns–Mitchell technique of dating cyclical turns, and of developing leading, coincident, and lagging indicators of these turns, can be said to work reasonably well in all ten nations is proof anew that Mitchell's initial concept of the business cycle still serves as an appropriate point from which to consider the nature of economic instability in the modern world. We must also remind the reader that the indicators included in this study constitute only the earliest of our experiments in developing growth cycle indicators in industrialized economies. We have made very few substitutions, deletions, or additions to our original list of indicators. We thus recognize the need for future adjustments in the selection of indicators for each of the foreign countries, corresponding to the continuing efforts to improve the system in the United States.

Our task in this chapter is to present the evidence and assess the record, turn by turn, indicator by indicator, and country by country. Supporting statistics can be found in Appendix 4B. The essential story in this chapter is provided in Appendix 4A, which shows the graphs of each of the ten countries. The results of the history, turn by turn, are summarized in the chapter tables.

THE UNITED STATES

Information essential for analyzing growth cycle indicators in the United States since World War II is provided in Figure 4A-1. The information contained in the graphs is particularly important because it enables us to make a direct comparison of indicators that are reasonably reliable at classical cycle turning points. Since very few countries outside the United States currently monitor classical cycles, it is essential to know whether indicators of classical turns are reliable indicators of growth turns. We have previously noted that growth cycle peaks tend to precede classical peaks, while troughs exhibit more or less the same timing (or perhaps a short lag). Because a direct comparison of the behavior of identical indicators at growth cycle and classical cycle turns over a long period can be made only for the United States, this step is critical in the appraisal of indicators in other economies. Where indicators behave differently we should, of course, like to know whether it is because the series chosen is a poor equivalent to the U.S. indicator we are attempting to approximate, or whether there is a real divergence between the United States and another country in terms of how the series behaves cyclically. The behavior of U.S. indicators during growth cycles is, therefore, of critical importance to this study.[2]

It is useful to recall that a major change in moving from classical cycle to growth cycle measurement for the United States was the addition of three "growth recessions" to the chronology between 1948 and 1971. Changes have also been made in the dating of turning points, notably at peaks.[3] Because there have been relatively few postwar classical cycles in the case of some other economies, the ability of the growth cycle measurement technique to identify new cyclical episodes (and thereby increase the number of turning points to be studied) is of considerable benefit in testing indicator behavior. It is, therefore, important to note that the three additional recessions—in 1951-52, 1962-64, and 1966-67—can be discerned in Figure 4A-1 in the behavior of most of the indicators. Among the roughly coincident indicators, which determine the growth cycle turns, the only series that fail to match all of the additional growth cycles are the unemployment rate and real personal income, both of which skipped the 1951-52 growth recession. The leading indicators conform about as well to the additional growth recessions as to the other recessions. The lagging indicators fail more often to reflect the additional recessions, doubtless reflecting the general insensitivity of lagging series.

Since the U.S. indicators were selected in 1966, it is of interest to see how they behaved in the decade of the 1970s. All of the indicators in each of the three timing categories reflect the 1973-75 recession. During the 1978-82 growth recession the stock market produced an early—therefore, extra—cycle, but failed to exhibit a peak near the 1978 peak. The ratio of price to unit labor cost produced several turns in the late 1970s. These turns were selected by the computer but were rejected judgmentally because of their small size and short duration. This leading indicator, therefore, displays a very early peak and a trough in 1980. All the coincident and lagging indicators reflect this recession.

These findings have led us to conclude that the technique for dating and measuring growth cycles has sufficient independent validity so that indicators selected on the basis of classical cycle behavior conform as well to recessions that are unique to the growth chronology as to those that are common to both the growth and the classical chronologies. Due to the absence of classical cycle chronologies for most market-oriented economies, and particularly because relatively little has been done to develop quantitative indicators of classical cycles abroad, this finding is important. It suggests the possibility that we can reason from growth cycles back to classical cycles. That is, if the indicators work well in dating and anticipating growth cycle turns in foreign countries, they could also be employed (as traditionally they have been employed in the United States) to date classical cycles and to lead and lag them in a similar manner.[4]

In this connection Mintz observed that "in all the series, the amplitudes of deviation [i.e., growth] cycles which correspond to classical business cycles are much larger than those of cycles which do not. . . ."[5] Thus, amplitudes in general were smaller in the 1960s than in the 1950s. Indeed it is only with the growth cycle technique that the interrelationships at work among the indicators during the 1960s can

Table 4-1. Leads and Lags at U.S. Growth Cycle Turns, Three Groups of U.S. Indicators, 1948-81.

| | *Median Lead (-) or Lag (+), in Months, at U.S. Growth Cycle Peaks (P) and Troughs (T)* | | | | | | | | |
	P 7/48	T 10/49	P 3/51	T 7/52	P 3/53	T 8/54	P 2/57	T 4/58	P 2/60	T 2/61
6 Lagging Indicators Inverted[a]	n.c.[b]	-15	-13	-6	-7	-11	-22	-9	-18	-8
12 Leading Indicators	-1	-5	-2	-10	-3	-9	-15	-2	-9	-1
6 Roughly Coincident Indicators	-2	0	-3	0	+1	0	0	0	0	0
6 Lagging Indicators	0	+4	+10	+1	+6	+8	+5	+4	+4	+5

Notes:

a. Median peaks in lagging group are compared with growth cycle troughs, and median troughs are compared with growth cycle peaks.

b. n.c. = no timing comparison.

Source: Appendix Table 4B-1.

be usefully examined at all. Moreover, the amplitudes of the 1970s appear more like those of the 1950s for a good many of the indicators, thus corroborating Mintz's original observation concerning the relative amplitudes of growth and classical cycles.[6]

The leads and lags of the twenty-six indicators included in Figure 4A-1 at each of the twenty U.S. growth cycle turning points are detailed in Appendix Table 4B-1. Table 4-1 summarizes this behavior by recording the median lead or lag for each of the three classifications of indicators at each growth cycle peak and trough. Where indicator turns cannot be matched with growth cycle turns, or where the data are not available, the number of indicators in each group from which medians can be derived is reduced. However, as a rule the median represents a reasonably large part of the total group of indicators.

The behavior of U.S. indicators summarized in Table 4-1 throws light on two major questions. First, how many exceptions to the rules governing the *timing* classification into leading, roughly coincident, or lagging indicators does the table reveal? That is, how often is a median for the leading indicators found not to lead, the median for

Table 4-1. continued

									Medians at		

Median Lead (–) or Lag (+), in Months,
at U. S. Growth Cycle Peaks (P) and Troughs (T) (continued)

P 5/62	T 10/64	P 6/66	T 10/67	P 3/69	T 11/70	P 3/73	T 3/75	P 12/78	P	T	P & T
-10	-24	-24	-12	-11	-14	-12	-8	-35	-13	-11	-12
-3	-9	-4	-8	-2	-1	-1	0	-2	-2	-5	-2
-2	0	-4	0	+1	0	+3	0	+3	0	0	0
+5	-4	+4	+6	+6	+16	+16	+10	+10	+6	+5	+5

the laggers found not to lag, and the median for the roughly coincident indicators found not to "roughly" coincide?[7]

Table 4-1 shows that there are only four (including zero timing) exceptions, one in each category. The median for the leading indicators is zero at the 1975 trough; and there is a four-month lead at the 1966 peak among the roughly coincident indicators and among the lagging indicators and zero timing at the 1948 peak and a four-month lead at the 1964 trough. Overall, then, the indicators conform to their designated classifications with a success rate of 96.5 percent (or 93.9% if one includes the zeros at the 1948 peak and the 1975 trough as exceptions). This conformity to expectations for the three groups of indicators is very high indeed, especially since it applies to a period extending well beyond 1966, when the indicators were selected and classified.

A second question is whether the *sequence* of turns shown by the three groups of indicators (excluding the turns of the inverted lagging indicators) is what we would expect.[8] That is, even if the median timing for all three groups showed a lag it could be said to conform to our expectations if these lags were +2, +4, and +6, with leaders showing the earliest turn, and laggers the latest. We find five exceptions in the table. Two of these exceptions occur early. At the 1948 peak the median timing for the roughly coincident indicators occurs before the turn in the leading indicators; at the 1951 peak the roughly coincident indicators also turn ahead of the leading indicators; at the 1964 trough the laggers show a median timing that occurs before that in the roughly coincident indicators; at the 1966 peak the leading and coincident groups show identical timing; and this is again the case at the 1975 trough.

Ignoring cases where two groups of indicators show identical median turns, we can therefore say that for the nineteen turning points studied, in only three instances (16%) do the groups fail to show the expected sequential pattern: at the 1948 peak, the 1951 peak, and the 1964 trough. For the three major indicator groups the expected sequence is visible among the medians for the groups 87 percent of the time (92% if medians showing the same timing are regarded as consistent with rather than contrary to the expected sequence of turns). By this test, the timing of the indicators at growth cycle turns is about as consistent as it is at classical cycle turns.

The behavior of the inverted laggers, shown at the top of the table, is another test of the indicator system. Many lagging indicators, especially those that reflect the costs of doing business, can be viewed as having an inverse effect on investment and other decisions. Hence, it is logical to treat their turns in inverted fashion with respect to the following turning point, which they lead. Lagging indicators at troughs can thus be viewed as leading the subsequent peak, and lagging indicators at peaks can be viewed as leading the subsequent trough. As Table 4-1 shows, inverted lagging indicators usually lead by intervals that are far longer than leading indicators do. Since 1948 there have been no failures to lead among the medians for inverted lagging indicators in the United States. This aspect of the sequence, which was observed in the 1950 study of classical cycles, as well as in subsequent studies, holds true for growth cycles as well.[9] If we include the inverted laggers the expected sequence of turns among the medians for each group appears 89 percent of the time (or 93% if tied medians are accepted as consistent with the "expected sequence").

The average duration of U.S. postwar growth cycles has been about three years, and it is clear that indicators will customarily reflect growth cycle turning points with turns of their own spread out at various points throughout the cycle. The full range around peaks (as shown in the averages) is from a lead of thirteen months for the inverted laggers to a lag of six months for the laggers, or nineteen months in all. The comparable range at troughs averages sixteen months. The Burns–Mitchell view, that business cycles are phenomena in which "one phase merges imperceptibly into the next," is thus an accurate one. Significant aspects of economic activity reflect or anticipate these phase changes throughout the growth cycle.

Having observed that indicators of classical cycles in the United States can indeed faithfully reflect growth cycle turning points,[10] we are now in a position to consider, turn by turn, how equivalents to these indicators perform in other economies.

CANADA

The growth cycle chronologies for Canada and the United States show that their economic swings are closely linked. Except for the Canadian growth recession in 1976-77 (which was not matched by a recession in the United States) both countries experienced roughly comparable recessions during the period covered in our study. The Canadian equivalents to the U.S. list of indicators (Figure 4A-2) exhibit a rather large percentage of skipped and extra cycles, but conformity to the expected *timing* among medians for the three groups of indicators is quite high. If we examine Table 4-2 to see whether Canadian leaders do, in fact, lead, laggers lag, and roughly coincident indicators turn within three months of the reference date, we find only twelve exceptions out of a total of fifty-eight observations. Among the leading indicators, there are short lags at the 1953, 1969, and 1976 peaks, and at the 1951, 1970, 1977, and 1980 troughs. Among the coincident indicators, we note three exceptions at the 1975, 1976, and 1979 turns. Among the lagging indicators, there are two exceptions—the leads at the 1953 and 1975 turns. We may conclude, however, that the timing averages among the Canadian indicators conform reasonably well to expectations based upon U.S. experience.

Table 4-2 also reveals six exceptions to the expected *sequential* order in Canada, but if one includes identical timing as perverse, the number of exceptions totals eight. Perverse timing occurs at the 1951 trough, the 1953 peak (twice), the 1969 peak, the 1970 trough, the 1975 trough, the 1979 peak and the 1980 trough. Identical timing occurs at the 1975 and 1980 troughs. These statistics produce a success rate of 84 percent if identical timing is not regarded as a failure. If we include identical timing in our definition of perverse timing the success rate is reduced to 79 percent. If one includes the inverted laggers, the success rate (excluding ties) rises to 89 percent, since there are no perverse timings among the seventeen sequences involving the inverted lagging and leading indicators. Including ties as perverse reduces the success rate to 85 percent. As was the case

Table 4-2. Leads and Lags at Canadian Growth Cycle Turns, Three Groups of Canadian Indicators, 1951-81.

	Median Lead (–) or Lag (+), in Months, at Canadian Growth Cycle Peaks (P) and Troughs (T)									
	P 4/51	*T* 12/51	*P* 3/53	*T* 10/54	*P* 10/56	*T* 8/58	*P* 11/59	*T* 3/61	*P* 3/62	*T* 5/63
6 Lagging Indicators, Inverted[a]	n.c.[b]	n.c.	n.c.	–25	–16	–11	–12	–14	–9	–13
12 Leading Indicators	–3	+1	+2	–4	–7	–8	–2	–4	–2	–2
6 Roughly Coincident Indicators	–1	0	0	–2	0	0	0	0	–1	0
6 Lagging Indicators	n.c.	n.c.	–6	+8	+11	+3	+2	+3	+1	+1

Notes:
a. Median peaks in lagging group are compared with growth cycle troughs, and medians and troughs are compared with growth cycle peaks.
b. n.c. = no timing comparison.
Source: Appendix Table 4B-2.

with median timings, most of these exceptions occur during the 1970s. Why the Canadian indicator system has, in general, behaved less well during the recent past ought to be a subject for future investigation.

THE UNITED KINGDOM

As can be observed in Figure 4A-3 and Table 4-3, all of the leading indicator medians for the United Kingdom lead at the reference turns. Only one of the roughly coincident indicators shows a median timing of more than three months lead or lag (a lead of four months at the 1955 peak), and all of the lagging indicator medians lag except for the exact coincidence at the 1966 peak. This is a very good record for expected timing among the indicator medians.

Concerning the expected temporal sequence at each turn, the patterns produced by the British indicator medians conform highly to predictions based on U.S. experience. Only one discrepancy appears before 1972—the identical timing for medians in the roughly coinci-

Table 4-2. continued

		Median Lead (–) or Lag (+), in Months,										
		at Canadian Growth Cycle Peaks (P) and Troughs (T) (continued)										
										Medians at		
P	T	P	T	P	T	P	T	P	T			
3/66	2/68	2/69	12/70	2/74	10/75	5/76	7/77	9/79	6/80	P	T	P & T
–33	–18	–8	–15	–15	–10	–12	–6	–12	–5	–12	–13	–12
–9	–8	+2	+4	–1	–6	+1	+2	–1	+1	–2	–3	–2
–1	0	0	0	0	–5	+4	+3	–6	+1	0	0	0
+5	+4	+7	+23	+10	–5	+8	+14	+4	+4	+5	+4	+4

dent and lagging indicator groups at the 1966 peak. At the 1973 peak, where one finds the only example of unexpected indicator behavior, the median for the leaders turns two months after the median for the roughly coincident indicators.

Of the thirty-seven sequences under review, the expected sequence appears 97 percent of the time. This figure would drop to 96 percent if one were to exclude inverted laggers. And if identical timing is regarded as perverse, the success rate would stand at 94 percent for all sequences; or 92 percent without the inverted laggers. This record conforms very closely to preliminary results obtained with a somewhat different chronology.[11]

In the present study, leaders lead and laggers lag by slightly longer periods, with the result that the spread among indicator turns is correspondingly increased. Beyond this, though, there appears to be no reason to alter Klein's original assessment that the experience of the United Kingdom during the past quarter century confirms and extends Ilse Mintz's finding that the NBER method of measuring business cycles can be successfully applied not only to growth cycles but to other industrial, market-oriented economies. The relationships involved appear to be as widely applicable, on this evidence at least, as Burns and Mitchell originally assumed.[12]

Table 4-3. Leads and Lags at British Growth Cycle Turns, Three Groups of British Indicators, 1951-81.

Median Lead (–) or Lag (+), in Months, at British Growth Cycle Peaks (P) and Troughs (T)

	P 3/51	T 8/52	P 12/55	T 4/58	P 3/61	T 2/63	P 2/66	T 8/67	P 6/69	T 2/72	P 6/73	T 8/75	P 6/79	Medians at P	T	P & T
6 Lagging Indicators, Inverted[a]	n.c.[b]	–11	–33	–18	–30	–21	–27	–18	–18	–20	–12	–17	–38	–28	–18	–19
12 Leading Indicators	n.c.	–2	–5	–4	–12	–8	–16	–6	–6	–10	+2	–3	–1	–6	–5	–6
6 Roughly Coincident Indicators	+1	+2	–4	0	0	0	0	–3	–5	0	0	+6	0	0	0	0
6 Lagging Indicators	+6	+7	+10	+5	+2	+9	0	+4	+12	+4	+12	+8	+6	+6	+6	+6

Notes:
a. Median peaks in lagging group are compared with growth cycle troughs, and median troughs are compared with growth cycle peaks.
b. n.c. = no timing comparison.
Source: Appendix Table 4B-3.

WEST GERMANY

When Mintz developed her original West German chronology, basing it largely on a collection of roughly coincident indicators, she summarized the evidence by noting, "Perhaps the most important feature brought out in these tables is the regularity with which all the indicators turn near all the business cycle turns."[13] This is perhaps still the most important finding with respect to the behavior of the coincident indicators, not only in the case of West Germany, but in the other economies under study as well. The performance of the indicator system in West Germany, however, is somewhat uneven (see Figure 4A-4 and Table 4-4.

Among the leading indicators, the median fails to conform twice—at the trough in 1963 (+1) and at the peak in 1955 (+14). Among the roughly coincident indicators, there are three exceptions—at the 1975 peak (-6) and the 1980 peak (-4) and at the trough in 1971 (+5). Among the lagging indicators, an exact coincidence appears at the 1970 peak.

The basic timing classification for the medians at all turns is as expected 87 percent of the time (and 84% of the time if we include the exact coincidence as perverse). If we exclude the lagging indicators in inverted form, we have thirty-one observations for West Germany, and the percentage of median timing conforming to expectations is 84 percent excluding the exact coincidences (or 81% including them). These percentages are about the same as for Canada.

When we ask whether the medians for the groups of indicators at each turn are in the appropriate sequence we find that among the inverted laggers versus the leading indicators there are no exceptions; among the leading versus the roughly coincident indicators, there are two failures to conform out of eleven comparisons, plus one case of identical timing. Among the roughly coincident versus lagging indicators, there is one instance of identical timing, but no perverse timing. In sum, 92 percent of the time the sequence is what we would expect (if we include the coincidences as perverse, the percentage is 84%). If we confine our attention to the three major indicator groups and ignore the behavior of the lagging indicators in inverted form, the success rate is 89 percent (78% including the identical timing as perverse).

In the case of West Germany, the success rate is equivalent to more than three-quarters of all the sequential observations that we can make. It is unfortunate that the exceptions are concentrated in the behavior of the leading indicators relative to the roughly coinci-

Table 4–4.   Leads and Lags at West German Growth Cycle Turns, Three Groups of West German Indicators, 1951–81.

Median Lead (-) or Lag (+), in Months, at West German Growth Cycle Peaks (P) and Troughs (T)

	P 2/51	T 2/54	P 10/55	T 4/59	T 2/61	P 2/63	P 5/65	T 8/67	P 5/70	T 12/71	T 8/73	T 5/75	P 2/80	Medians at P	Medians at T	Medians at P & T
5 Lagging Indicators, Inverted[a]	n.c.[b]	n.c.	n.c.	n.c.	n.c.	n.c.	-19	-17	-29	-19	-14	-14	-56	-24	-17	-19
7 Leading Indicators	n.c.	n.c.	+14	-6	-10	+1	-3	-4	-9	-4	-6	-6	-14	-8	-4	-7
7 Roughly Coincident Indicators	0	0	+2	+1	0	0	0	+3	0	+5	-6	+1	-4	0	+1	0
5 Lagging Indicators	n.c.	n.c.	n.c.	n.c.	n.c.	+8	+10	+4	0	+6	+7	+2	n.m.[c]	+7	+5	+6

Notes:
a. Median peaks in lagging group are compared with growth cycle troughs, and median troughs are compared with growth cycle peaks.
b. n.c.   = no timing comparison.
c. n.m. = no matching turn.
Source: Appendix Table 4B–4.

dent indicators. In forecasting economic activity this is the very comparison likely to receive the most attention. It is well to recall, however, that the virtual absence of classical recessions in West Germany until the 1970s made conventional analysis of cyclical behavior in general, as well as indicator analysis in particular, all but impossible for the postwar period. In a sense, therefore, the German evidence is the clearest thus far in suggesting that the sequence of turns in leading, roughly coincident, and lagging indicators is transferable from classical to growth cycles. It might have been argued, for example, that this transferability occurs only because roughly coterminous classical cycles accompany the growth cycles. In Germany the expected results appear even during periods when there are virtually no classical cycles. As will be seen, this is equally true of Japan, and it underscores one of the useful properties of growth cycle analysis: there are times when it is a prerequisite to any cyclical analysis at all.

FRANCE

The basic information with which to assess the behavior of the indicator system in France is given in Figure 4A-5 and summarized in Table 4-5. With France we encounter the first serious obstacle to testing the indicator system in another country, because thus far we have been able to find only two series to include in the lagging indicator group. We have (reluctantly) placed these two series in the form of a composite index, but not because we have great confidence in any composite index based on so few series. However, not only are confirming indicators necessary to test the three basic indicator groups fully, but the lagging indicators in inverted form are, as we have seen, one of the best early indicators of subsequent cyclical changes in direction. Despite this drawback and for the sake of comparing French cyclical behavior with that in the other countries, we have decided to deal with what information we have. As Table 4-5 suggests, the incentive to find more lagging indicators should be high. Even the little information we have conforms quite as we would expect—the inverted laggers show (mostly) long leads, and the lagging indicators show median lags at each growth cycle turn. In terms of whether the median timing in each indicator group conforms to the basic timing expected, the data indicate a positive correlation for all turns involving the lagging indicators, both in their inverted and regular form. The leading indicators show leads with but one exception (the 1971 trough) while the roughly coincident indicators display one discrepancy from the required turn of three months (or less) from the growth cycle turn. The exception is at the peak in

Table 4-5. Leads and Lags at French Growth Cycle Turns, Three Groups of French Indicators, 1957-81.

Median Lead (−) or Lag (+), in Months, at French Growth Cycle Peaks (P) and Troughs (T)

	P 8/57	T 8/59	P 2/64	T 6/65	P 6/66	T 5/68	P 11/69	T 11/71	P 5/74	T 6/75	P 8/79	Medians at P	T	P & T
2 Lagging Indicators, Inverted[a]	n.c.[b]	n.c.	n.c.	n.c.	n.c.	n.c.	−17	−20	−18	−7	−44	−18	−14	−18
6 Leading Indicators	−1	−16	−5	−12	−4	−4	−2	+4	−11	−4	−2	−3	−4	−4
5 Roughly Coincident Indicators	−2	−1	+2	−3	0	0	−12	+3	0	0	0	0	0	0
2 Lagging Indicators	n.c.	n.c.	n.c.	n.c.	n.c.	+1	+4	+12	+6	+6	n.m.[c]	+5	+6	+6

Notes:
a. Median peaks in lagging group are compared with growth cycle troughs, and median troughs are compared with growth cycle peaks.
b. n.c. = no timing comparison.
c. n.m. = no matching turn.
Source: Appendix Table 4B-5.

1969. This gives the French indicator system a success rate of 93 percent (or 94% if we include the lagging indicators in inverted form).

If we consider whether the French indicator system displays the expected sequence of turns for the groups of indicators of each growth cycle turn, data show that the only discrepancies occur in the relationship between the leading and roughly coincident indicators. Three exceptions out of eleven sequences can be observed. They occur at 1957 peak, the 1969 peak, and the 1971 trough. This relationship is the one most widely watched in any indicator system, and it is unfortunate that in France the success rate is only 73 percent. This poor showing underscores the importance of enriching the indicator system in France, because if we include the lagging indicators in the sequences to be monitored we find that the French performance is what is expected in 81 percent of the sixteen sequences (and 86% if we include the inverted lagging indicators and increase the observations to twenty-one). While expected indicator behavior in France is slightly lower than that observed generally in the countries considered earlier, it is still quite high. An increase in the number of indicators in the future can be expected to improve the representativeness of the indicator system as a reflection of French economic activity.

ITALY

As was the case in France, there are but two lagging indicators in the system we have developed for Italy. The basic information with which to judge the Italian economy is presented in Figure 4A-6 and is summarized in Table 4-6. The figure suggests that the system's performance is remarkably good in view of the anomalous behavior of a number of the indicators. There is, for one thing, tremendous volatility in several of these individual indicators. Industrial production, for example, a series frequently used by economists as the sole measure of cyclical activity, displays six computer-selected turning points that have been eliminated according to our judgment because of their relatively small amplitudes. (Some of these turns are even reflected in the composite index, but the amplitude is very small and the recessions have been rejected judgmentally.) There is clearly more ambiguity emerging from the computer-selected turns in the case of Italy than has been the case in any of the countries thus far analyzed. Why this should be so is still a question for future research.

It is remarkable that, despite inadequate or volatile data, the Italian indicator system works as well as it does. The median timing for the indicator groups at individual turning points conforms within an

Table 4-6.   Leads and Lags at Italian Growth Cycle Turns, Three Groups of Italian Indicators, 1956–81.

Median Lead (−) or Lag (+), in Months, at Italian Growth Cycle Peaks (P) and Troughs (T)

	P 10/56	T 7/59	P 9/63	T 3/65	P 8/69	T 9/72	P 4/74	T 5/75	P 12/76	T 12/77	P 2/80	Medians at P	T	P & T
2 Lagging Indicators, Inverted[a]	n.c.[b]	n.c.	n.c.	n.c.	n.c.	−27	−13	−7	−13	−12	−14	−13	−12	−13
5 Leading Indicators	+12	−10	−2	−6	−8	−10	−5	−5	0	−1	−14	−4	−6	−5
5 Roughly Coincident Indicators	0	−4	+1	0	0	+4	0	0	0	−2	0	0	0	0
2 Lagging Indicators	n.c.	n.c.	n.c.	n.c.	+10	+6	+6	+6	0	+12	n.c.	+6	+6	+6

a. Median peaks in lagging group are compared with growth cycle troughs, and median troughs are compared with growth cycle peaks.

b. n.c. = no timing comparison.

Source: Appendix Table 4B-6.

acceptable range to the definition for each timing classification. Out of eleven turns, the median timing among the leading indicators shows some lead at all the turns except the 1956 peak and 1976 peak, when the median is zero. The roughly coincident indicators show two of the medians falling outside the three-month range considered appropriate for "rough coincidence." The exceptions are the four-month lead at the 1959 trough, and the four-month lag at the 1972 trough. (Since 1972 the roughly coincident indicators have all behaved quite well for Italy, a finding that is noteworthy in view of the tendency in some countries, such as Canada, West Germany, and France, for coincident indicators to behave less well in the past dozen years or so.) The lagging indicators in Italy all lag, with the exception of a median timing of zero at the 1976 peak. In sum, the percentage of "correct" observations totals 82 percent (or 85% if we include the inverted laggers, which all display long leads).

But what about the record of sequential turns among the four groups of indicators for Italy? The leading indicators display a median that precedes the median for the roughly coincident indicators at all the reference turns except for the first peak in 1956, and trough in 1977. At the 1976 peak the two medians show identical timing. The median for lagging indicators follows the median in the roughly coincident indicators at all turns except again in the 1976 peak, when the two groups of indicators turned together. Ignoring the inverted lagging indicators, the success rate for the sequences is 88 percent (excluding the cases of identical timing) and 76 percent if identical timing is included among the perverse timing sequences. If we consider the inverted lagging indicators, the number of sequences increases from seventeen to twenty-three. Ignoring the identical timings, the success rate is 91 percent; regarding identical timing as perverse reduces the percentage to 83 percent, which is still rather high. In general, then, the results for the Italian indicator system are remarkably good, particularly in view of the difficulties with data availability and performance. Improving the data base with respect to both the quantity and quality of information is a matter to which attention must be directed in future studies of Italian business cycles.

BELGIUM

The system of economic indicators for Belgium was not developed until fairly recently, thus making the task of establishing Belgian equivalents to the 1966 U.S. indicator list more difficult than was

Table 4-7. Leads and Lags at Belgian Growth Cycle Turns, Three Groups of Belgian Indicators, 1964-81.

	Median Lead (-) or Lag (+), in Months, at Belgian Growth Cycle Peaks (P) and Troughs (T)							Medians at		
	P 10/64	T 7/68	P 9/70	T 7/71	P 7/74	T 10/75	P 6/79	P	T	P & T
2 Lagging Indicators, Inverted[a]	n.c.[b]	n.c.	-16	-20	-26	-9	-35	-26	-14	-20
6 Leading Indicators	-3	-4	-14	-2	-2	-2	+2	-2	-2	-2
4 Roughly Coincident Indicators	-1	-1	0	-1	-2	-4	-17	-2	-1	-1
2 Lagging Indicators	n.c.	+10	+2	+10	+6	+9	+16	+6	+10	+10

Notes:
a. Median peaks in lagging group are compared with growth cycle troughs, and median troughs are compared with growth cycle peaks.
b. n.c. = no timing comparison.
Source: Appendix Table 4B-7.

the case in the economies already discussed. Available data are presented in Figure 4A-7 and summarized in Table 4-7.

The Belgian experience provides a good example of the difficulties that can emerge in selecting an appropriate turning point for growth cycles since the measures of aggregate economic activity (which are all presumably reflected in the growth cycle chronology) fail to turn within a narrow time frame. In the early 1970s the index of industrial production turned a full year before the trough in the coincident composite index was reached. Retail sales turned even earlier than the index of production, while only unemployment—a series which not infrequently lags at growth cycle turns—exhibits a trough near the coincident composite index. We have placed the turn in 1971—the time when most of the components of the composite index turn rather than when the composite index turns.

Despite these difficulties, we may note that the median timing for each of the indicator groups falls within the range we would expect. At six of the seven turns available, the medians lead for the leading indicators. Medians for the roughly coincident indicators also turn within three months of the selected reference turns in five of seven instances. There is no failure to lag among the lagging indicators in the six cases available.

If we examine the relationship between the median timing for leading and roughly coincident indicators (a total of seven comparisons), there are two cases of perverse timing (1975, 1979). We find that the median for leaders does indeed turn before the median for the roughly coincident indicators, in four cases, but in one case there is identical timing. There are no failures of the median for lagging indicators to turn after the median for leading indicators. Moreover, in the five instances available, the inverted laggers invariably lead the leading indicators by a fairly wide margin. Despite the paucity of data, the two lagging indicators also behave as expected. Because it is clear that the indicators we do have do behave reasonably well the case for developing a larger and better group of lagging indicators for Belgium is strong indeed and we would hope that this can soon be done. Indeed one of the overall byproducts from analyzing an indicator system in other countries is to suggest the usefulness to that country of improving the quantity and quality of the indicators available in cases, as Belgian experience illustrates, where the indicator system seems to work.

Analysis of Table 4–7 reveals that among the sequential relationships just considered we find a success rate of 85 percent if we exclude the five lagging inverted indicators, or 89 percent if we consider all of the sequential relationships that can be compared. If we include the one tie as perverse the percentages fall to 77 percent and 83 percent. Such success rates, based as they are on limited data, encourage continued monitoring of Belgian business cycles. Further development of the indicator system, with particular attention paid to the identification of lagging indicators, however, is clearly necessary for a fuller understanding of this small, though highly industrialized, economy.

THE NETHERLANDS

The authors have been able to acquire quite a number of equivalents to the 1966 U.S. list of reliable indicators in their research on the Netherlands. And while an adequate chronology has been developed, difficulties with the data and indicator performance have led to results that are in certain respects less satisfactory than results obtained

Table 4–8. Leads and Lags at Dutch Growth Cycle Turns, Three Groups of Dutch Indicators, 1950-81.

Median Lead (-) or Lag (+), in Months, at Dutch Peaks (P) and Troughs (T)

	P 7/50	T 6/52	P 10/56	T 5/58	P 3/61	T 2/63	P 11/65	T 8/67	P 11/70	T 8/72	P 8/74	T 7/75	P 9/76	T 11/77	P 12/79	Med P	Med T	Med P&T
3 Lagging Indicators, Inverted[a]	n.c.[b]	n.c.	-10	-6	-12	-31	-15	-14	-15	-19	-8	-7	-6	-12		-13	-11	-12
9 Leading Indicators	+9[c]	+6	-8	-1	0	+3	-2	-6	-6	-4	-1	+2	+4		-4	-2	-1	-1
5 Roughly Coincident Indicators	+4[c]	+2	0	0	0	0	+3	0	0	0	0	0	0	-4	0	0	0	0
3 Lagging Indicators	n.c.	+9	+6	0	0	+8	+3	+3	+3	0	+7	+8	+12	+2[c]	+3	+3	+8	+6

Notes:

a. Median peaks in lagging group are compared with growth cycle troughs, and median troughs are compared with growth cycle peaks.

b. n.c. = no timing comparison.

c. Only one indicator turn.

Source: Appendix Table 4B-8.

for countries already reviewed. Why this should be the case is unclear, but we shall attempt an explanation based on the evidence in Figure 4A–8 and Table 4–8.

We do have an unusually long growth cycle chronology for the Netherlands. If we consider leading indicators, we find that, out of fifteen possible observations, five medians exhibit perverse timing behavior (lags). Of these, three occur at peaks; two at troughs. Clearly, leading indicators behaved badly at the beginning of the period under review, but there has more recently been pervserse behavior as well among the leading indicators. If we define "success" as any lead at all, however, the leading indicators performed as expected in two-thirds of the cases examined. Among the roughly coincident indicators, there are only two that must be termed perverse, but again they occur very early and very late in the period under consideration. This gives a success rate of 87 percent for the roughly coincident indicators, which compares well with what has been found earlier in the case of other countries. The large number of exact coincidences in timing for these medians suggests strongly that the same indicators that track growth cycles in other market-oriented economies give reasonably unambiguous results for the Netherlands as well. The record increases our confidence in the growth cycle chronology that we have devised for the Netherlands, and we believe that it is a reasonably appropriate one against which to attempt the development of reliable leading and lagging indicators.

In the case of lagging indicators, of the thirteen growth cycle turns for which a median timing can be calculated ten produce a lag and three show exact coincidences. No breakdown in the performance of lagging indicators appears either at the beginning or the end of the period we are studying, and the exceptions to expected timing occur more or less at random in the middle of the period.

If we next consider the median of the timing comparisons at all the individual turns, the results are very similar to those observed in the behavior of the composite indicators summarized in Chapter 3. Very short leads exist for the leading indicators at both peaks and troughs; adequately long lags at peaks as well as troughs can be observed for the lagging indicators. The overall success rate among the three groups of indicators is 77 percent. This rate approximates the percentages calculated for countries previously discussed, but, as we have said, the Dutch leading indicators do not exhibit very long leads.

We should now consider the sequential performance of the four groups of indicators (including the lagging indicators in inverted form). The relationship between inverted laggers and leaders reveals no perverse sequences or ties—a perfect success rate. Among leading and roughly coincident indicators, less satisfactory results might be anticipated because of the short leads among the leaders. Out of fifteen possible observations, eight are in the direction we would expect, five are perverse (with the roughly coincident median timing preceding the median timing for the leading indicators), and two are ties. Excluding the ties the success rate is 53 percent. But if we include the ties this rate climbs to 67 percent.

Thirteen comparisons of the timing between roughly coincident and lagging indicators result in ten cases that are in the expected direction, for a success rate of 77 percent. There are three ties (23% of the cases) and no cases of perverse behavior. Thus, if we consider the ties as successful (that is, as not being perverse) the roughly coincident/lagging sequence achieves a 100 percent success rate.

If we ignore the inverted laggers and if the identical timing cases are regarded as perverse, there are twenty-eight sequential observations, and they produce a success rate of 64 percent. If identical timing is not regarded as perverse, the success rate increases to 82 percent. When we include the inverted indicators, we arrive at forty sequential observations, thirty of which behave as expected (not including the cases of identical timing), for a success rate of 75 percent. If ties are not regarded as perverse, the success rate overall rises to 88 percent.

Many researchers tie the fortunes of the Dutch economy to West Germany. Comparison of Table 4–8 to Table 4–4 suggests that, despite some degree of parity in growth cycle chronologies between the two countries, very few similarities in the lapses from the expected sequence exist among the indicator groups. There are, of course, differences in the essential organization of the two economies, and it is probably fair to say that the West German economy is considerably more market-oriented than the Dutch. Whether divergence from full reliance on the market affects the potential usefulness of an indicator system is one of the questions that in a sense underlies the whole of this book. While there are considerable differences among the ten countries under review, all appear to be sufficiently "market-oriented" to fall well within the Mitchellian rubric of "nations that organize their work mainly in business enterprises." Hence, degree of market orientation does not appear to be a promising avenue to explore in accounting for the instances of "failure" in the indicator system for the Netherlands. We have seen that the success rate is well within the range found for other economies and that the essential integrity of the indicator approach is supported once again with the Dutch data under review. The Dutch success rate also suggests that the next stage in our work—improving the performance of the indicator system in each country by developing indicators especially sensitive to growth fluctuations—is especially important in the case of the Netherlands. This is particularly true for the leading indicators, which do not in general present leads long enough to be very useful in economic forecasting. While there is much to be said for an international indicator system based on a common set of business indexes, there is also much to be said for tailoring this effort, when necessary, on a country-by-country basis in order to produce the most sensitive indicator systems possible.

SWEDEN

Sweden further tests the application first questioned in connection with our discussion of the Netherlands, of the term "market-oriented" as an ingredient essential to the Mitchellian analysis of international economic indicators.

A total of seventeen series in Sweden were regarded as roughly equivalent (in deflated form) to the twenty-six series derived from the U.S. 1966 list of reliable indicators, which served as our basis for collecting data. One of the Swedish leaders, though, housing starts, an industry highly regulated by the national authorities, proved to have no discernible growth cycle turning points and so could not be matched with a growth cycle chronology. While the Swedish government in recent years has swung away from central planning and moved again toward a market-orientation, it is nonetheless interesting to consider how an indicator system derived from the Burns-Mitchell methodology (and duplicating as closely as possible the indicators found reliable in the United States) will behave in a country that has, during the post–World War II period, pursued "the middle way."

Figure 4A-9 illustrates the behavior of the leading, roughly coincident, and lagging indicators for Sweden at each of the six growth cycle turns we have identified. A summary of this behavior appears in Table 4-9, which describes the median timing for the three basic groups of indicators, as well as for the laggers in inverted form, at each of the three peaks and troughs in the Swedish chronology.[14]

Table 4-9 suggests that the Swedish data reveal a success rate of 78 percent. If we ignore the inverted lagging indicators, the median for all the indicators classified into the three basic timing groups

Table 4-9. Leads and Lags at Swedish Growth Cycle Turns, Three Groups of Swedish Indicators, 1965-81.

| | *Median Lead (−) or Lag (+), in Months, at Swedish Growth Cycle Peaks (P) and Troughs (T)* | | | | | | Medians at | | |
	P 2/65	T 7/67	P 7/70	T 7/72	P 6/74	T 7/78	P	T	P & T
4 Lagging Indicators, Inverted[a]	n.m.[b]	−19	−22	−24	−13	−48	−18	−24	−22
7 Leading Indicators	−3	+7	−3	0	+4	−7	−3	0	−2
6 Roughly Coincident Indicators	0	0	0	−1	+5	−2	0	−1	0
4 Lagging Indicators	+10	+10	0	+10	+1	+6	+1	+10	+8

Notes:
a. Median peaks in lagging group are compared with growth cycle troughs, and median troughs are compared with growth cycle peaks.
b. n.m. = no matching turn.
Source: Appendix Table 4B-9.

falls in the expected category fourteen out of eighteen times. The median for the leaders produces two lags—one of four months at the 1974 peak, and one of seven months at the 1967 trough. Among the coincident indicators, a five-month median lag occurs at the 1974 peak. Laggers lag except at the 1970 peak. If we include the inverted laggers, a total of twenty-two observations results, and because inverted laggers consistently lead as expected, the total success rate rises to 19 out of 23 possible cases, or 83 percent of the time. This rate is well within the limits of cases reviewed earlier. It is, in fact, as good, and possibly a bit better, than the behavior of the composite indexes covered in Chapter 3.

Turning our attention to the question of whether or not expected sequences are discernible among the various medians for the indicator groups, we find once again that the results line up reasonably close to those in other countries. If we confine our attention to the three major timing classifications, we observe twelve sequences among the medians for the Swedish indicators. Of these, there are four instances of perverse timing, excluding one instance of identical timing—a "success rate" of 67 percent. If identical timing is regarded as perverse, the rate drops to 58 percent. Perverse timings occur between the leading and coincident indicators at the 1967 trough and the 1972 trough and the 1974 peak, as well as between coincident and lagging indicators at the 1974 peak.[15] (Timing is identical at the 1970 peak.)

We can, as before, improve the performance of the system overall by including the inverted lagging indicators. The overall success rate for the Swedish indicator system can thus be raised to 71 percent if identical timing is regarded as perverse, and to 76 percent if it is not. The lagging indicators in inverted form produce five observations, and in all these cases the inverted lagging index turns before the leading index, although there are two instances in which there is no match.

The success rate for Sweden is, therefore, quite similar to that for the Netherlands, but once again we find that, with few exceptions, the median leads for leading indicators are disappointingly short. Lagging indicators show reasonably long lags. We can conclude then, that while the Swedish record corroborates yet again the overall feasibility of the cyclical approach, search for more sensitive indicators should be undertaken to enhance our understanding of this country's market forces.

JAPAN

We saw in Chapter 3 that U.S. and Canadian growth cycle chronologies are closely related. The Japanese economic record, while broadly comparable to North America, appears to be a bit closer to the European economies, if not in timing, then in the number of growth cycles experienced in the period since the early 1950s. During the past thirty years Japan, like West Germany, experienced six growth cycles. Canada and the United States, for a roughly comparable period, experienced eight. Japan's rapid growth during the 1950s and 1960s precluded cyclical declines in aggregate economic activity, yet the indicator behavior expected from the evidence of classical cycles in the United States was substantially reproduced in Japanese growth cycles.

Table 4-10, summarizes the median timing for indicators at each growth cycle turning point. The findings are essentially the same as those we have come to expect—exceptions, however, occur among the roughly coincident indicators at the 1980 peak, which shows a twelve-month lead. There are no exceptions among the leading indicators, and only one among the lagging indicators (a four-month lead

Table 4-10. Leads and Lags at Japanese Growth Cycle Turns, Three Groups of Japanese Indicators, 1953–81.

Median Lead (−) or Lag (+), in Months, at Japanese Growth Cycle Peaks (P) and Troughs (T)

	P 12/53	T 6/55	P 5/57	T 1/59	P 1/62	T 1/63	P 7/64	T 2/66	P 6/70	T 1/72	P 11/73	T 3/75	P 2/80	Medians at P	T	P & T
6 Lagging Indicators, Inverted[a]	n.c.[b]	n.c.	−12	−8	−21	−6	−14	−15	−34	−5	−15	−7	−51	−18	−7	−14
10 Leading Indicators	−1	−9	−4	−4	−6	−6	−10	−6	−5	−1	−6	−2	−14	−6	−4	−4
6 Roughly Coincident Indicators	−2	0	0	0	−2	0	−2	+1	0	0	0	0	−12	−2	0	0
6 Lagging Indicators	n.c.	+11	+12	+15	+6	+5	+4	+9	+3	+8	+8	+8	−4	+5	+8	+8

Notes:
a. Median peaks in lagging group are compared with growth cycle troughs, and median troughs are compared with growth cycle peaks.
b. n.c. = no timing comparison.
Source: Appendix Table 4B-10.

of the 1980 peak). This represents a success rate of 95 percent. If we include the inverted lagging indicators, appropriate behavior among Japanese indicators occurs in 96 percent of the observations.

If we examine whether the groups of indicators turn in the expected sequence regardless of the absolute timing, we find that the Japanese record is almost as impressive. The median for leading indicators occurs earlier than the median for roughly coincident indicators at all turns, with the exception of the very first peak in 1953 (when leaders turned one month after roughly coincident indicators). Relationships between the roughly coincident indicators and the lagging indicators performed as expected in every instance, except the 1980 peak when the coincident group turned eight months after the lagging group. Thus, the success rate among the three major indicator groups is 92 percent. If we include the inverted lagging indicators, we encounter the expected timing at all turns, with the exception of the 1963 trough when the inverted lagging and leading indicators have identical median timing. For all four indicator groups the success rate is 94 percent (or 92% if we count ties among the perverse timing observations).

SUMMARY AND CONCLUSIONS

Having summarized the timing behavior of leading, roughly coincident, and lagging indicators at growth cycle turning points for ten different countries, the evidence of aggregate economic activity appears to strongly support the fundamental hypothesis of this book—namely, that the Burns–Mitchell approach to cyclical analysis can be adapted to monitor growth cycles not only in the United States, but in other market-oriented economies as well.

We will now concentrate on the median timing of each group of indicators at growth cycle peaks or troughs in the countries under study. Does the median for each group of indicators at each turn, in fact, conform to the timing classification rules for indicators? How consistently do leading indicators lead, lagging indicators lag, and roughly coincident indicators turn within the prescribed three months of each growth cycle turn? To what extent does the median timing for all indicator groups adhere to the expected sequence? To answer this third question, we considered all the possible sequential observations available, including or excluding the sequences involving the inverted laggers vis-à-vis the leaders (on the grounds that inverted laggers lead by so long that it is truly rare for the median timing of turns in that group not to precede the leaders), and paid particular attention to cases where the median timing in two groups of indicators was identical. These "ties," if regarded as examples of "perverse timing," can be excluded from the "successful sequences." We thus reduce the definition of success in the sequential patterns to the minimum.

The timing sequences considered in the previous tables of this chapter are summarized in Table 4-11. If we include the inverted laggers, the table suggests that overall the expected sequence occurred 88 percent of the time in the nine foreign countries. This compares to 82 percent for the United States. If we exclude the inverted laggers and consider simply the sequences for leading, roughly coincident, and lagging indicators, the expected sequences occurred at turns in 83 percent of the cases outside the United States, compared to 87 percent for the U.S. data.

This suggests that there are countries outside the United States—where the technique for the classification of indicators originated, where the system actually behaves better than in the United States along with cases where the contrary is the case. It should, of course, be borne in mind that the results just given are based on the behavior of median timing patterns, and there are a far larger number of exceptions in the behavior of individual indicators at individual turns.[16] But that kind of a test would also reveal a large number of exceptions if we considered the behavior of individual indicators at classical cycles.[17]

Moreover, the figures in this chapter form an indispensable part of the total picture because they do indeed show the behavior of each individual indicator on a turn by turn basis. The general conformity to the growth cycle chronology postulated, as well as the exceptions, is visibly displayed there for the interested reader.

Having commented on the overall success with which the indicators we have collected perform, we ought, nonetheless, to pause to consider why the indicator system performs notably better in some countries than in others. One observation is certainly in order. In general, the indicator system often performs less well in the initial periods for which data in foreign countries became available. Time after time exceptions, both in the median timing for a group of indicators and in the sequential behavior, was poorer at the first turn or two than subsequently. Whether this can be explained entirely on grounds that the data are of lesser quality is uncertain. Certain countries have undeniably undergone important economic changes, i.e., they have become more or less "market-oriented." In any case it is doubtful whether the successfulness of the indicator system can be correlated with the degree of market-dominance with any precision. Certainly, the indicator system appears to work somewhat more con-

Table 4-11. Summary, Percent "Success" Rate in Median Timing of Growth Cycle Indicators, for Ten Countries.

Country	Number of Observed Sequences[a]	Percent Expected Sequences		Number of Observed Sequences Excluding Inverted Laggers	Percent Expected Sequences	
		All Sequences	Excluding "Ties"		All Sequences	Excluding "Ties"[b]
United States	56	89	93	38	87	92
Canada	55	85	89	35	84	79
United Kingdom	37	94	97	25	92	96
West Germany	25	84	92	18	78	89
France	21	86	86	16	81	81
Italy	23	83	91	17	83	91
Belgium	18	83	89	13	77	85
Sweden	17	75	88	12	58	75
Netherlands	40	71	76	28	64	82
Japan	36	92	94	25	88	92
Mean (Excluding U.S.)	30	84	89	21	78	77
Median (Excluding U.S.)	25	85	89	18	78	85

Notes:
a. Including inverted laggers.
b. Cases where two groups of indicators show identical median timing are "ties." In this column they are treated as consistent with the "expected" sequence.

sistently for some of the larger countries than is the case in some of the smaller economies, although why the results for the Netherlands, for example, where it works relatively poorly, should be so disparate to the results for Belgium, where it works relatively well, is not at all clear. Overall, the results were least encouraging in the case of Sweden and the Netherlands, but on the other hand the performance appears better than in the United States, in the United Kingdom, Belgium, and perhaps, Japan.

One other finding is perplexing. The number of exceptions was somewhat greater not only at the beginning, but also, in the case of a number of countries, during the most recent few growth cycle turns. This tendency, though not pronounced, is noticeable. Even in the United States the success rate was higher prior to the last few growth cycle turns. We have, of course, already commented on the necessity for constant review of indicator performance with the object of updating and revising the short lists of "most reliable indicators" on which for the sake of efficiency many countries now rely. The comments made here underscore the importance of this while we remind the reader of our earlier finding that indicators for the United States historically have only rarely exhibited any fundamental change in their timing characteristics. Certainly, they have only rarely been reclassified from one group to another.

There are other anomalies. Again with respect to the Dutch performance, it is interesting to note that the success rate is in the same general range as is that of West Germany which (among the major countries) has a somewhat lower success rate than the other countries. The Dutch often comment on the degree to which cyclical developments in their country follow those in West Germany. We have begun to explore indicators related directly to foreign trade in an effort to test the usefulness of the indicator system in forecasting these international developments. (See Chapter 7 for a preliminary discussion of these possibilities.) What remains to be done is to consider whether there may be countries in which the domestic operation of an indicator system can be systematically changed by the influences from outside. That is, could the interrelationships mirrored in the indicator system be systematically affected in enterprise economies heavily dependent on developments in another economy? The answer is not clear, but the possibility is certainly real that the performance of indicators which otherwise lead or lag with some degree of consistency in countries that are both enterprise-oriented and largely self-sufficient could be significantly affected in a country with a large dependence on an outside economy. Such a possibility might explain the performance of the Dutch indicators, but the question of why German performance is poorer than that of the United Kingdom, Italy, Canada, or Japan, remains largely open. A systematic and continuing reevaluation of the performance of the indicators in each country is always in order, perhaps employing some variant of the scoring systems used in recent years for U.S. indicators.[18]

NOTES TO CHAPTER 4

1. Cf. A.F. Burns and W.C. Mitchell, *Measuring Business Cycles* (New York: NBER, 1946), p. 3.

2. Before examining the figures in the appendixes the reader should be reminded of the notation used. Asterisks denote turning points selected by the computer or by judgmental analysis. Circled asterisks identify turns selected by the computer but rejected in judgmental analysis. Asterisks inside a square identify turning points added by judgmental analysis. In this way divergences from the computer-selected turns, based on a codification of the basic "rules" for turning point selection, can be easily seen.

3. The current growth cycle chronology represents a more up-to-date version of the chronology developed by Mintz, "Dating United States Growth Cycles," *Explorations in Economic Research* 1, no. 1 (Summer 1974). For 1948–1969, ten out of the fifteen turning points in Mintz's U.S. chronology are the same in the present chronology. Some of the differences are the result of our use of the Bry-Boschan technique; Mintz measured long-term trend directly as a centered, seventy-five-month moving average. These differences, however, are relatively minor.

4. This was found to be the case in the 1973–76 "classical" recession. See Geoffrey H. Moore and Philip A. Klein, "New Measures of Recession and Recovery in Seven Nations," *Across the Board* (October 1976). Also, "A New Index for the Summit," *New York Times* (May 1, 1977), Financial Section, p. 18; and "Appraising Recent Economic Recovery in Three Countries," *Economic Outlook USA* (University of Michigan, Survey Research Center) 4, no. 3 (Summer 1977): 38–39.

5. Ilse Mintz, "Dating United States Growth Cycles," p. 46.

6. For illustration of this point, examine the coincident composite index for the United States (Figure 3-1).

7. By definition, leading indicators must show a lead of at least one month, the laggers must lag by at least one month, and the roughly coincident indicators must turn within three months of the reference turn. A somewhat more lenient rule would count exact coincidences (zero timing) as "not exceptional" in the leading and lagging indicator groups. In either interpretation, there is some overlapping possible—that is, a one-month lead is not exceptional in the leading indicators or in the roughly coincident category. As a rough measure of conformity to the timing classification, however, the overlapping possibility is not serious. In the following discussion the percentage of exceptions to the rules in each

country are shown by counting zero timing as not exceptional and in parentheses counting zeros as exceptions.

8. This test is more stringent than the previous test for timing because there can be no overlapping in the classification of "success." It is true, however, that examining the sequence of turns in all timing classes permits of "success" even when all groups show leads or lags.

9. See G.H. Moore's *Statistical Indicators of Cyclical Revivals and Recessions* (New York: NBER, Occasional Paper No. 31, 1950), pp. 54-57; and "Generating Leading Indicators from Lagging Indicators," *Western Economic Journal* (June 1969): 137-44. Also Phillip Cagan, "The Influence of Interest Rates on the Duration of Business Cycles," in Jack M. Guttentag and Phillip Cagan, eds., *Essays on Interest Rates*, Vol. 1 (New York: NBER, 1969); and Kathleen H. Moore, "The Comparative Performance of Economic Indicators in the United States, Canada, and Japan," *Western Economic Journal* (December 1971): 419-28.

10. Concerning the record of leading indicators derived from the analysis of classical cycles, Mintz "Dating United States Growth Cycles," pp. 69-72, pointed out that in some ways their performance is even better at U.S. growth cycle turning points. One of the objections raised over the performance of leading indicators during classical cycles is that they sometimes give "false signals"— that is, they indicate a classical turn that in fact fails to materialize. As Mintz points out, however, when the same series is analyzed in growth cycle terms many of these false signals become accurate: a weakening in a series, which does not become severe enough to produce an absolute decline in the level of activity, can nonetheless show up as growth recession. Hence, leading indicators, even though derived from classical cycle analysis, may in fact have a better track record in accurately predicting growth cycle turns. She also found that oftentimes the variability of the lead around growth cycle turning points was reduced.

11. Compare Table 4-3 to Table 6 in Philip A. Klein, "Postwar Growth Cycles in the United Kingdom—An Interim Report," *Explorations in Economic Research* 3, no. 1 (Winter 1976): 103-46.

12. Ibid., p. 129.

13. Ilse Mintz, *Dating Postwar Business Cycles: Methods and their Application to Western Germany, 1950-67* (New York: NBER, Occasional Paper No. 197, 1969), p. 28.

14. For an earlier analysis of Swedish growth cycles, see Philip A. Klein, *Analyzing Growth Cycles in Postwar Sweden*, Economic Research Report Number 44 (Stockholm: Swedish Federation of Employers, Swedish Industrial Publications, August 1981).

15. At this point, the reader is reminded of the earlier discussion (Chapter 3) concerning the spread among coincident indicators at the 1974 turning point, and the consequent difficulty in selecting an appropriate growth cycle turn. The spread among most of the indicators was about a year, although unemployment lagged twenty-nine months.

16. The reader may refer to the actual timing of each indicator in each country given in Appendix B.

17. Geoffrey H. Moore and Julius Shiskin devised a scoring system in connection with their 1966 list of indicators—the list, in fact, on which the international work reported here was based. With 100 percent representing perfection, the twelve leading indicators scored between 44 percent and 87 percent with respect to their timing at available classical cycle turning points, or generally lower than the results we have found here for our international growth cycle indicators. The roughly coincident indicators scored between 12 percent and 87 percent, while the lagging indicators scored between 25 percent and 94 percent. The scores refer to our question one, rather than to the sequences referred to in the text. But the evidence is suggestive of the definition of "success" which was reasonable to adhere to in the analysis of U.S. indicators for classical cycle analysis. Geoffrey H. Moore and Julius Shiskin, *Indicators of Business Expansions and Contractions*, National Bureau of Economic Research, 1967, p. 68.

18. In addition to the Moore–Shiskin scoring system already referred to, Zarnowitz and Boschan utilized much the same system in connection with their 1975 revision of the U.S. short list. *Business Conditions Digest* (May and November 1975).

APPENDIX 4A

FIGURES SHOWING ALL INDICATORS SELECTED FOR
TEN MARKET-ORIENTED ECONOMIES

Figure 4A-1.   United States, Components of Leading Index.

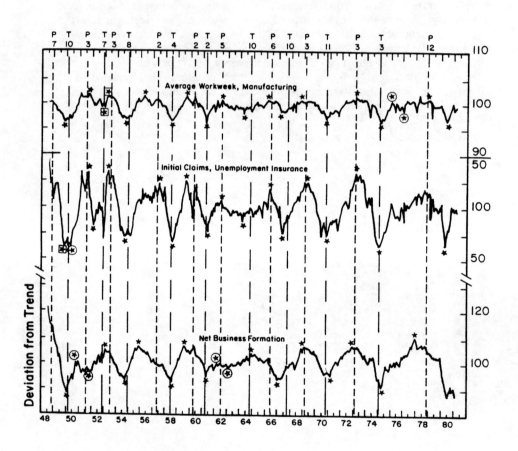

Figure 4A-1. United States (*continued*)

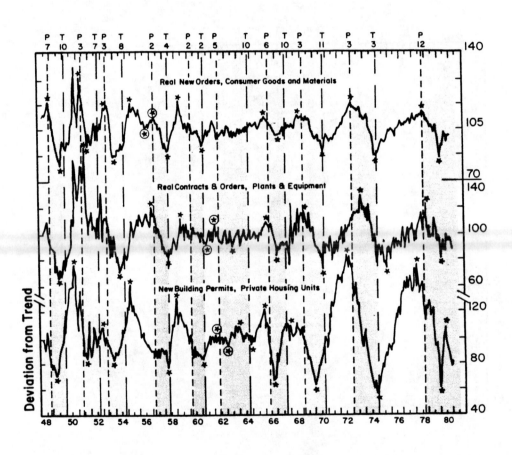

Figure 4A-1. United States (*continued*)

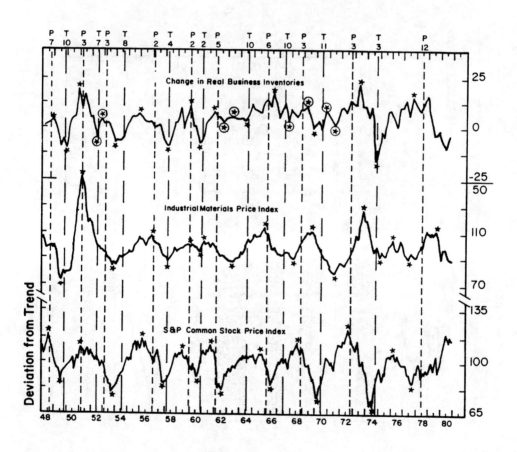

Figure 4A-1. **United States** (*continued*)

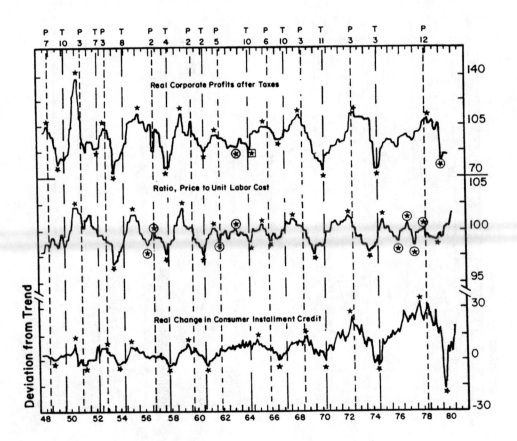

Figure 4A-1. **United States** *(continued)*

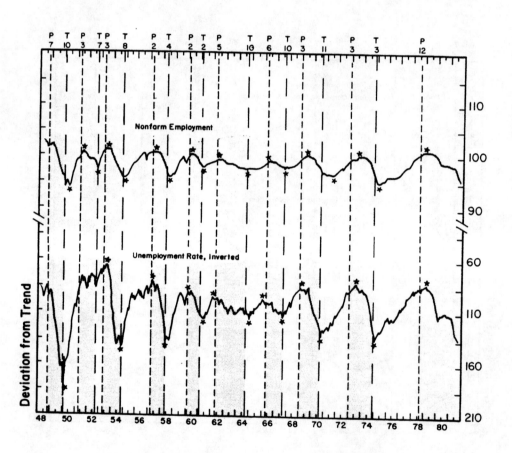

Figure 4A-1. United States (*continued*)

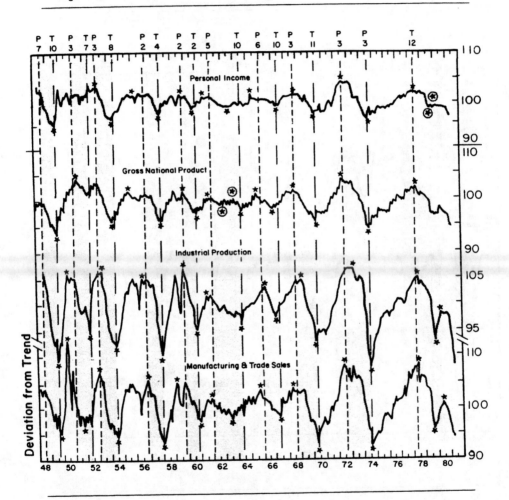

Figure 4A-1.   United States (*continued*)

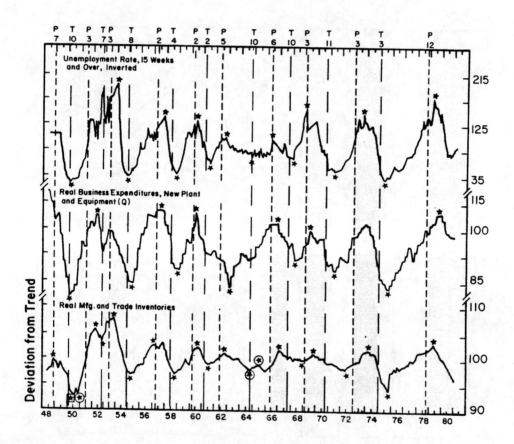

Figure 4A-1. **United States** (*continued*)

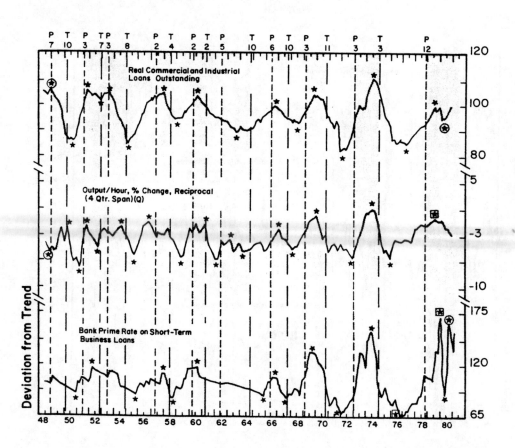

Figure 4A-2. Canada, Components of Leading Index.

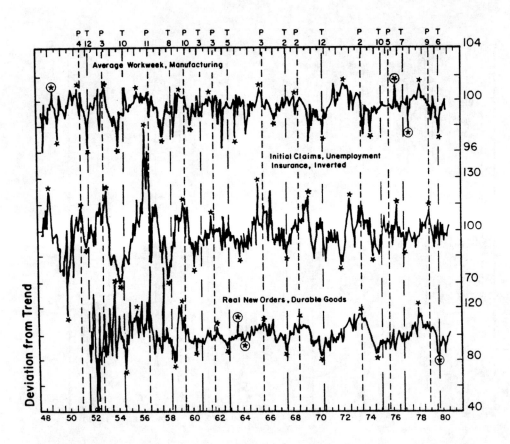

Figure 4A-2.   Canada (*continued*)

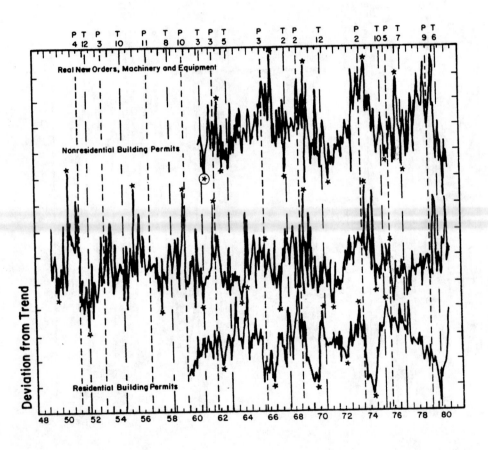

Figure 4A–2. Canada (*continued*)

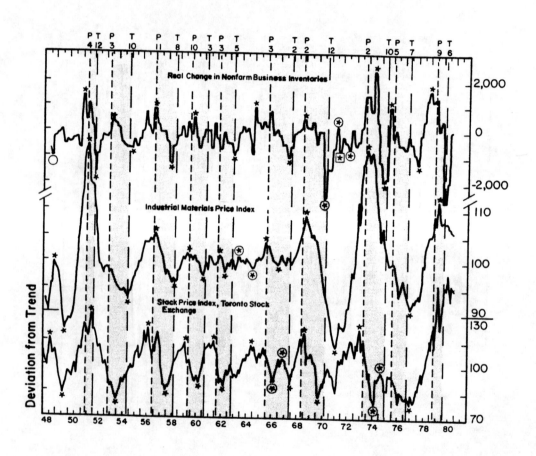

Figure 4A-2. Canada (*continued*)

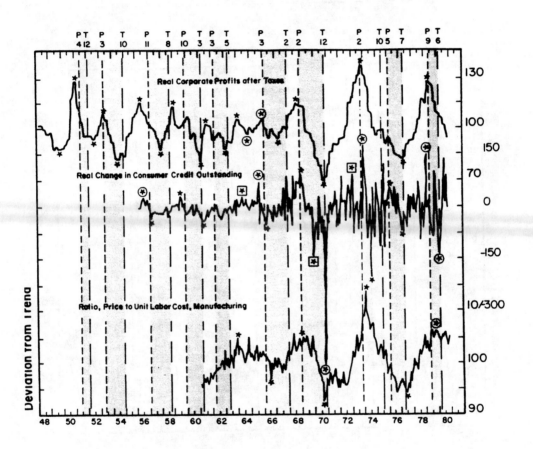

Figure 4A-2.   Canada (*continued*)

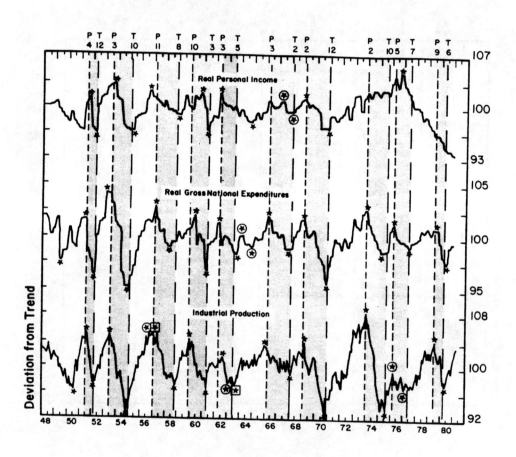

Figure 4A-2.   Canada (*continued*)

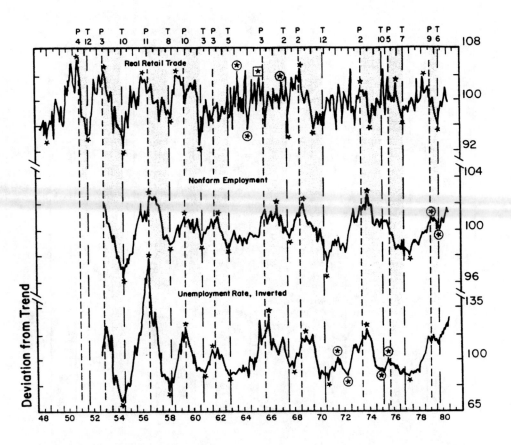

Figure 4A-2. Canada (*continued*)

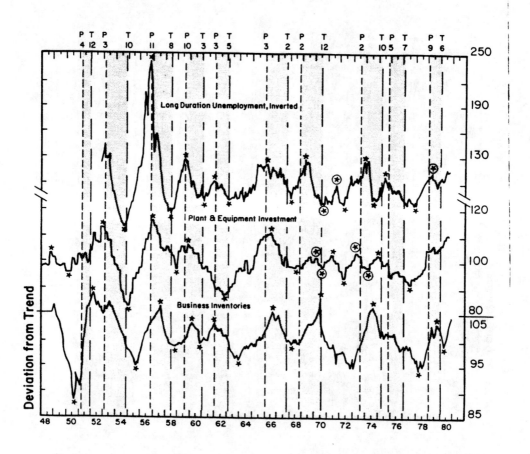

Figure 4A-2. Canada (*continued*)

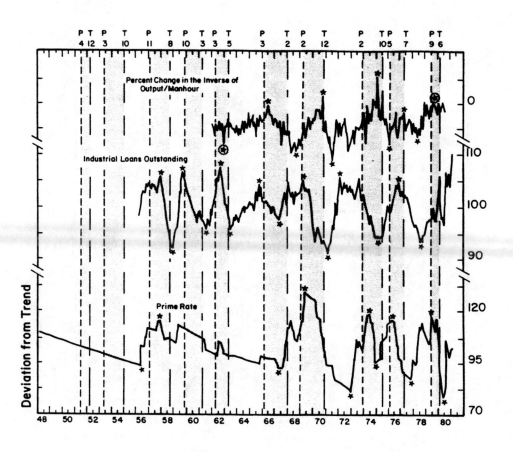

Figure 4A-3. United Kingdom, Components of Leading Composite Index.

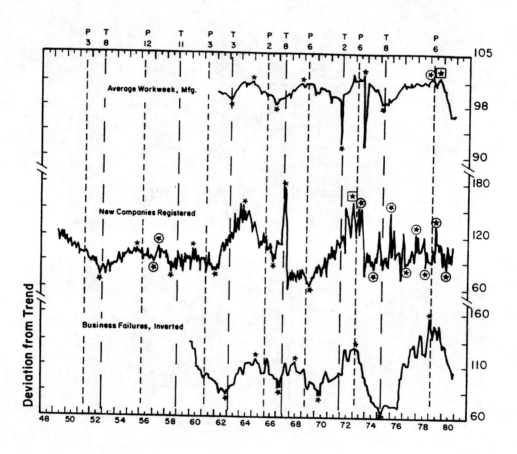

Figure 4A-3.   United Kingdom (*continued*)

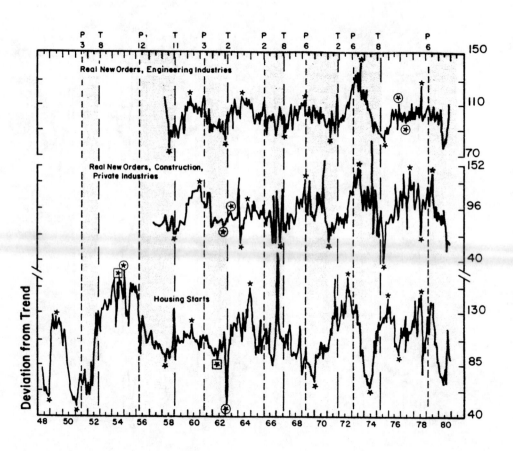

Figure 4A-3. United Kingdom (*continued*)

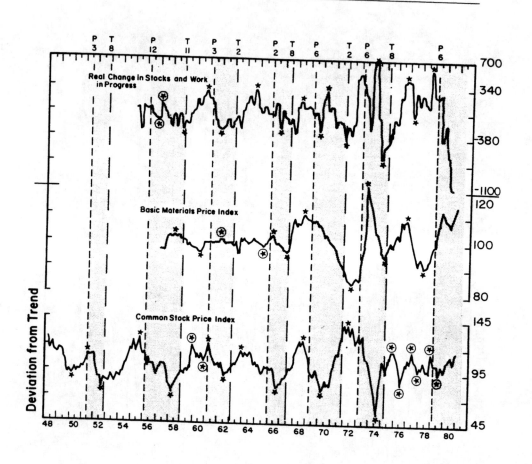

Figure 4A-3. United Kingdom (*continued*)

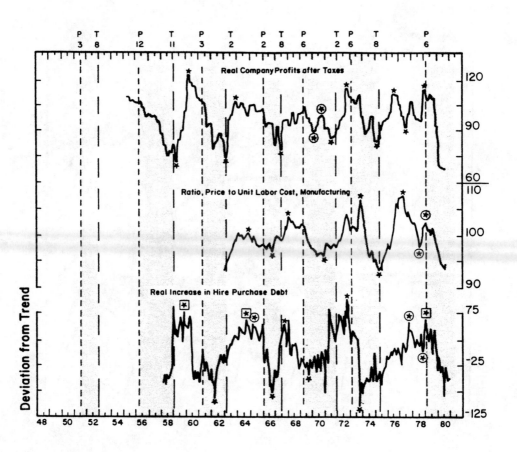

Figure 4A-3. United Kingdom (*continued*)

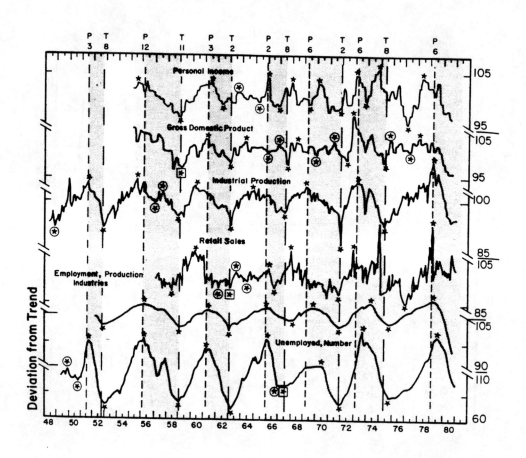

Figure 4A–3. United Kingdom (*continued*)

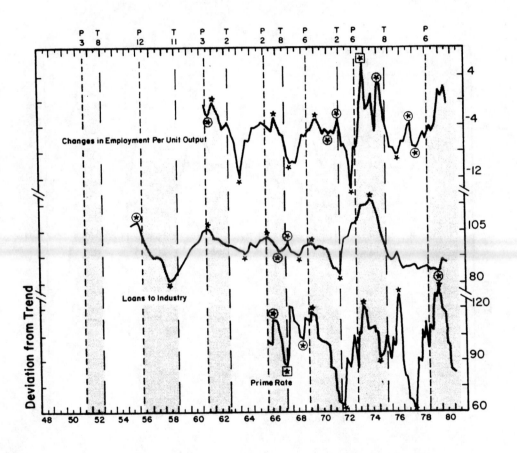

Figure 4A-3. United Kingdom (*continued*)

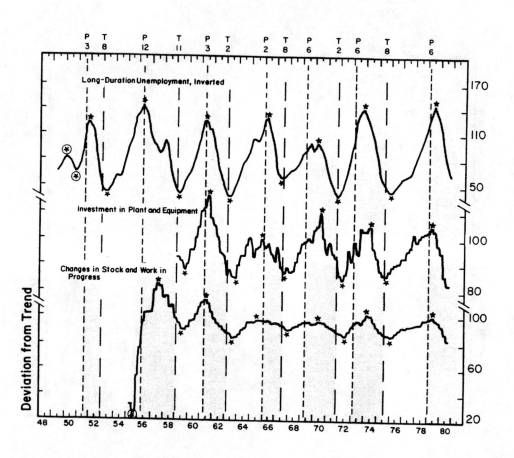

Figure 4A-4. West Germany, Components of Leading Composite Index.

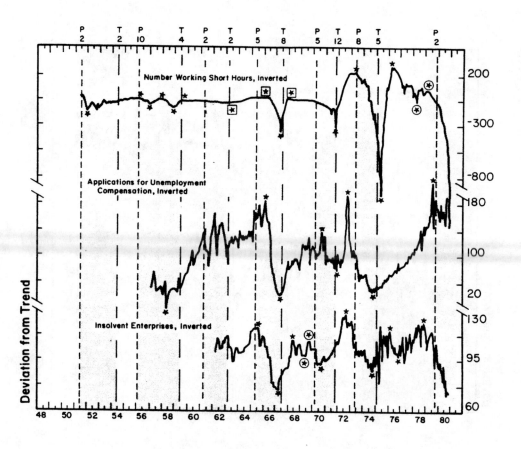

Figure 4A-4. West Germany (*continued*)

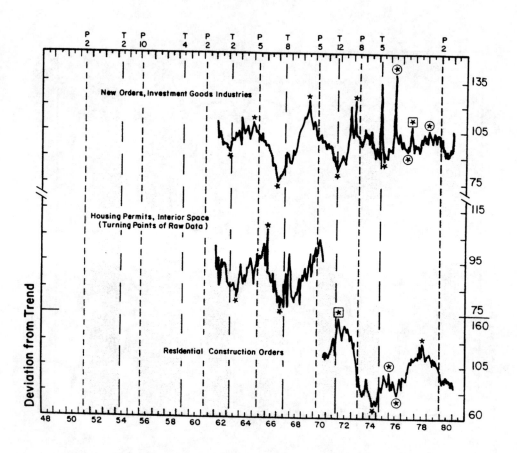

Figure 4A-4. West Germany (*continued*)

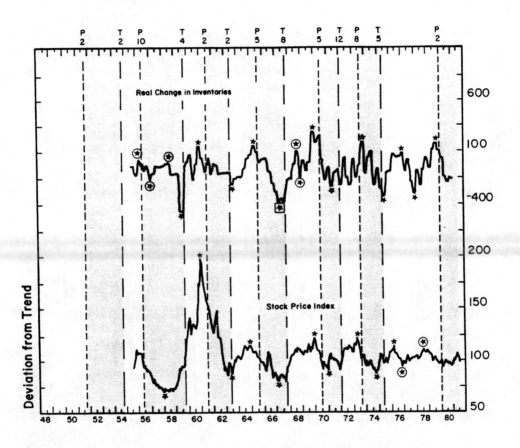

Figure 4A-4. West Germany (*continued*)

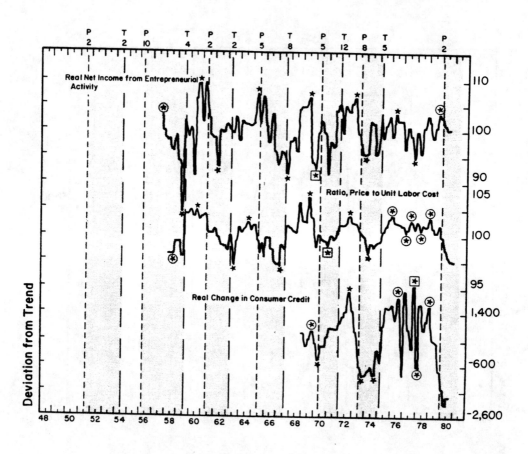

Figure 4A-4. West Germany (*continued*)

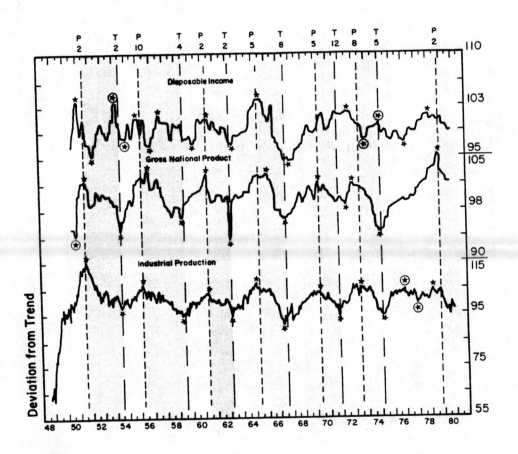

Figure 4A-4. West Germany (*continued*)

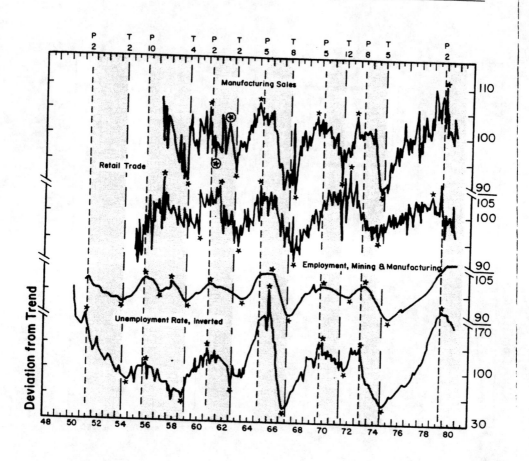

Figure 4A-4. West Germany (*continued*)

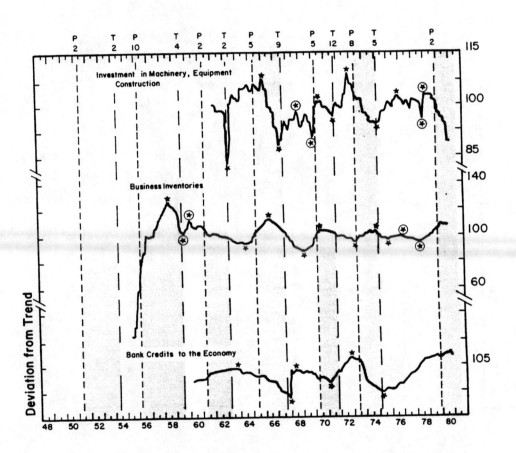

Figure 4A–4. West Germany (*continued*)

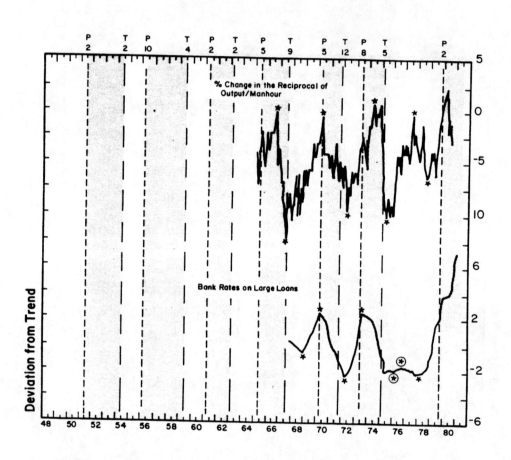

Figure 4A-5. France, Components of Leading Index.

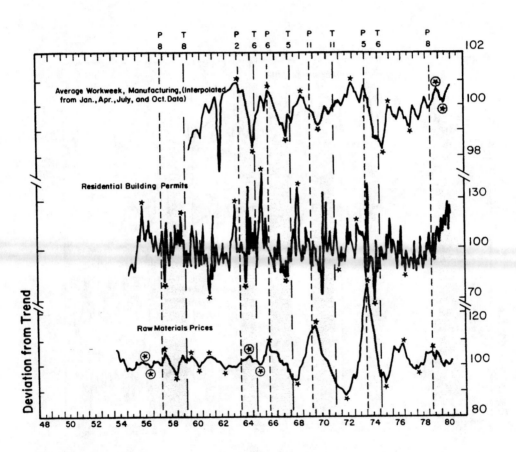

Figure 4A-5.   France (*continued*)

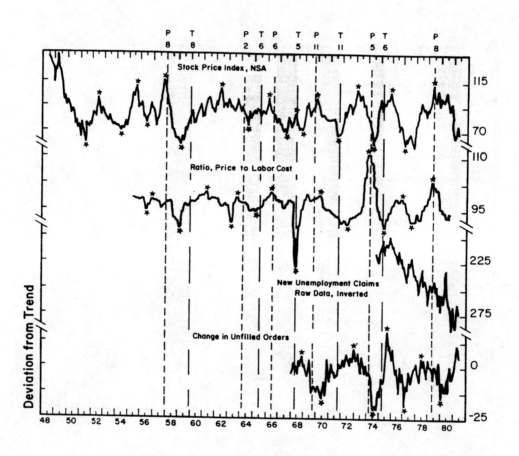

Figure 4A-5.   France (*continued*)

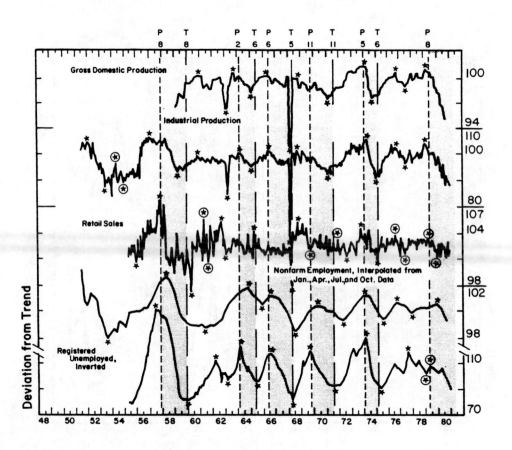

Figure 4A–5. France (*continued*)

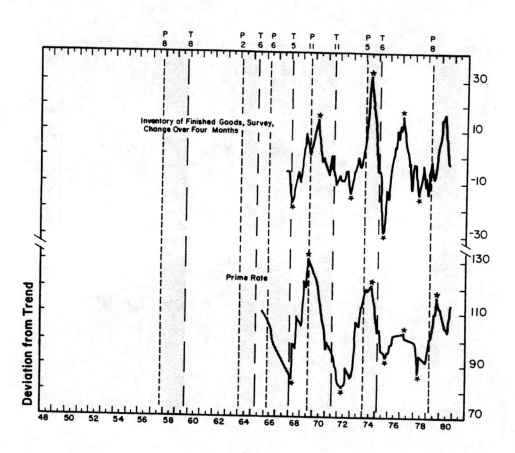

Figure 4A-6. Italy, Components of Coincident Composite Index.

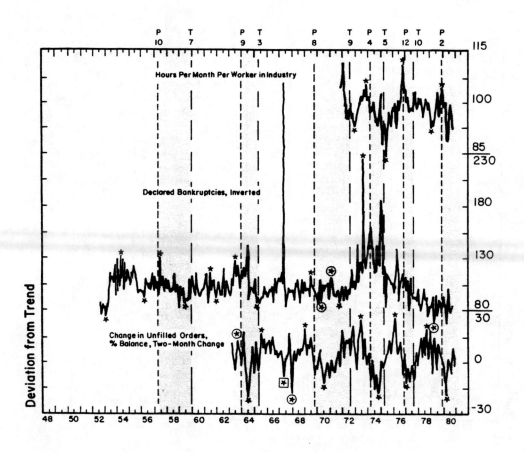

Figure 4A-6. Italy *(continued)*

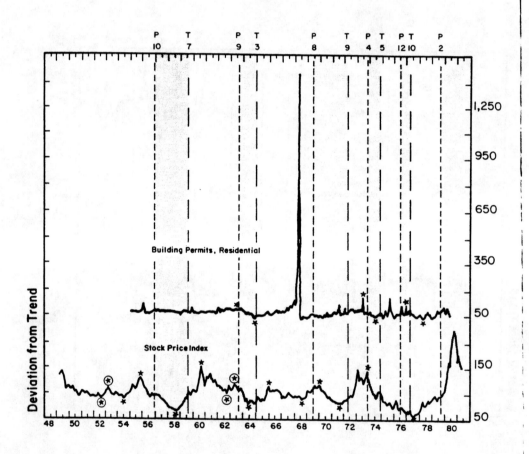

Figure 4A-6. Italy *(continued)*

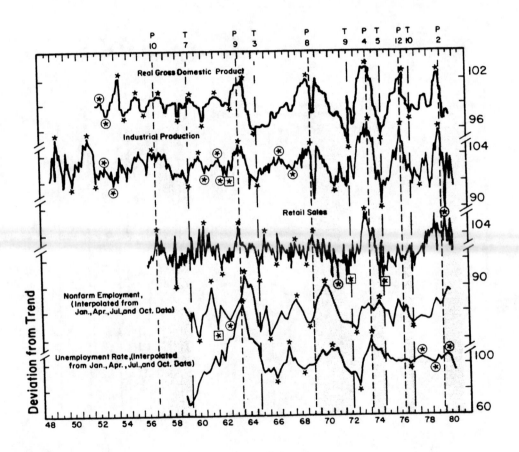

Figure 4A–6.   Italy (*continued*)

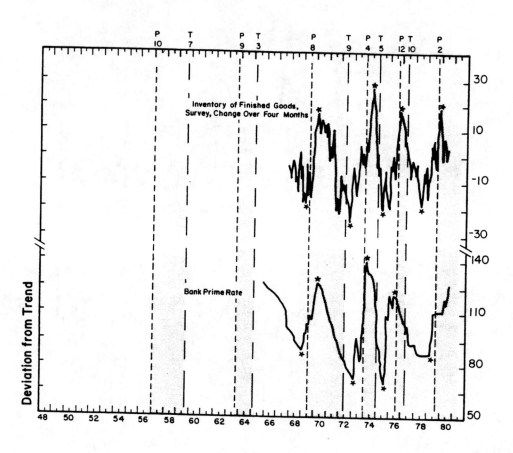

Figure 4A-7.   Belgium, Components of Leading Composite Index.

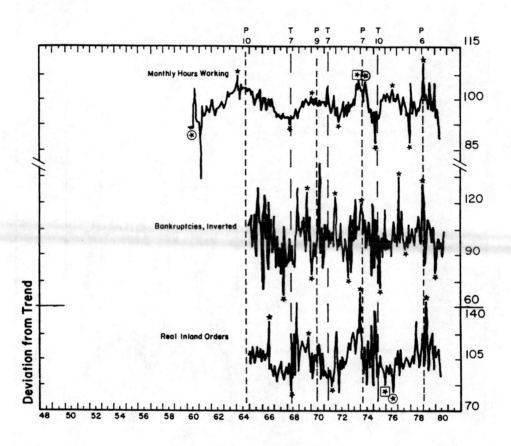

Figure 4A-7.   Belgium (*continued*)

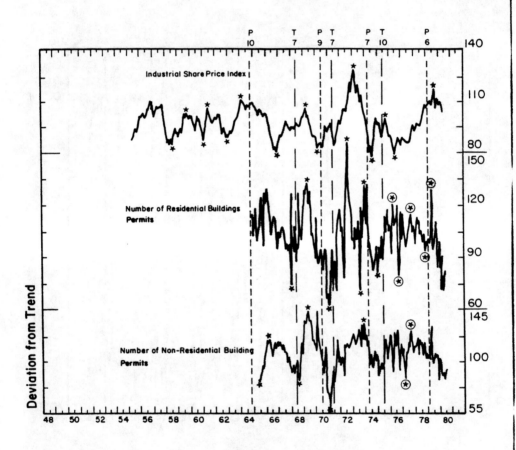

Figure 4A-7.   Belgium (*continued*)

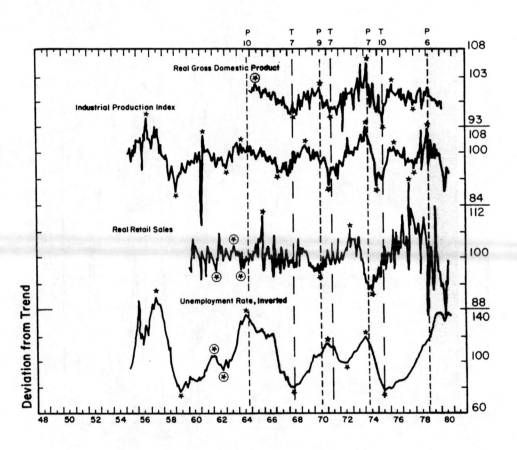

Figure 4A-7. Belgium (*continued*)

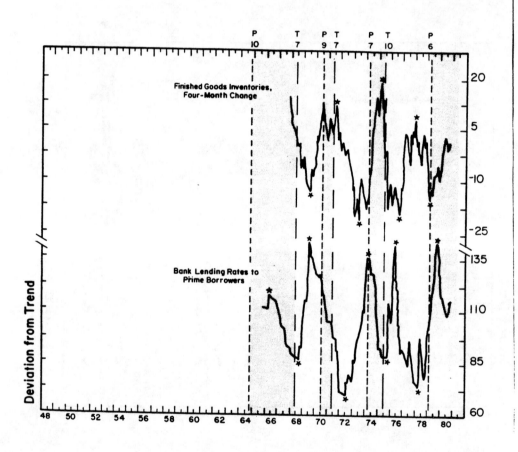

Figure 4A-8. Netherlands, Components of Leading Index.

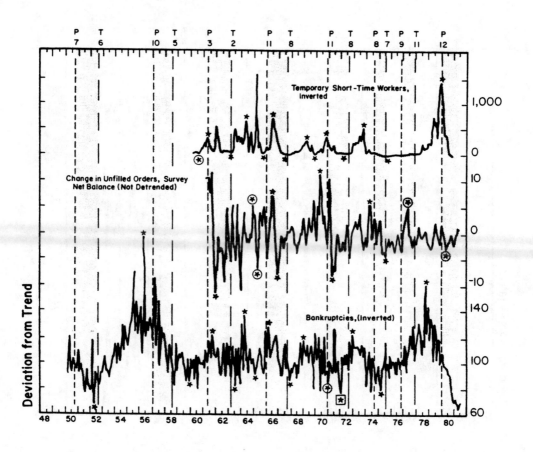

Figure 4A-8. Netherlands (*continued*)

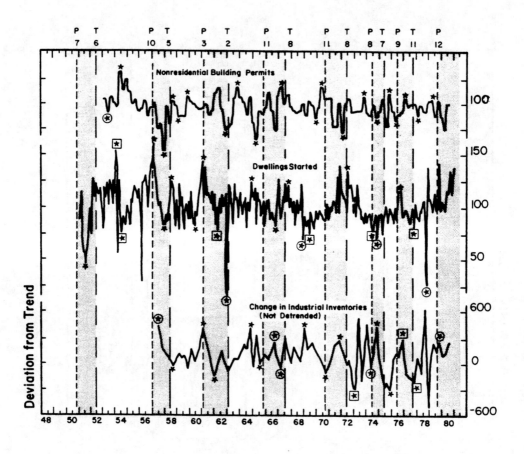

Figure 4A-8.   Netherlands (*continued*)

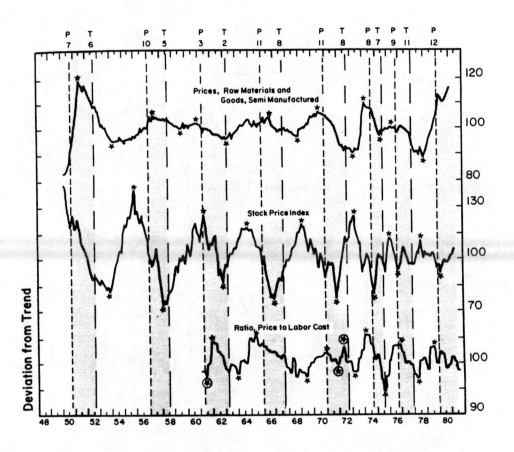

Figure 4A-8. Netherlands (*continued*)

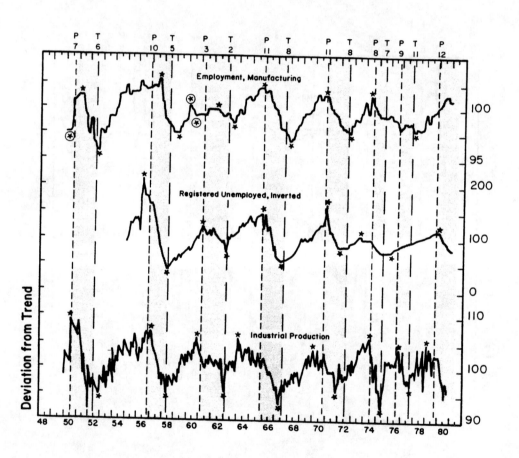

Figure 4A–8.   Netherlands (*continued*)

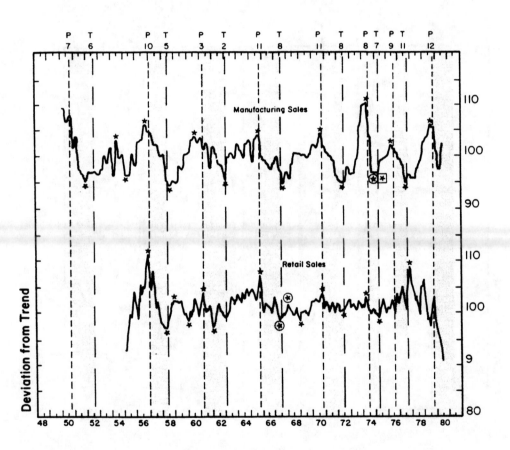

Figure 4A-8. Netherlands (*continued*)

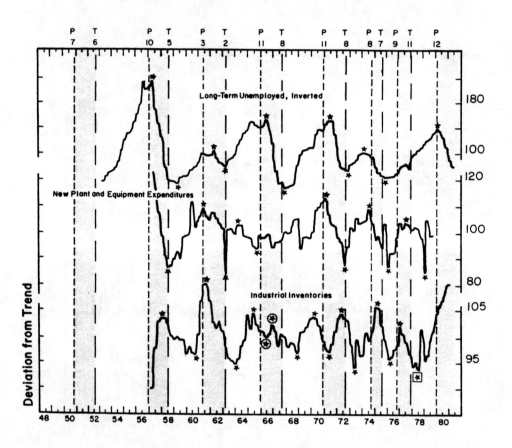

Figure 4A-9. Sweden, Components of Leading Composite Index.

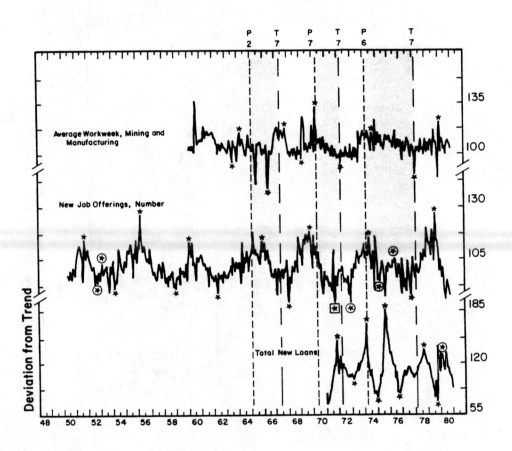

Figure 4A–9. Sweden (*continued*)

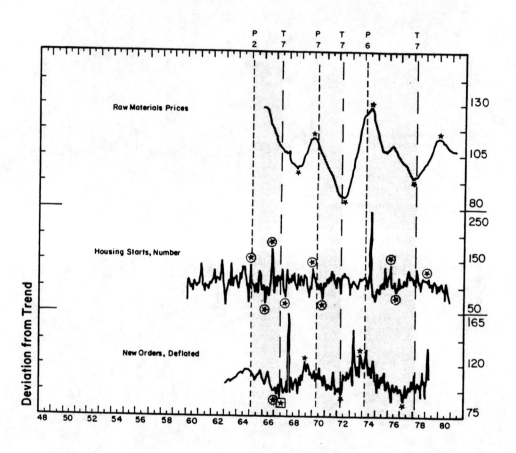

Figure 4A-9. **Sweden** (*continued*)

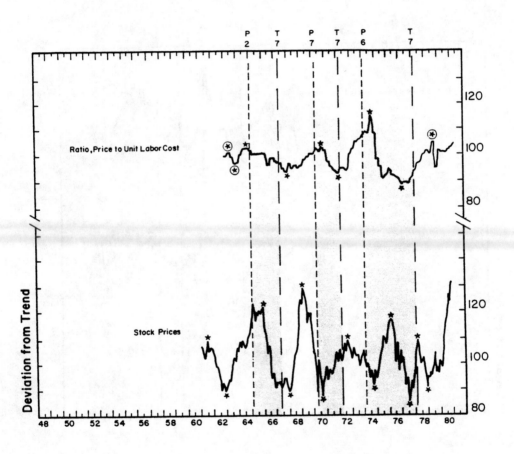

Figure 4A-9. Sweden (*continued*)

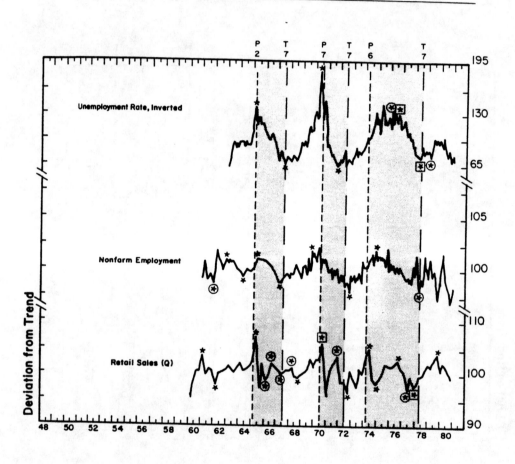

Figure 4A-9. Sweden (*continued*)

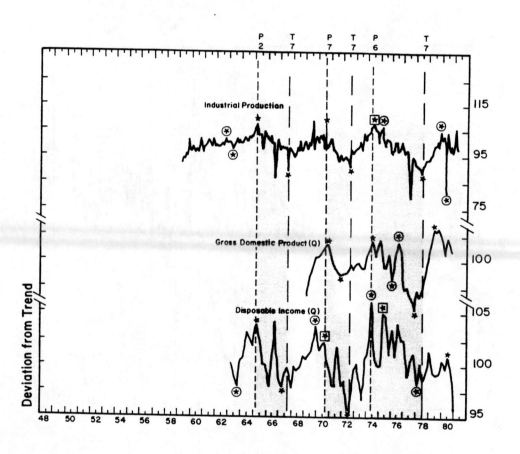

Figure 4A-9.   Sweden (*continued*)

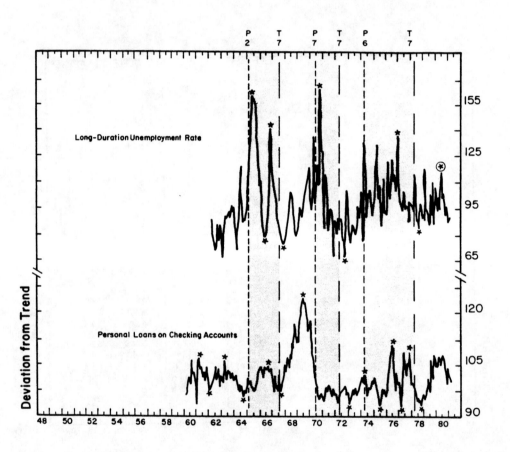

Figure 4A-9.   Sweden (*continued*)

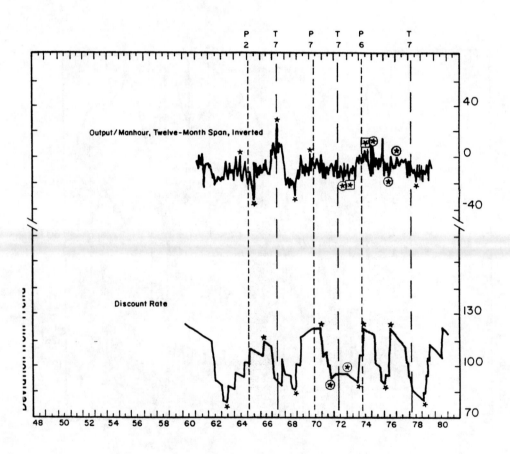

Figure 4A-10. Japan, Components of Leading Index.

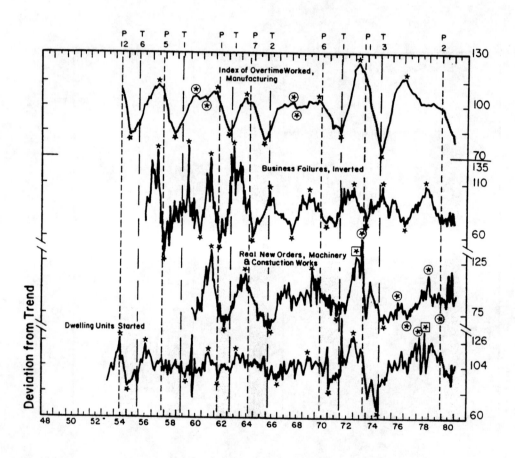

Figure 4A–10. Japan (*continued*)

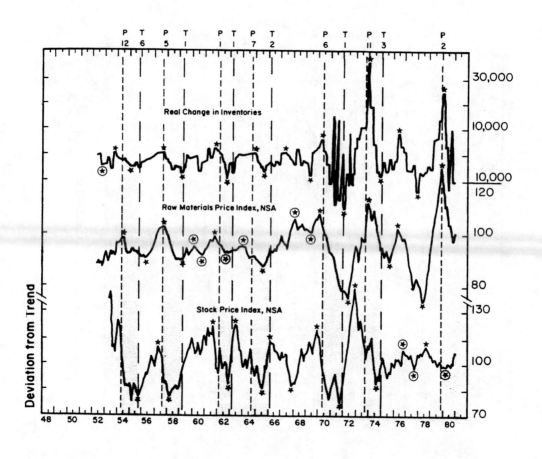

Figure 4A-10.   Japan (*continued*)

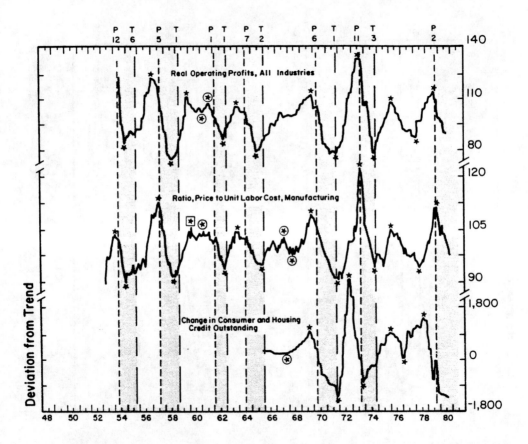

Figure 4A-10. Japan (*continued*)

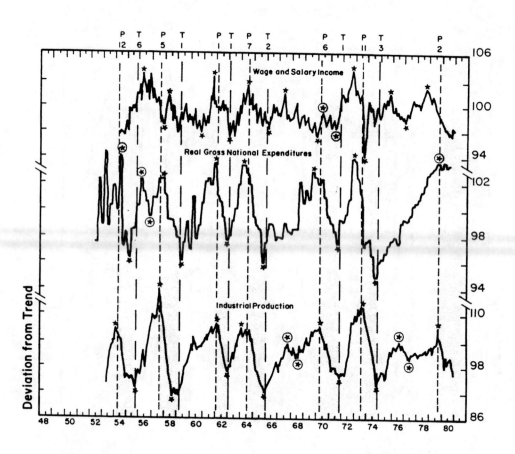

Figure 4A–10.   Japan (*continued*)

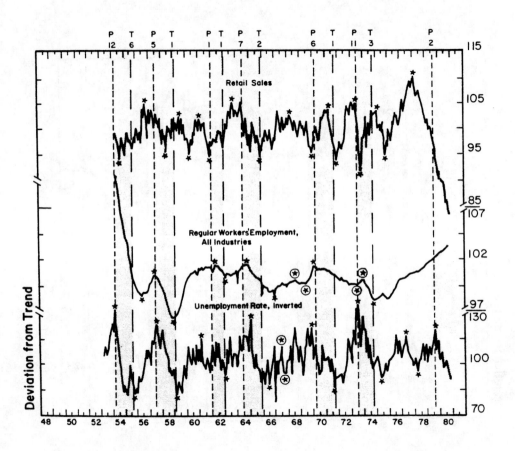

Figure 4A-10. Japan (*continued*)

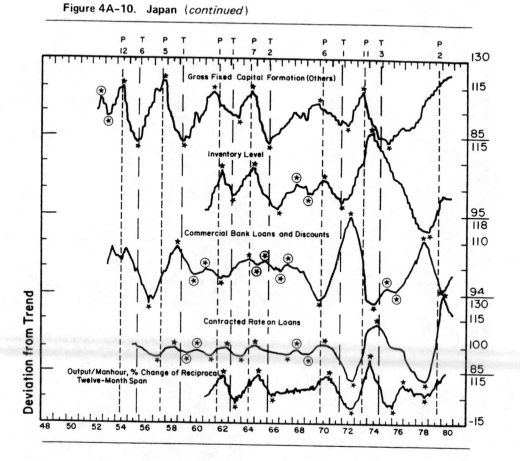

APPENDIX 4B
TIMING OF INDIVIDUAL INDICATORS AT GROWTH CYCLE TURNING POINTS, TEN MARKET-ORIENTED COUNTRIES
(pages 204 through 223)

The numbers in the far left column identify the series and are based on the United States 1966 classification of indicators. They appear as 1.0, 2.0, etc. For other countries, the decimal place digit is zero when the equivalent series in other countries is identical to the United States series. When the decimal place digit is 1 or 2 this indicates a different series was the closest equivalent to the United States series. For example, 3.1 in Canada refers to New Orders, durable goods, the closest Canadian equivalent to the United States series: 3.0, New Orders, consumer goods and materials.

Table 4B-1. Individual Indicators and Composite Indexes, Lead (-) or Lag (+) at Growth Cycle Turning Points, in Months, United States.

	Peaks									
	7/48	3/51	3/53	2/57	2/60	5/62	6/66	3/69	3/73	12/78
Leading Indicators										
1.0 Average workweek, manufacturing	n.a.	+1	-3	-15	-9	-1	-4	-5	+1	-1
2.0 Initial claims, unemployment insurance (inverted)	n.a.	0	-4	+1	-10	-1	-2	+1	-1	-2
4.0 Net business formation	n.a.	n.m.	-6	-20	-11	n.m.	-20	-2	-5	-12
3.0 New orders, consumer goods and materials	-1	-2	-2	-23	-12	n.m.	-3	-4	0	+1
5.0 Contracts and orders, plant and equipment	n.a.	+2	n.m.	-3	-11	n.m.	-4	+1	+7	+3
6.0 New building permits, private housing units	n.a.	-8	-5	-24	-15	+21	-5	-12	-3	-6
7.0 Change in business inventories (q)	+1	-4	n.m.	-15	0	-3	+5	n.m.	+8	-10
8.0 Industrial materials price index	n.a.	-1	n.m.	-2	-1	-12	-3	+10	+12	+14
9.0 Stock price index, 500 S&P common	-1	-1	n.m.	-10	-7	-5	-5	-3	-2	n.m.
10.0 Corporate profits after taxes (q)	-2	-4	-1	-15	-9	-3	-4	-4	+2	+2
11.0 Ratio, price/unit labor cost, nonfarm business (q)	n.a.	-7	n.m.	-21	-9	-6	-7	-10	-4	-40
12.0 Change in consumer installment credit	n.a.	-8	0	-23	-6	n.m.	-14	-1	-2	-6
Roughly Coincident Indicators										
17.0 Personal income	n.a.	n.m.	0	-4	-1	-5	-9	0	-1	0
15.0 Gross national product (q)	n.m.	+4	n.m.	-16	-1	-1	-5	-2	-2	+1
16.0 Industrial production	n.a.	-7	+4	0	-1	-5	+4	+5	+6	+3

18.0 Manufacturing and trade sales	n.a.	-7	0	0	-9	-2	-3	-4	-1	+3
13.0 Employees on nonfarm payrolls	n.a.	+1	0	+1	+2	0	0	+4	+8	+3
14.0 Unemployment ratio (inverted)	n.a.	n.m.	+3	+1	0	-3	-4	+2	+7	+5
Lagging Indicators										
19.0 Unemployment rate, 15 weeks and over (inverted)	n.a.	n.m.	+7	+7	+3	+5	0	0	+9	+7
20.0 Business expenditures, new plant and equipment, deflated (q)	n.a.	+11	n.m.	+3	+3	n.m.	+5	+5	+11	+14
21.0 Manufacturing and trade inventories	0	+10	+4	-3	+5	+5	+9	+7	+15	+7
23.0 Commercial and industrial loans outstanding	n.a.	+3	+1	+7	+4	n.m.	+2	+9	+18	+9
22.0 Output per hour, percentage change of reciprocal (q)	n.m.	+2	+14	-6	+12	+9	+8	+11	+20	+11
24.0 Prime rate on short-term business loans	n.m.	+10	n.m.	+7	+5	n.m.	+3	+5	+16	+16
Composite Indexes										
Inverted Lagging	n.a.	-11	n.m.	-24	-18	-10	-19	-12	-12	-36
Leading	n.a.	-2	n.m.	-17	-9	n.m.	-3	-1	-1	+3
Roughly Coincident	n.a.	-2	+2	+1	0	-1	-3	0	+8	0
Lagging	n.a.	n.m.	+2	+7	+3	+3	+5	+7	+16	+16

Note:
n.a. = Data not available.
n.m. = No matching turn.

Table 4B-1. continued

					Troughs				
	10/49	7/52	8/54	4/58	2/61	10/64	10/67	11/70	3/75
Leading Indicators									
1.0 Average workweek, manufacturing	-6	0	-4	-2	-2	-9	-8	-2	0
2.0 Initial claims, unemployment insurance (inverted)	-6	-11	-5	0	0	-10	-6	-1	0
4.0 Net business formation	-3	n.m.	-5	0	-1	n.m.	-11	+3	-1
3.0 New orders, consumer goods and materials	-4	-10	-10	0	-1	n.m.	-7	0	0
5.0 Contracts and orders, plant and equipment	-6	n.m.	-5	-1	n.m.	-15	-9	-1	+9
6.0 New building permits, private housing units	-9	-12	-11	-2	-2	+2	-11	-10	0
7.0 Change in business inventories (q)	+1	n.m.	-9	-2	-3	-2	n.m.	-9	-1
8.0 Industrial materials price index	-4	n.m.	-10	0	-2	-16	+9	+13	+4
9.0 Stock price index, 500 S&P common	-4	n.m.	-11	-4	-4	-24	-12	-5	-3
10.0 Corporate profits after taxes (q)	-5	-2	-9	-2	0	+1	-5	0	-1
11.0 Ratio, price/unit labor cost, nonfarm business (q)	n.a.	n.m.	-9	-2	0	+1	-14	-9	-7
12.0 Change in consumer installment credit	-11	-12	-5	-2	+2	n.m.	-8	0	0
Roughly Coincident Indicators									
17.0 Personal income	0	n.m.	-1	0	-2	-11	0	+11	0
15.0 Gross national product (q)	+2	n.m.	-2	-1	+1	+2	-4	+10	0
16.0 Industrial production	0	0	+1	0	0	0	-3	0	0

18.0 Manufacturing and trade sales	+2	−7	0	0	0	−11	0	0	0
13.0 Employees on nonfarm payrolls	+4	0	0	+1	+2	0	0	+9	+3
14.0 Unemployment ratio (inverted)	0	n.m.	+1	0	+3	+4	0	+1	+2
Lagging Indicators									
19.0 Unemployment rate, 15 weeks and over (inverted)	+1	n.m.	0	+4	+5	+1	+5	+8	+4
20.0 Business expenditures, new plant and equipment, deflated (q)	+1	n.m.	+6	+7	n.m.	−20	+7	+9	+8
21.0 Manufacturing and trade inventories	+4	+1	+6	+4	+4	+15	+15	+20	+9
23.0 Commercial and industrial loans outstanding	+7	+1	+2	+4	n.m.	−14	+9	+16	+26
22.0 Output per hour, percentage change of reciprocal (q)	n.m.	−2	+9	+10	+12	−8	+4	+27	+11
24.0 Prime rate on short-term business loans	+10	n.m.	+11	+4	n.m.	+13	0	+16	+25
Composite Indexes									
Inverted Lagging	n.a.	n.m.	−15	−7	−9	−26	−11	−13	−8
Leading	−4	n.m.	−9	−2	−2	n.m.	−6	0	0
Roughly Coincident	0	0	0	0	0	−11	0	0	0
Lagging	+6	n.m.	+6	+4	+5	+1	+5	+16	+9

Note:
n.a. = Data not available.
n.m. = No matching turn.

Table 4B-2.   Individual Indicators and Composite Indexes, Lead (-) or Lag (+) at Growth Cycle Turning Points, in Months, Canada.

	Peaks									
	4/51	3/53	11/56	10/59	3/62	3/66	2/69	2/74	5/76	9/79
Leading Indicators										
1.0 Average workweek, manufacturing	-3	+2	-11	-5	-3	-3	-3	-16	n.m.	-9
2.0 Initial claims, unemployment insurance (inverted)	+1	+2	-5	-2	-3	-5	+9	-12	+8	0
3.1 New orders, durable goods	n.a.	+10	-14	-3	+3	-1	0	-2	n.m.	-12
5.1 New orders, machinery and equipment	n.a.	n.a.	n.a.	n.a.	+3	+10	+7	+5	+9	n.a.
5.2 Nonresidential building permits	-10	n.m.	-15	-2	-1	+1	+5	+3	+1	n.a.
6.0 Residential building permits	n.a.	n.a.	n.a.	n.a.	n.a.	-16	+10	-3	-3	n.a.
7.0 Change in nonfarm business inventories (q)	-5	+2	0	+4	n.m.	-13	0	+9	-3	-4
8.0 Industrial Materials Price Index	0	n.m.	+2	-1	+2	-1	+4	+2	n.m.	+4
9.0 Stock price index Toronto Stock Exchange	+6	n.m.	-4	-3	-3	-14	+3	-4	n.m.	n.a.
10.0 Corporate profits after taxes (q)	-5	-1	-9	-11	-7	-25	-3	0	n.m.	-1
11.0 Ratio price to unit labor cost, manufacturing	n.a.	n.a.	n.a.	n.a.	n.a.	-27	+1	+3	n.m.	n.a.
12.0 Change in consumer credit outstanding	n.a.	n.a.	n.a.	-4	n.m.	-21	0	-10	+1	n.a.
Roughly Coincident Indicators										
17.0 Personal income (q)	+1	+2	-6	+10	-1	n.m.	0	n.m.	+6	n.m.
15.0 Gross National Expenditure (q)	-2	-4	0	+4	-1	-1	0	0	0	-1
16.0 Industrial production	0	0	0	0	+4	-3	+1	0	n.m.	0

18.1 Retail trade	−2	0	−4	−8	n.m.	−3	0	0	+7	−6
13.0 Nonfarm employment	n.a.	n.a.	0	0	+3	+12	+2	+6	n.m.	n.m.
14.0 Unemployment rate (inverted)	n.a.	n.a.	−1	−5	−3	+3	+5	+4	n.m.	n.a.
Lagging Indicators										
19.0 Long term unemployment	n.a.	n.a.	0	+1	+1	+4	+7	+6	−2	n.a.
20.0 Plant and equipment, Real Canadian dollars	n.m.	−1	+3	+4	n.m.	+9	n.m.	+18	n.m.	n.a.
21.0 Business Inventories, Real Canadian dollars	n.a.	−10	+11	+7	0	+10	+21	+10	n.m.	+8
22.1 Percentage change in the inverse of O/MH	n.a.	n.a.	n.a.	n.a.	n.a.	+5	+22	+15	n.m.	n.a.
23.0 Industrial loans in Real Canadian dollars	n.a.	n.a.	+12	−2	+6	−5	+3	−21	+9	n.a.
24.0 Canada Prime Rate	n.a.	n.a.	+12	n.m.	n.m.	n.m.	+5	+8	+3	+1
Composite Indexes										
Lagging index, inverted	−7	−16	−23	−11	−9	−28	−3	−15	n.m.	−19
Leading index	−2	n.m.	−8	−2	−4	−2	+1	+1	n.m.	+4
Roughly coincident index	−2	0	−1	0	0	0	0	0	0	0
Lagging index	n.m.	0	+2	+5	+6	+4	+9	+5	n.m.	+7

Note:
n.a. = Data not available.
n.m. = No matching turn.

Table 4B-2. continued

	Troughs									
	12/51	10/54	8/58	3/61	5/63	2/68	12/70	10/75	7/77	6/80
Leading Indicators										
1.0 Average workweek, manufacturing	0	-5	-8	-10	+7	-11	+2	-10	n.m.	+1
2.0 Initial claims, unemployment insurance (inverted)	-2	-4	-2	-7	+11	-1	+18	-6	+2	n.m.
3.1 New orders, durable goods	+7	+1	+3	-5	-2	0	-1	-6	n.m.	n.m.
5.1 New orders, machinery and equipment	n.a.	n.a.	n.a.	n.a.	-6	-1	+7	+3	0	n.m.
5.2 Nonresidential building permits	+2	n.m.	-9	+1	+12	-7	+9	-7	0	n.m.
6.0 Residential building permits	n.a.	n.a.	n.a.	n.a.	-7	-14	+22	-11	n.a.	n.a.
7.0 Change in nonfarm business inventories (q)	-1	+1	-6	n.m.	0	-3	+14	-2	+10	n.a.
8.0 Industrial Materials Price Index	n.a.	-2	-3	-2	-7	-11	+12	n.m.	+3	n.a.
9.0 Stock price index Toronto Stock Exchange	n.m.	-10	-8	-5	-8	+1	-6	n.m.	+3	n.a.
10.0 Corporate profits after taxes (q)	+5	-5	-9	-1	-3	-9	-1	n.m.	-2	n.a.
11.0 Ratio price to unit labor cost, manufacturing	n.a.	n.a.	n.a.	n.a.	n.a.	-18	0	n.m.	+2	n.a.
12.0 Change in consumer credit outstanding	n.a.	n.a.	-19	+1	n.m.	-21	-11	-11	-2	n.a.
Roughly Coincident Indicators										
17.0 Personal income (q)	-1	+1	0	-1	+15	n.m.	-1	n.m.	n.a.	n.a.
15.0 Gross National Exchange (q)	-1	-5	-6	-1	+3	-3	-1	-5	+1	+2
16.0 Industrial production	0	-3	+1	0	-1	0	0	0	n.m.	+1

18.1 Retail trade	+1	0	+1	-2	n.m.	0	-8	-10	0	0
13.0 Nonfarm employment	n.a.	0	0	0	0	+1	+4	n.m.	+6	n.a.
14.0 Unemployment rate (inverted)	n.a.	-3	-2	+2	0	+4	+4	n.m.	+5	n.a.
Lagging Indicators										
19.0 Long term unemployment	n.a.	+1	+1	+3	+1	+5	+23	-5	+14	n.a.
20.0 Plant and equipment, Real Canadian dollars	n.m.	+4	+6	n.m.	-3	+10	n.m.	n.m.	+7	n.a.
21.0 Business Inventories, Real Canadian dollars	n.a.	+11	+3	-2	+10	+4	+32	n.m.	+15	+5
22.1 Percentage change in the inverse of O/MH	n.a.	n.a.	n.a.	n.a.	n.a.	+8	+10	+7	n.m.	n.a.
23.0 Industrial loans in Real Canadian dollars	n.a.	n.a.	+3	+4	+1	-8	+5	-5	+16	n.a.
24.0 Canada Prime Rate	n.a.	+17	n.m.	n.m.	n.m.	-10	+27	-7	+7	+3
Composite Indexes										
Lagging index, inverted	n.m.	-17	-19	-19	-8	-19	-13	-15	n.m.	-2
Leading index	n.m.	-7	-9	-4	-6	-3	+1	n.m.	+2	+2
Roughly coincident index	-1	0	0	-1	+2	0	-1	0	+6	0
Lagging index	n.m.	+2	+4	+3	+1	+9	+23	n.m.	+7	+3

Note:
n.a. = Data not available.
n.m. = No matching turn.

Table 4B-3. Individual Indicators and Composite Indexes, Lead (–) or Lag (+) at Growth Cycle Turning Points, in Months, United Kingdom.

	Peaks							Troughs					
	3/51	12/55	3/61	2/66	6/69	6/73	6/79	8/52	11/58	2/63	8/67	2/72	8/75
Leading Indicators													
1.0 Average workweek, manufacturing	n.a.	n.a.	n.a.	-14	-5	+6	+7	n.a.	n.a.	+1	-9	0	-3
4.1 New companies registered	n.a.	-5	-12	-22	-20	-3	n.a.	-1	-6	-13	-10	-28	n.m.
4.2 Business failures (inverted)	n.a.	n.a.	n.a.	-8	-9	0	-1	n.a.	n.a.	-12	-4	-19	-1
5.1 New orders, engineering industries	n.a.	n.a.	-13	-22	-1	+6	-7	n.a.	-5	-2	+2	-8	+4
5.2 New orders, construction, private industry	n.a.	n.a.	-5	-16	-1	+4	+4	n.a.	+1	+13	-3	-9	+3
6.0 Housing starts, thousands	n.m.	-19	-11	-15	n.m.	-6	-6	n.m.	-9	-10	n.m.	-23	-11
7.0 Change in stocks and work in progress (q)	n.a.	n.a.	-4	-15	-10	+14	-4	n.a.	0	-12	+6	0	-6
8.0 Basic materials price index	n.a.	+28	n.m.	+3	-6	+7	n.m.	n.a.	+19	n.m.	-1	+8	-2
9.0 Common stock price index	+1	-5	+1	-26	-5	-10	n.m.	-2	-9	-7	-9	-20	-8
10.0 Companies' profits less U.K. taxes (q)	n.a.	n.a.	-13	-27	+2	-4	-1	n.a.	-3	0	0	-3	-3
11.0 Ratio, price to unit labor cost, manufacturing	n.a.	n.a.	n.a.	-15	-14	+9	-22	n.a.	n.a.	n.a.	-9	-12	+1
12.0 Increase in hire purchase debt	n.a.	-19	-16	-19	-19	-5	0	n.a.	n.a.	-11	-10	-27	-19

Roughly Coincident Indicators

17.0 Personal disposable income (q)	n.a.	-7	+2	0	-14	-1	-10	n.a.	0	-9	-6	-3	+21
15.0 Gross domestic product (q)	n.a.	n.a.	-1	-21	-10	-4	-13	n.a.	+3	0	-7	+6	0
16.0 Industrial production	0	-7	-12	-14	0	0	0	0	-1	-1	0	0	0
18.1 Retail sales	n.a.	n.a.	-11	+3	-15	-3	0	n.a.	-6	0	-9	-1	+22
13.0 Employment in production industries	n.a.	+1	+1	-1	+6	+14	+2	+2	+2	0	+8	+1	+6
14.0 Unemployed (inverted)	+2	0	0	0	+14	+6	+6	+3	0	+1	0	+1	+6

Lagging Indicators

19.0 Long-term unemployment, inverted	+6	+3	0	+5	+13	+10	+7	+7	+4	+2	-1	+2	+8
20.0 Investment in plant and equipment	n.a.	n.a.	+5	0	+17	+17	+5	n.a.	+9	+9	+3	+6	+6
21.0 Changes in stock and work in progress	n.a.	+17	+2	-6	+14	+14	+5	n.a.	+6	+6	+6	+9	+9
22.0 Changes in employment per unit output	n.a.	n.a.	+8	+9	+11	+8	n.m.	n.a.	n.a.	+12	+6	+12	+15
23.0 Loans to industry	n.a.	n.a.	+2	0	+5	+14	n.m.	n.a.	-9	+15	+12	0	n.m.
24.0 Prime rate	n.a.	n.a.	n.a.	n.a.	+3	+5	+9	n.a.	n.a.	n.a.	-1	+3	-4

Composite Indexes

Lagging index, inverted	n.a.	-18	-26	-30	-22	-14	-39	n.a.	-33	-19	-13	-30	-15
Leading index	n.a.	n.a.	-12	-15	-10	-3	+5	n.a.	-5	-11	-9	-11	-1
Coincident index	n.a.	0	0	0	-1	+14	0	0	0	0	+3	0	+3
Lagging index	n.a.	+3	0	+5	+13	+8	+10	n.a.	+4	+9	+10	+2	+8

Note:
n.a. = Data not available.
n.m. = No matching turn.

Table 4B–4. Individual Indicators and Composite Indexes, Lead (–) or Lag (+) at Growth Cycle Turning Points, in Months, West Germany.

	Peaks							Troughs					
	2/51	10/55	2/61	5/65	5/70	8/73	2/80	2/54	4/59	2/63	8/67	12/71	5/75
Leading Indicators													
1.1 Number working short hours, inverted	n.a.	0	–17	+10	–27	–1	–43	–41	–6	+1	–2	0	+3
2.0 Applications for unemployment compensation, inverted	n.a.	n.a.	n.a.	+10	+6	–7	–2	n.a.	–13	n.m.	–2	+2	–4
4.1 Insolvent enterprises, inverted	n.a.	n.a.	n.a.	+4	–22	–8	–9	n.a.	n.a.	n.a.	–4	–14	–4
5.1 New orders, investment goods industrial	n.a.	n.a.	n.a.	–4	–9	–3	–14	n.a.	n.a.	0	–7	0	+3
Housing permits, interior space	n.a.	n.a.	n.a.	+10	n.a.	n.a.	n.a.	n.a.	n.a.	+8	–3	n.a.	n.a.
6.1 Residential construction orders	n.a.	n.a.	n.a.	n.a.	n.a.	–18	–15	n.a.	n.a.	n.a.	n.a.	n.a.	–6
7.0 Inventory change	n.a.	+27	–5	–4	–5	+4	–4	n.a.	–1	+2	–5	–8	+4
9.0 Stock price index	n.a.	n.a.	–6	–9	–6	–5	–47	n.a.	–22	0	–8	–13	–8
10.1 Net income from entrepreneurial activities	n.a.	n.a.	–6	0	–10	–3	n.m.	n.a.	–2	–12	+3	–22	–15
11.0 Ratio, price to unit labor cost	n.a.	n.a.	–9	–9	–9	–9	n.m.	n.a.	n.a.	+3	–6	–10	–12
12.0 Change in consumer credit	n.a.	n.a.	n.a.	n.a.	–9	–9	–33	n.a.	n.a.	n.a.	n.a.	–19	–18

Roughly Coincident Indicators

17.0 Disposable income (real)	-6	-5	0	0	n.m.	-9	-9	-27	+10	+3	+6	n.m.	+24
15.0 Gross national product (real)	0	+7	0	+9	0	-6	0	0	-2	0	0	+8	0
16.0 Industrial production	0	0	0	-4	-1	0	-7	+1	+3	0	+3	0	+2
18.1 Manufacturing sales	n.a.	n.a.	-2	-4	-6	-7	+3	n.a.	-1	0	+5	0	-2
18.2 Retail trade	n.a.	+18	+9	-1	n.m.	-12	-9	n.a.	+11	+4	+5	n.m.	-5
13.1 Employment in mining and manufacturing	n.a.	+1	+1	+11	+3	+3	n.m.	-3	+1	+9	+3	+9	+8
14.0 Unemployment rate	n.a.	+4	0	+10	+4	+1	+2	+6	-2	0	-3	+5	+1

Lagging Indicators

20.0 Investment in machinery, equipment, and construction	n.a.	n.a.	n.a.	+9	+3	-6	-36	n.a.	n.a.	0	-3	-1	0
21.0 Level of inventories	n.a.	+28	n.m.	+12	+3	+18	n.m.	n.a.	n.a.	+15	+18	+17	+9
23.1 Bank credits to the economy	n.a.	n.a.	n.a.	-21	-24	-8	n.a.	n.a.	n.a.	n.a.	+4	-9	-1
22.0 Percentage change in the reciprocal of output/manhour	n.a.	n.a.	n.a.	+16	0	+11	n.m.	n.a.	n.a.	n.a.	-2	+6	+3
24.1 Bank rates on large loans	n.a.	n.a.	n.a.	n.a.	0	+3	n.m.	n.a.	n.a.	n.a.	+18	+6	+36

Composite Indexes

Lagging index, inverted	n.a.	n.a.	n.a.	n.a.	-35	-12	-12	n.a.	n.a.	n.a.	n.m.	-18	-18
Leading index	n.a.	n.a.	-6	-4	-9	-7	-9	n.a.	-2	+2	-2	-4	-6
Roughly coincident index	0	0	0	-1	+2	-6	0	-27	-2	0	0	+7	+3
Lagging index	n.a.	n.a.	n.a.	+9	+1	+3	+3	n.a.	n.a.	n.a.	-2	+8	+4

Note:
n.a. = Data not available.
n.m. = No matching turn.

Table 4B-5. Individual Indicators and Composite Indexes, Lead (−) or Lag (+) at Growth Cycle Turning Points, in Months, France.

	Peaks						Troughs				
	8/57	2/64	6/66	11/69	5/74	8/79	8/59	6/65	5/68	11/71	6/75
Leading Indicators											
1.0 Average workweek, manufacturing	n.a.	−1	+1	−6	−13	n.m.	n.a.	−2	−4	−14	+4
6.0 Building permits, residential	−21	−5	−6	−11	−9	n.m.	−21	−12	−7	+4	−5
8.0 Wholesale price index, raw materials	+3	n.m.	0	+5	−1	+1	−9	n.m.	+5	+9	+4
9.0 Index of stock prices	−1	−23	−5	+2	−12	+1	−13	−12	−10	−1	−9
11.0 Ratio, price to unit labor cost, manufacturing (q)	n.a.	−37	−4	+3	−3	−5	−16	−15	−3	+4	−3
3.1 Change in unfilled orders, total	n.a.	n.a.	n.a.	−11	−13	−10	n.a.	n.a.	n.a.	−16	−8
Roughly Coincident Indicators											
15.0 Gross Domestic Production (q)	n.a.	−6	−1	−12	0	0	n.a.	−4	0	−6	−4
16.0 Industrial production	−10	+2	0	−12	+3	−1	−6	−3	0	−6	−1
18.1 Retail sales	0	+14	n.m.	−12	−4	n.m.	0	n.m.	0	+12	0
13.0 Employment, nonfarm	+5	+8	+1	+8	0	+8	+20	+6	+3	+9	+7
14.0 Registered unemployed (inverted)	−4	0	+3	0	0	−19	+2	0	+1	0	+3
Lagging Indicators											
21.1 Inventory of finished goods, survey, change over four months	n.a.	n.a.	n.a.	+9	+6	n.m.	n.a.	n.a.	+1	+15	+4
24.0 Commercial banks, prime rate	n.a.	n.a.	n.a.	−1	+7	+6	n.a.	n.a.	+1	+9	+8
Composite Indexes											
Lagging index, inverted	n.a.	n.a.	n.a.	−17	−18	−44	n.a.	n.a.	n.a.	−20	−7
Leading index	−1	−5	−4	−2	−11	−2	−16	−12	−4	+4	−4
Roughly coincident index	−2	+2	0	−12	0	0	−1	−3	0	+3	0
Lagging index	n.a.	n.a.	n.a.	+4	+6	n.m.	n.a.	n.a.	+1	+12	+6

Note: n.a. = Data not available; n.m. = No matching turn.

Italy.

	Peaks						Troughs				
	10/56	9/63	8/69	4/74	12/76	2/80	7/59	3/65	9/72	5/75	10/77
Leading Indicators											
1.1 Hours per month per worker in industry	n.a.	n.a.	n.a.	-3	0	+1	n.a.	n.a.	+4	+3	+19
4.1 Declared bankruptcies (inverted)	+2	-5	-2	-6	n.m.	n.m.	-7	-2	-11	n.m.	n.m.
3.1 Change in unfilled orders, total	n.a.	n.a.	-8	-9	-8	-14	n.a.	-11	-26	-6	-7
6.0 Building permits, residential	n.a.	-2	n.m.	-4	+5	0	n.a.	-2	n.m.	-5	+12
9.0 Stock price index	-13	-36	+8	0	n.m.	n.m.	-12	-7	-10	n.m.	+2
Roughly Coincident Indicators											
15.0 Gross Domestic Product (q)	+4	+5	-3	-2	+2	0	-8	-1	-1	0	+1
16.0 Industrial production	-3	0	-1	0	0	0	0	0	-14	0	+10
18.1 Retail sales	0	-2	0	-5	n.m.	n.a.	-13	0	-13	-1	n.a.
13.0 Nonfarm employment	n.a.	+4	+11	+9	-5	n.a.	+9	+10	+4	+8	0
14.0 Unemployment rate (inverted)	n.a.	+1	+18	0	n.a.	n.a.	n.a.	+16	+7	n.a.	-3
Lagging Indicators											
21.1 Inventory of finished goods, survey, change over 4 months	n.a.	n.a.	+10	+8	+3	+3	n.a.	n.a.	+4	+5	+14
24.0 Commercial banks, prime rate	n.a.	n.a.	+11	+3	-2	n.m.	n.a.	n.a.	+9	+8	+23
Composite Indexes											
Lagging index, inverted	n.a.	n.a.	-5	-15	-13	-14	n.a.	n.a.	-24	-5	-7
Leading index	n.a.	-35	0	-9	n.a.	n.m.	-12	-2	-10	n.a.	+6
Coincident index	n.a.	+1	+7	0	0	0	n.a.	+10	+6	0	0
Lagging index	n.a.	n.a.	+13	+8	+3	n.m.	n.a.	+48	+4	+6	+14

Note: n.a. = Data not available; n.m. = No matching turn.

Table 4B–7. Industrial Indicators and Composite Indexes, Lead (–) or Lag (+) at Growth Cycle Turning Points, in Months, Belgium.

	Peaks				Troughs		
	10/64	9/70	7/74	6/79	7/68	7/71	10/75
Leading Indicators							
1.1 Monthly hours working	–8	–5	–3	+1	–1	+12	–2
4.1 Bankruptcies, inverted	n.a.	n.m.	–1	0	–8	n.m.	+2
3.1 Real inland orders	+22	–8	–2	+4	–1	+5	+7
9.1 Industrial share price index	–9	–16	–13	+8	–18	–14	–10
6.1 Number of residential building permits	n.a.	–14	0	n.a.	–5	–2	–5
5.2 Number of nonresidential building permits	+14	–14	–4	n.a.	–2	–2	n.m.
Roughly Coincident Indicators							
15.0 Real Gross Domestic Product	n.a.	0	0	–34	+1	0	+1
16.0 Industrial production	–7	–14	–1	0	–15	–2	–6
18.1 Real retail sales	+14	n.m.	–17	–17	n.a.	–11	–11
14.0 Unemployment rate, inverted	–1	+7	–2	n.a.	–1	+15	–1
Lagging Indicators							
21.1 Finished goods, inventories, change over 4 months	n.a.	+15	+13	+23	+16	+27	+15
24.1 Bank lending rates to prime borrowers	+20	–12	0	+9	+4	+14	+3
Composite Indexes							
Lagging index, inverted	n.m.	n.m.	–22	–10	–18	n.m.	–9
Leading index	n.a.	–14	–6	+4	–5	–3	0
Roughly coincident index	–7	+3	–6	–7	–2	+12	+1
Lagging index	+27	–1	+6	+11	+3	+14	+4

Note: n.a. = Data not available; n.m. = No matching turn.

Table 4B-8.   Individual Indicators and Composite Indexes, Lead (−) or Lag (+) at Specified Turning Points: Netherlands.

	Peaks								Troughs						
	7/50	10/56	3/61	11/65	11/70	8/74	9/76	12/79	6/52	5/58	2/63	8/67	8/72	7/75	11/77
Leading Indicators															
1.1 Temporary short-time workers (inverted)	n.a.	n.a.	−1	+7	−1	−10	n.m.	0	n.a.	n.a.	0	−4	−5	+2	n.m.
3.1 Change in unfilled orders	n.a.	n.a.	n.a.	+6	−7	−5	n.m.	n.m.	n.a.	n.a.	−16	−10	−17	0	n.m.
4.1 Bankruptcies, inverted	n.a.	−8	+4	+3	−23	−20		−14	−5	+16	+3	0	−8	−5	n.m.
5.1 Nonresidential building permits (q)	n.a.	−29	−16	+18	−3	−6	+8	−4	n.a.	−6	−3	+30	−3	−5	+6
6.1 Dwellings started	n.a.	+3	−1	−11	n.m.	−22	+2	n.m.	−12	−7	−10	−9	n.m.	−9	+3
7.0 Change in industrial inventories (q)	n.a.	n.a.	−1	n.m.	n.m.	+6	+5	n.m.	n.a.	+3	−12	n.m.	+9	+7	+3
8.1 Prices, raw materials and semi-manufactured goods	+9	+7	−7	+7	−4	−4	−5	n.m.	+19	+14	0	+16	+8	−1	+13
9.0 Stock price index	n.a.	−13	+1	−13	−21	−16	−7	−15	+15	−5	−4	−8	−9	−8	−13
11.0 Ratio, price to labor cost, (q)	n.a.	n.a.	+8	−6	0	−6	+2	−4	n.a.	n.a.	+9	+21	+6	+1	+6
Roughly Coincident Indicators															
13.1 Employment, manufacturing (q)	+7	+10	+14	0	0	0	n.m.	n.m.	+2	+9	+6	+6	+3	n.m.	+3
14.1 Registered unemployed, number (inverted)	n.a.	−5	0	+1	+3	−9	n.m.	0	n.a.	0	0	0	−6	+7	n.m.
16.0 Industrial production	0	+4	−3	−20	−8	0	0	−8	+6	−1	0	−3	−8	0	0
18.1 Manufacturing sales (q)	n.a.	−2	−7	0	0	0	−1	−1	−7	+3	0	+3	0	+1	0
18.2 Retail sales	n.a.	0	0	0	0	0	−2	−22	n.a.	−1	−12	+18	0	0	n.m.

(Table 4B-8. continued overleaf)

Table 4B-8. continued

	Peaks								Troughs						
	7/50	10/56	3/61	11/65	11/70	8/74	9/76	12/79	6/52	5/58	2/63	8/67	8/72	7/75	11/77
Lagging Indicators															
19.0 Long-term unemployed (inverted), (q)	n.a.	+4	+11	+6	+6	−6	n.m.	+2	n.a.	+9	0	+3	+3	+4	n.m.
20.0 New plant equipment expenditures (q)	n.a.	n.a.	+2	n.m.	+3	0	+11	n.a.	n.a.	0	0	n.m.	0	+7	+15
21.1 Industrial inventories (end of q)	n.a.	+14	+6	−5	−8	+7	+6	n.m.	n.a.	+28	+10	+16	+10	+8	+10
Composite Indexes															
Inverted lagging index	n.a.	−31	n.m.	−33	n.m.	n.m.	−7	−10	n.a.	n.a.	−21	−13	n.m.	n.m.	−9
Leading index	n.a.	−13	−1	−12	−3	−4	+5	+2	+20	−6	0	−9	−9	+2	+3
Roughly coincident index	+1	−1	0	0	+2	0	0	+2	0	0	0	+3	+3	0	+9
Lagging index	n.a.	+2	+8	+8	−3	+5	+5	+2	n.a.	+3	0	+6	0	+7	+15

Note:
n.a. = Data not available.
n.m. = No matching turn.

Table 4B-9. Individual Indicators and Composite Indexes, Lead (–) or Lag (+) at Growth Cycle Turning Points, in Months, Sweden.

	Peaks			*Troughs*		
	2/65	7/70	6/74	7/67	7/72	7/78
Leading Indicators						
1.1 Number of hours worked (in industry)	– 11	0	+ 4	– 12	0	0
2.1 Number of new job offerings	+ 10	- 6	+ 4	+ 8	– 6	– 5
3.1 Value of new orders, constant prices	– 3	– 12	– 4	+ 2	0	– 12
6.1 Number of housing starts	—	—	–·	—	—	—
8.0 Raw material prices	n.a.	– 3	+ 5	+ 16	+ 1	– 3
9.0 Stock price	+ 11	– 14	– 18	+ 7	– 20	– 7
11.0 Ratio, price to ULC	– 3	+ 7	+ 8	+ 7	– 2	– 11
12.1 New loans to households	n.a.	+ 19	– 2	n.a.	+ 9	– 19
Coincident Indicators						
13.0 (Nonfarm) employment	+ 5	– 7	+ 8	– 4	+ 6	n.m.
14.0 Unemployment rate	0	– 1	+ 29	+ 1	– 8	0
15.0 Gross Domestic Product	n.a.	+ 1	– 1	n.a.	– 8	– 8
16.0 Industrial production index	– 1	0	0	0	0	– 1
17.0 Disposable income, 1975 prices	0	0	+ 11	– 5	– 2	n.m.
18.1 Retail sales, volume	+ 3	+ 4	+ 2	+ 16	+ 4	– 2
Lagging Indicators						
19.0 Long duration unemployment rate, inverted	+ 3	+ 4	+ 32	+ 4	+ 4	+ 4
22.1 O/MH, 12-month span, inverted	– 7	– 3	+ 6	+ 17	+ 11	+ 5
23.1 Personal loans on checking accounts	+ 18	– 12	0	+ 1	+ 8	+ 6
24.1 Discount rate	+ 16	+ 7	+ 2	+ 18	+ 20	+ 11
Composite Indexes						
Inverted lagging index	– 24	n.m.	– 6	– 27	n.m.	– 20
Leading index	0	– 6	– 2	+ 9	0	– 5
Roughly coincident index	0	0	– 1	0	– 2	– 1
Lagging index	+ 21	– 12	– 1	+ 3	+ 17	+ 9

Note:
n.a. = Data not available.
n.m. = No matching turn.

Table 4B–10. Individual Indicators and Composite Indexes, Lead (−) or Lag (+) at Growth Cycle Turning Points, in Months, Japan.

	Peaks							Troughs					
	12/53	5/57	1/62	7/64	6/70	11/73	2/80	6/55	1/59	1/63	2/66	1/72	3/75
Leading Indicators													
1.1 Index of overtime workers manufacturing	n.a.	−4	−3	−4	−4	−5	−36	−9	−7	−3	−5	−2	0
4.1 Business failures (inverted)	n.a.	−5	−8	−15	−12	−9	−14	n.a.	−18	−11	−16	−13	−14
5.0 New orders, machinery and construction works	n.a.	n.a.	−6	−3	−8	−4	n.m.	n.a.	n.a.	−6	+2	−3	+4
6.1 Dwelling units started	0	−14	−9	−12	−12	−8	−15	−8	+5	−11	+10	−11	−2
7.0 Change in inventories (q)	−7	−3	−5	+4	−1	+3	+3	−10	−2	−5	−6	+1	−1
8.0 Raw materials price index	+3	0	−5	n.m.	−3	+3	0	+6	−1	n.m.	−7	+6	+8
9.0 Stock price index	n.a.	−4	−6	−15	−5	−10	−13	−1	−13	−3	−7	−2	−5
10.0 Operating profits, all industries (q)	n.a.	−13	−33	−15	−5	−7	−1	−15	−11	−9	−11	0	−2
11.0 Ratio, price to unit labor cost, manufacturing	−2	0	−23	−8	−5	+2	+2	−10	−2	−1	−4	0	0
12.1 Change in consumer and housing credit outstanding (q)	n.a.	n.a.	n.a.	n.a.	−7	−9	−12	n.a.	n.a.	n.a.	n.a.	+1	0
Coincident Indicators													
17.1 Wage and salary income	−20	n.m.	−5	0	n.m.	−9	−12	n.m.	+8	0	n.a.	+1	−13
15.0 Gross national expenditures (q)	n.a.	+3	−2	−5	−7	−9	n.m.	n.m.	+1	0	+2	n.m.	−13
16.0 Industrial production	−2	0	0	−5	0	+3	0	0	−7	−1	0	0	0

18.1 Retail sales	n.a.	-10	n.m.	-8	+14	0	-19	0	-8	n.m.	-1	+3	-11
13.0 Regular workers' employment, all industries	n.a.	0	+4	+4	0	n.m.	n.m.	+9	-2	+2	+13	n.m.	+1
14.0 Unemployment rate (inverted)	0	+1	-10	+8	-3	+1	0	+1	+2	+2	+7	-1	+7
Lagging Indicators													
20.0 Gross fixed capital formation (others)	+2	0	-5	+1	-4	0	n.m.	-1	+1	+7	0	+7	+8
21.0 Inventory level	n.a.	n.a.	+4	+4	+2	+9	n.m.	n.a.	n.a.	+1	+9	+1	+50
23.1 Commercial bank loans and discounts	n.a.	+16	n.m.	-1	n.m.	-11	-14	+11	n.m.	-10	+50	n.m.	-7
24.1 Contracted rate on loans	n.a.	+12	+9	+7	+4	n.m.	+6	+19	+29	+8	+18	+14	n.m.
22.1 Output/manhour, percentage change of reciprocal, 12-month span	n.a.	n.a.	+7	+9	+7	+8	n.m.	n.a.	n.a.	+5	+7	+10	+14
Composite Indexes													
Lagging index, inverted	n.a.	-9	-29	-13	-46	-14	-12	n.a.	-17	-8	-15	-14	-8
Leading index	-2	-4	-5	-9	-4	+3	0	-10	-7	-3	-6	+1	-1
Roughly coincident index	n.a.	0	-5	0	-7	-1	0	0	0	0	+1	+3	-1
Lagging index	n.a.	+3	+4	+4	+5	+8	+6	+14	+7	+5	+7	+8	+47

Note:
n.a. = Data not available.
n.m. = No matching turn.

Chapter 5

QUALITATIVE INDICATORS OF GROWTH CYCLE DEVELOPMENTS

The 1966 U.S. list of indicators that served as the initial focus of our efforts to develop growth cycle chronologies in nine foreign countries was composed of "quantitative," as opposed to "qualitative," indicators. Quantitative indicators record cyclical changes in economic magnitudes measured in terms of physical units, constant prices, percentages, and so on. As such, they are designed to reflect the complex of economic interrelationships that constitute the fabric of "aggregate economic activity" on which Mitchell originally based his research.

Qualitative indicators, on the other hand, issue from surveys of entrepreneurs or consumers concerning their attitudes toward either what has happened or what is expected to happen regarding particular economic variables. Thus, the European Economic Commission now coordinates surveys of entrepreneurs in eight of its member countries. These surveys are designed to elicit information concerning production expectations, stocks of finished goods, the state of order books, selling-price expectations, views of production trends, and so forth. The entrepreneurs may be asked to report actual numbers, but usually the information requested is subjective in nature. Businessmen may be asked whether orders have been above or below "normal," or how they expect orders to behave in the coming months. Information of this sort bears a strong resemblance to the

This chapter draws heavily on a report prepared for the European Economic Commission by Philip A. Klein entitled *Monitoring Growth Cycles with Qualitative Indicators: A Study of Business Surveys in EEC Countries* (1980).

index of consumer sentiment long utilized by the University of Michigan's Survey Research Center, which reports the opinions and buying plans of consumers. Just as the EEC surveys reflect the confidence in the immediate economic future held by entrepreneurs, consumer surveys reflect the psychological state of consumers.

Qualitative indicators can be useful in analyzing unfolding cyclical developments and can be related to a number of business cycle theories. While purely psychological theories no longer earn our primary attention, most theories providing insight into the workings of business cycles continue to place some emphasis on subjective appraisals among entrepreneurs. Mitchell's use of changing profit expectations, Keynes's attention to the collapse of the marginal efficiency of investment, Harrod's warranted rate of growth, and Lucas's rational expectations affirm the importance of psychological attitudes among participants in market-oriented economies. Economic analysis in general abounds with discussions of self-fulfilling prophesies—if, for example, enough investors believe the stock market will collapse, then the likelihood that the market will in fact collapse is enormously enhanced. The line between the "objective state of an economy" and the subjective view toward that economy taken by consumers or entrepreneurs has always been a murky one at best.

There is no reason, then, for not marshalling all the information that may augment our understanding of unfolding cyclical developments. This would involve not only tracking the changes in significant economic magnitudes, but tracking the changing attitudes of players in the economic game as well. The degree of subjectivity in these qualitative indicators varies, of course. A survey asking entrepreneurs to state whether their order books are up or down compared to the previous month or quarter will naturally deal in data that is more objective than a survey dependent upon a businessman's notion of "normal" order levels. Between these two extremes are questions concerning plans—for example, a plan to expand a factory or buy new equipment—that reflect the participant's view of the future economy as it affects that participant's own business activity, a view that may or may not conform to what in fact the participant subsequently does. Survey methods and the phrasing of questions must, therefore, be thoroughly understood before responses can be analyzed.

Qualitative indicators have long been popular in European countries, and in recent years they have been effectively adopted by Asian countries as well. In some cases, recourse to qualitative indicators has reflected, no doubt, a paucity of quantitative information. In other cases, a conscious decision to develop attitudinal information had been reached. While this chapter will focus on the behavior of cyclical turning points as they are reflected in both qualitative and quantitative indicators, the information contained in the qualitative indicators is frequently regarded as significant in its own right. This, for example, is clearly the belief of the EEC. Knowing what entrepreneurs think about a variety of unfolding economic developments—particularly when their views are "harmonized" by surveying entrepreneurs in a number of countries with the same questionnaire and analyzing the replies by means of common techniques and assumptions—can provide information on developments within the community that is useful in and of itself.

If Mitchell and his co-workers concentrated their attention on quantitative indicators, it was no doubt because their view of what happens during business cycles focused on actual economic interrelationships. But cycles are clearly determined by what participants *think* is going to happen as well. There is merit in collecting and analyzing both quantitative and qualitative indicators. Researchers must be careful, however, in what they claim for either type of indicator. The EEC indicators had their genesis in the business surveys developed after World War II in Munich by the IFO-Institute, and J.-D. Lindlebauer recently described these surveys:

> The IFO-Institute has succeeded in creating completely new instruments for cyclical observations by means of its surveys of businessmen. For the first time, they enable the judgments and anticipations of businessmen to be determined and represented in the form of time series . . . the results of the IFO surveys seemed to be predestined to act as business cycle indicators from the onset.[1]

The business surveys undertaken by the IFO-Institute became the prototype for similar surveys coordinated in other member countries through the EEC. In the United Kingdom, such surveys have, for the past quarter century, been carried out by the Confederation of British Industry (CBI).

Qualitative indicators may have achieved their greatest popularity in Europe, but they have by no means been neglected in the United States. As long ago as 1957 the National Bureau of Economic Research undertook a conference devoted to "The Quality and Economic Significance of Anticipations Data."[2] This conference, analyzing major surveys of consumers and entrepreneurs, dealt specifically with the Federal Reserve Board's Survey Research Center, the Department of Commerce's survey of investment intentions, and such private efforts as the McGraw-Hill and Dun & Bradstreet surveys of entrepreneurial anticipations.

In this chapter we shall concentrate on results obtained by surveys collected and coordinated by the EEC and the Confederation of British Industry. Surveys taken by the Japanese Planning Agency, as well as some U.S. agencies, will be referred to briefly. We are also limiting the basis of our discussion to surveys taken of entrepreneurs active in the manufacturing sector of the major EEC countries. The survey questions of immediate concern to us cover the following points:

1. Production trends in the recent past: up, unchanged, down?
2. Production expectations for the month ahead: up, unchanged, down?
3. Order books: above normal, normal, below normal?
4. Export order books: above normal, normal, below normal?
5. Stocks of finished goods: above normal, normal, below normal?
6. Selling-price expectations in the months ahead: up, unchanged, down?

The CBI survey in the United Kingdom asks for essentially the same information, but in slightly different form, and we shall introduce these CBI questions as appropriate. We shall also be concerned with the possibilities of utilizing qualitative indicators in monitoring growth cycles, and for this we shall present charts of the survey data for Germany and make timing comparisons for Germany, France, Italy, and the United Kingdom.

METHODOLOGICAL PROBLEMS

The rest of this chapter will focus on how turning points in time series derived from entrepreneurial responses compare to turning points based on quantitative indicators. In the case of "expected changes in production," for example, how do the turning points in such a survey-derived series compare to the turning points actually exhibited by production?

All of the survey responses dealt with in this chapter are analyzed in the form of "net balances," which are found by subtracting the percentage of respondents who reply "down" or "decrease" or "below normal" from the percent who reply "up" or "increase" or "above normal." This approach also implicitly takes into account the number who reply "no change." For example, if those who reply "up" later reply "no change," the net balance declines.

Two problems must be faced initially. The first involves the question of dating the replies. The EEC surveys refer to "the months ahead," which is ambiguous. Since replies are probably not all received at the same time, even if the time interval were precise it would be applied to different periods by the respondents. We have handled this problem by interpreting "the months ahead" in the way explicitly assumed in the CBI surveys, which ask respondents to comment on what they feel has happened during the past four months or what they expect in the next four months. Questions sent out at the end of, say, September, are answered in October and refer, therefore, to the October–February period. We date the replies in the center of the period, that is, December, and label the results as "four months, centered." This is important in determining how to relate the timing of the survey questions to the growth cycle chronologies for each of the four countries under consideration, and to the quantitative data with which the survey data are to be compared. It also enables us to interpret the U.K. data derived from the CBI survey in the same way as the EEC survey results.

Another problem in interpreting the net balances is more complicated. We have noted that some of the questions ask whether the variable is above or below "normal." When the question is so posed we assume that the variable has, in effect, been "trend-adjusted" mentally by the respondent. The net balance of the replies is equivalent to a trend-adjusted level in the corresponding quantitative variable. If we wish to compare survey results to the rate of change in this quantitative variable, it is necessary to take the first difference of the net balances as originally observed. These measures, along with others discussed below, are summarized in Table 5-1.

The above treatment applies to the EEC survey questions concerning finished goods stocks and order books (total and export). But the CBI treats these categories in terms of the trend in the past four months and the expected trend for the next four months, to which respondents are asked to reply "up," "same," or "down." The critical point to note is that when the question is phrased in this way the net balances are *not* equivalent to *levels* of orders or stocks but are analogous to *rates of change* in quantitative indicators of these variables. Thus, if we wish to compare the two kinds of indicators, the qualitative results must first be cumulated. Alternatively, one could take the first difference of the quantitative indicators and compare them with the net balances of the survey replies. Unless these adjustments are made, the lead in turning points reported for qualitative indicators over comparable quantitative indicators may simply reflect the earlier timing of first differences. One can produce earlier turns in most economic series by taking first differences.[3]

The other questions analyzed (production and prices) take the form of responses indicating that the variable has increased or de-

Table 5-1. Method of Treating Survey Statistics and Corresponding Quantitative Variables.

Variable[a]	Survey Question	Survey Statistic	Comparable Quantitative Statistic
1. Order books (stock of unfilled orders)	Above or below normal	1.1. Net balance	1.1.1. Level of unfilled orders 1.1.2. Ratio of unfilled orders to sales 1.1.3. Trend-adjusted level of unfilled orders
		1.2. First difference of net balance	1.2.1. Change in unfilled orders 1.2.2. New orders 1.2.3. New orders, trend-adjusted
2. Stocks of finished goods	Above or below normal	2.1. Net balance	2.1.1. Level of finished goods inventories 2.1.2. Trend-adjusted level of finished goods inventories 2.1.3. Ratio of finished goods inventories to sales
		2.2. First difference of net balance	2.2.1. Change in finished goods inventories 2.2.2. Change in ratio of finished goods inventories to sales
3. Production, selling prices, CBI survey of new orders, stocks of raw materials, stocks of finished goods, profits calculated from average prices less average costs, business confidence, Dun & Bradstreet survey of profits.	Up or down, actual in past or anticipated ahead	3.1. Net balance, diffusion index	3.1.1. Change during corresponding interval
		3.2. Cumulated net balance, placed at the end of interval	3.2.1. Level at end of corresponding interval

Note:
a. Variables refer to the EEC surveys except as indicated.

creased in the recent past, or is expected to do so in the coming months. When so posed the replies in net-balance form are treated as explained above for orders. Either the net balances are compared to the rate of change in production or prices, or the cumulated net balances are compared to the levels of the quantitative variable.

A final difficulty arises from the fact that the EEC survey refers to order books, that is, to total unfilled orders, whereas often the only available quantitative data refer to new orders. We assume that the change in unfilled orders is a proxy for new orders, and use the first differences of the net balances to compare with new orders. Table 5-1 sets forth all these relations.

In all the comparisons in this chapter, therefore, we shall indicate whether survey results are being compared to levels of variables (such as the volume of production) or to rates of change over time. In each case we shall refer to the variables according to the classification of Table 5-1. We shall also analyze the results for Germany in some detail and make summary reports for France, Italy, the United Kingdom, and the United States.

ORDER BOOKS

Since analysis of German order books is typical of the techniques utilized in treating other survey results, it is well to elaborate the approach to data for West Germany at this point. For the "quantitative equivalent" of the survey data we use a series compiled by German government sources regarding *actual* new orders for each month. This quantitative indicator is different from survey results primarily because it is not based on subjective impressions, i.e., whether order books are greater or less than "normal." Furthermore, the EEC questionnaire deals with stocks of unfilled orders (order books), whereas the quantitative series is restricted to new orders. In quantitative form, the change in unfilled orders equals new orders minus sales. By differencing the net balances we have put them into a form as comparable as possible to the flow of new orders.

Figure 5-1 records the level of order books in West Germany according to the EEC survey, and Figure 5-2 shows the first differences derived from this series. Actual new orders, trend-adjusted, appear in Figure 5-3.

It is clear from Figure 5-1 that the level of order books has conformed quite consistently to the growth cycle, with roughly coincident timing. Not surprisingly, the turns are shifted and the series becomes more volatile when the series is first differenced, but it is these turning points (shown in Figure 5-2) to which the quantitative

Figure 5-1. West Germany, Timing at Growth Cycle Turns, Level of Order Books, Total (1.1), Survey Net Balance, 1968-79.

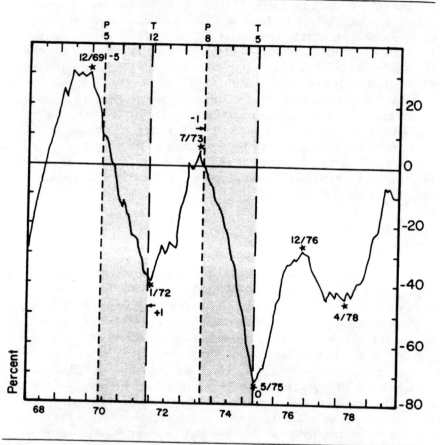

Note:
Vertical lines represent peaks (P) and troughs (T) of growth cycles, and entries above and below the dates on the charts are the number of months lead (-) or lag (+) vis-a-vis the growth cycle. The figure in parentheses in the title refers to the type of statistic described in Table 5-1.

Selected turns are indicated by asterisks. Where they differ from turns selected by the computer, the asterisks are enclosed in a square. Where computer-selected turns have been deleted, the asterisk is circled.

Figure 5-2. West Germany, Timing at Growth Cycle Turns, Change in Level of Order Books, Total (1.2), First Difference of Survey Net Balance, 1968-79.

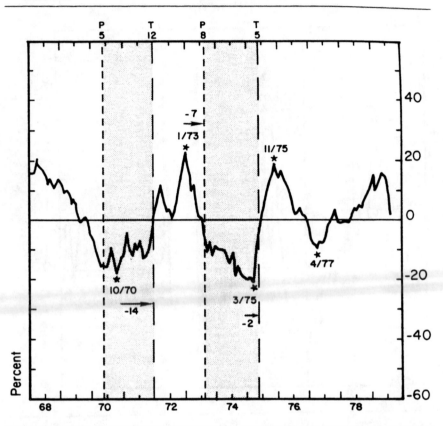

series (new orders) must be compared. The quantitative series itself leads at peaks but not at troughs (Table 5-2, Col. 7). The number of turning point comparisons between actual new orders and the survey replies on changes in order books is very limited, but suggests that in this case the survey results lead actual new orders (Table 5-2, Col. 8). This is somewhat unexpected because we have found that, in general, survey results do *not* lead their corresponding quantitative indicators. One difficulty, which may account here for the lead, involves the degree to which changes in order books can appropriately be used as a proxy for new orders. Changes in order books are obviously the result of not only new orders, but of the rate at which orders are filled, which may itself be cyclically sensitive. If sales exceed new

Figure 5-3.   West Germany, Timing at Growth Cycle Turns, New Orders, Total Trend-Adjusted (1.2.3), Quantitative Series, 1968-79.

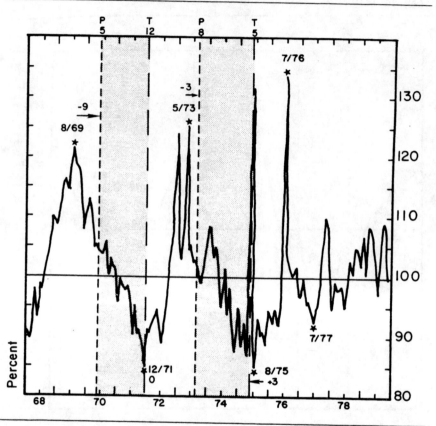

orders, the level of order books will drop even though new orders are increasing.

Entrepreneurs may also interpret this question in terms of whether their stock of unfilled orders is high or low relative to sales. In this case the proper comparison of the net balance would be to the ratio of unfilled orders to sales. Unfortunately, such a quantitative series does not exist for West Germany. We raise the possibility of this interpretation because it might explain why the survey results lead the volume of new orders. The ratio might lead new orders also. The survey results do suggest, however, that a generally better forecasting system can be achieved by utilizing both qualitative and quantitative indicators.

Table 5-2. West Germany, Timing at Growth Cycle Turns, Three Measures of Orders, 1966-79.

Part A. Dates of Peaks and Troughs

Growth Cycle Chronology (1)		EEC Survey Level of Order Books, Net Balance (1.1) (2)		EEC Survey, Change in Order Books (1.2) (3)		Quantitative Series, New Orders (Trend-Adjusted) (1.2.3.) (4)	
P	T	P	T	P	T	P	T
5/65	8/67						
5/70	12/71	12/69	1/72		10/70	8/69	12/71
8/73	5/75	7/73	5/75	1/73	3/75	5/73	8/75
		12/76	4/78	11/75	4/77		

Part B. Lead (−) or Lag (+), in Months

Growth Cycle Chronology (1)		Level of Order Books vs. Chronology (2) vs. (1) (5)		Change in Order Books vs. Chronology (3) vs. (1) (6)		New Orders vs. Chronology (4) vs. (1) (7)		EEC Survey, Change in Order Books (1.2) vs. New Orders (1.2.3.) (3) vs. (4) (8)	
P	T	P	T	P	T	P	T	P	T
5/65	8/67								
5/70	12/71	−5	+1		−14	−9	0		−14
8/73	5/78	−1	0	−7	−2	−3	+3	−4	−5

Average Timing at:	Level of Order Books (5)		Change in Order Books (6)		New Orders (7)		EEC Survey (8)	
	P	T	P	T	P	T	P	T
P	−3		−7		−6		−4	
T		0		−8		+2		−10
P+T	−1		−8		−2		−8	

Figure 5-4. West Germany, Timing at Growth Cycle Turns, Levels of Export Order Books, (1.1), Survey Net Balance, 1968-79.

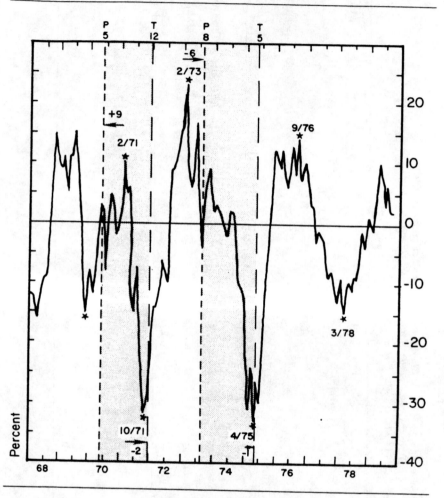

In the case of export orders for West Germany, we find that EEC survey results conform well to growth cycles but display longer leads than total order books do (Figure 5-4 and Table 5-3). Figure 5-5 and the accompanying Table 5-4 also show that the lead of export orders versus growth cycles is increased when the series is first differenced—that is, by expressing the results in the form of the change in export order books rather than their level. Export orders ought, in principle, to reflect the cycles of one's trading partners, not necessar-

Figure 5-5. West Germany, Timing at Growth Cycle Turns, Change in Level of Export Order Books, (1.2), Survey Net Balance, 1968-79.

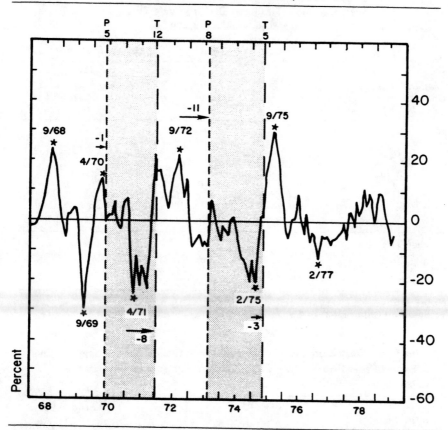

ily domestic cycles. The cyclical conformity of West German export orders is probably the result of a general synchronization of growth cycles in EEC countries in recent years.

Our analysis of German order books reveals that when survey results are analyzed as *levels*, the turns in the replies correspond reasonably well to growth cycle turns, but when analyzed as *flows*, replies lead at both peaks and troughs and also lead the quantitative series on new orders.

We do not have actual quantitative series regarding orders in France, so we shall confine our analysis to the survey results for total orders and export orders. Table 5-5 summarizes our findings with respect to the behavior of the net balances (analogous to order book levels—Col. 2), and to changes in the new balances (analogous to new

Table 5-3. West Germany, Timing at Growth Cycle Turns, Level of Export Order Books, (1.1), Survey Net Balance, 1968–79.

				Lead (–) or Lag (+), in Months			
Growth Cycle Chronology (1)		Survey (2)		Survey vs. Chronology (3)		Export Order Books vs. Total Order Books[a] (4)	
P	T	P	T	P	T	P	T
	8/67						
5/70		2/71		+9		+14	
	12/71		10/71		–2		–3
8/73		2/73		–6		–5	
	5/75		4/75		–1		–3
		9/76					
			3/78				–1
Average Timing at:							
P				+2		+2	
T					–2		–2
P + T				0		0	

Note:
a. Based on Column (2) of Table 5-2.

Table 5-4. West Germany, Timing at Growth Cycle Turns, Change in Level of Export Order Books, (1.2), First Difference of Survey Net Balance, 1968–79.

				Lead (–) or Lag (+), in Months	
Growth Cycle Chronology		Survey			
P	T	P	T	P	T
	8/67				
5/70		4/70		–1	
	12/71		4/71		–8
8/63		9/72		–11	
	5/75		2/75		–3
		9/75			
			2/77		
Average Timing at:					
P				–6	
T					–6
P + T				–6	

Table 5-5. France, Results of Survey Order Book Behavior at Growth Cycle Turns, 1968–79.

Part A. Turning Points

Growth Cycle Chronology (1) P	T	Level of Order Books (1.1), Total Survey Net Balance (2) P	T	Change in Level of Order Books (1.2) First Difference of Column (2) (3) P	T	Level of Export Order Books (1.1), Survey Net Balance (4) P	T	Change in Level of Export Order Books (1.2), First Difference of Column (4) (5) P	T
5/68	11/69	7/69	12/70	9/68	5/70	2/70	1/72	8/69	8/70
8/71	7/74	11/73	8/75	4/73	11/74	11/73	9/75	8/72	11/74
6/75		9/76	1/78	12/75	5/77			11/75	6/77
				11/78					

Part B. Timing Comparisons, Lead (–) or Lag (+), in Months

Growth Cycle turn	(2) vs. (1) (6)	(3) vs. (1) (7)	(4) vs. (1) (8)	(5) vs. (1) (9)
5/68		-14	+2	-3
11/69	-4			
8/71	-8	-18	-8	-23
7/74		-7	+3	-7
6/75	+2			
Average Timing at:				
P	-6	-14	-2	-13
T	-3	-11	+4	-11
P + T	-4	-13	+1	-10

orders or the change in unfilled orders—Col. 3). The survey of French total order book levels produces only four cycle comparisons. Three of these do lead the growth cycle turns, but the leads are not consistently long. As was the case with the West German data, the leads can be regarded as significantly long only when viewed as the change in order books, that is, as the net flow of new orders.

Columns 4 and 5 of Table 5-5 summarize the behavior of the export order books. Clearly, there is no strong tendency for the levels to lead or lag, based on the few observations. Overall, the timing behavior is similar to that found for West Germany. The change in the net balances, which are viewed as reflecting the net flow of new export orders, exhibits leads that are considerably longer for France than was the case for West Germany.

For Italy, the results in Table 5-6 are strikingly similar to those for France. The survey on order books analyzed as levels shows an average lead of four months at all growth cycle turns (Col. 2), an average lead of thirteen months at all turns for the change in order books (Col. 3), and an average lead of eleven months for the change in export order books (Col. 5). Only the average timing of the level of export order books in Italy—a three-month lead (Col. 4)—diverges from the timing in France.

For the United Kingdom, it will be recalled that we are utilizing surveys conducted by the Confederation of British Industry.[4] While the information elicited over the years by the CBI has been essentially similar to that acquired by the EEC (indeed, the CBI now conducts the harmonized survey for the EEC in the United Kingdom), the form of the questions was earlier somewhat different. Regarding orders, for example, the CBI questionnaire asked whether the "trend in the past four months" or "the expected trend for the next four months" was "up, down or unchanged" (3.1 in Table 5-1), instead of whether order books were "above or below normal" (1.1 in Table 5-1), as in the EEC questionnaire. Unlike the EEC surveys, the original CBI surveys produced net balances that were analogous to changes in a quantitative series of new orders. These net balances must be cumulated to be analogous to the level of new orders.

Table 5-7 summarizes our findings based on CBI surveys of order books in the United Kingdom, covering a twenty-year period. The results differ from the West German pattern. In West Germany turns in the survey series precede turns in the quantitative series at peaks and troughs, on average, by eight months (compare Table 5-2). In the United Kingdom the survey tended to lag the quantitative series by about eight months at both peaks and troughs (Table 5-7, Col. 8).

Table 5-6. Italy, Results of Survey Order Book Behavior at Growth Cycle Turns, 1968-79.

Part A. Turning Points

Growth Cycle Chronology (1)		Level of Order Books (1.1), Total Survey Net Balance (2)		Change in Level of Order Books (1.2), First Difference of Column (2) (3)		Level of Export Order Books (1.1), Survey Net Balance (4)		Change in Level of Export Order Books (1.2), First Difference of Column (4) (5)	
P	T	P	T	P	T	P	T	P	T
2/70	9/72	8/69	10/71	10/68	6/70	9/69	10/71	11/68	6/70
4/74	5/75	11/73	5/75	6/73	11/74	8/73	7/75	6/73	11/74
12/76	12/77	10/76	3/78	2/76	4/77	9/76	7/78	5/76	8/77
		3/79		9/78		3/79		9/78	

Part B. Timing Comparisons, Lead (-) or Lag (+), in Months

		(2) vs. (1) (6)		(3) vs. (1) (7)		(4) vs. (1) (8)		(5) vs. (1) (9)	
P	T	P	T	P	T	P	T	P	T
2/70	9/72	-6	-11	-16	-27	-5	-11	-15	-27
4/74	5/75	-3	0	-10	-6	-8	+2	-10	-6
12/76	12/77	-2	+3	-10	-8	-3	+7	-7	-4

Average Timing at:

	(6)	(7)	(8)	(9)
P	-4	-12	-5	-11
T	-3	-14	-1	-12
P + T	-3	-13	-3	-12

Table 5-7.   United Kingdom, New Orders Behavior at Growth Cycle Turns, 1958–79.

Part A.   Turning Points

Growth Cycle Chronology (1)		New Orders Cumulated Net Balance (3.2) CBI Survey (2)		Volume Index (3.2.1) (3)		New Orders Net Balance (3.1), CBI Survey (4)		Change in Volume Index (3.1.1) (5)	
P	T	P	T	P	T	P	T	P	T
3/61	11/58	8/60	3/59	2/60	6/58	2/59	12/61	9/59	6/61
2/66	2/63	6/65	4/63	4/64	12/62	4/64	12/66	2/63	2/65
6/69	8/67	5/70	11/67	5/69	1/67	4/68	4/71	2/68	1/71
6/73	2/72	3/74	3/72	12/73	6/71	8/73	2/75	7/73	8/74
8/75	8/75		2/76		10/75	11/76	5/78	5/76	3/77

Part B. Lead (−) or Lag (+), in Months

Turn date	(2) vs. (1) (6) P	(6) T	(3) vs. (1) (7) P	(7) T	(2) vs. (3) (8) P	(8) T	(4) vs. (1) (9) P	(9) T	(5) vs. (1) (10) P	(10) T	(4) vs. (5) (11) P	(11) T
11/58		+4		−5		+9		−14		−20		+6
3/61	−7		−13		+6		−25		−18		−7	
2/63		+2		−2		+4		−8		n.m.		+22
2/66	−8		−22		+14		−22		n.m.ᵃ		+14	
8/67		+3		−7		+10		−10		−13		+3
6/69	+11		−1		+12		−14		−16		+2	
2/72		+1		−8		+9		−6		−12		+6
6/73	+9		+6		+3		+2		+1		+1	
8/75		+6		+2		+4						+14
Average Timing at:												
P	+1		−8		+9		−15		−11		+3	
T		+3		−4		+7		−10		−15		+10
P + T	+2		−6		+8		−12		−13		+6	

Note:
a. n.m. = No matching turn.

Figure 5-6.   United Kingdom, Timing at Growth Cycle Turns, Changes in Volume, Index of New Orders, (3.1.1), 1958-79.

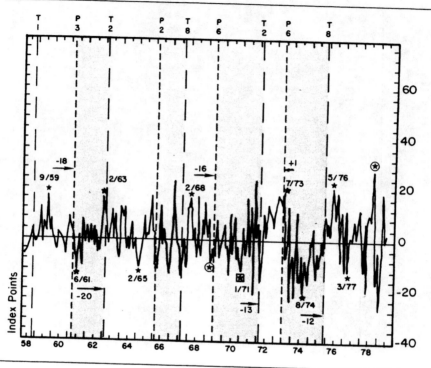

The quantitative series on new orders led growth cycle turns in both countries, but by a somewhat longer margin in the case of Britain. The U.K. survey pattern is also roughly similar to the pattern for France and Italy, although the latter two countries averaged a very slight lead at growth cycle turns.

In terms of changes in the level of new orders over four-month spans, the U.K. experience (Table 5-7, Col. 4) also largely duplicates the pattern in the other countries, with the exception of West Germany: a lead of about a year for both the CBI survey results and the actual order changes.[5]

In the United Kingdom the turns in actual orders precede the survey turns by about six months (Col. 11). Individual turns exhibit a great deal of variation, although the actual order changes lead the surveys at all but one of the ten turns studied. The British actual changes in orders, however, is a highly volatile series, seriously reducing its potential for forecasting growth cycle turns (see Figure 5-6).

One of the principal strengths of the survey replies is their greater smoothness. This characteristic, together with the tendency of survey results to be available before the quantitative equivalents, constitutes one of the major reasons for considering qualitative indicators along with quantitative indicators in developing indicators for forecasting.

FINISHED GOODS INVENTORIES

Actual finished goods inventories in the United States tend to lag by long intervals at growth cycle peaks and troughs, while raw materials inventories lag by short intervals or roughly coincide. In the case of West German survey results, which report whether inventories are above or below normal, finished goods inventories also lag at growth cycle turning points. Due to the long length of the interval, the series can best be viewed as "inverted." Figure 5-7 and Table 5-8 reveal that troughs in inventories correspond almost precisely to growth cycle peaks, while inventory peaks correspond to growth cycle troughs.

There is economic logic to this situation. If the survey responses really refer to the ratio of inventories to sales, a peak in this ratio signals the point at which sales finally stop decreasing faster than inventories, thus suggesting to entrepreneurs that they may have reduced production (which is the essence of the recession) sufficiently. The beginning of decline in the inventory/sales ratio makes it feasible for production to increase. When entrepreneurs are no longer worried that production will outrun sales, they anticipate when they might once more expand production. The longer inventory liquidation continues, the more reasonable production increases look to producers. Hence, inventories reflect both the past growth cycle turn and anticipate the subsequent turn.

We should also note that the survey net balances for West Germany, if interpreted as representing the level of inventories, can be transformed to represent inventory investment (the net flow of goods into inventories). Figure 5-8 and Table 5-9 illustrate this transformation and suggest that investment in finished goods stocks lags, but now the lags are relatively short. The rate of change in inventories is, of course, a record of inventory investment, which is a component of output. Inventory change represents a flow of goods, just as total output does.

Tables 5-10 and 5-11 summarize the survey results dealing with inventory behavior in France and Italy. In the case of France, the economic logic detailed in connection with West German inventories can be applied in a similar manner. Levels of finished goods inven-

Figure 5-7. West Germany, Timing at Growth Cycle Turns, Change in Finished Goods Stocks, (2.2), First Difference of Survey Net Balance, 1968–79.

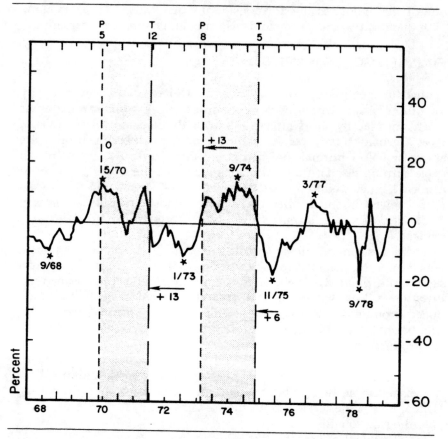

tories, when compared to the growth cycle chronology positively (Table 5–10, Col. 2), show a very long lag, but when compared invertedly to the chronology, they show a lead (Col. 3). Change in finished goods inventories, customarily regarded as a lagging indicator, performed in France (Col. 4) as it did in West Germany.

In Italy, the behavior of finished goods stocks is precisely what one would expect (Table 5–11). If levels of these stocks are related positively to the growth cycle chronology, one finds a lag of more than a year on average (Col. 2), longer at troughs than at peaks. If, however, stock levels are analyzed on an inverted basis, the lag becomes a short lead (Col. 3). On the other hand, changes in finished

Table 5-8. West Germany, Timing at Growth Cycle Turns, Levels of Finished Goods Inventories, (2.1), Survey Net Balance, 1968-79.

Growth Cycle Chronology		Survey		Lead (−) or Lag (+), in Months	
P	T	P	T	P	T
		Part A. Results for Survey Related Positively			
	8/67		11/69		+27
5/70		12/71		+19	
	12/71		7/73		+19
8/73		6/75		+22	
	5/75		11/76		+18
		1/78			
Average Timing at:					
P				+20	
T					+21
P + T				+21	
		Part B. Results for Survey Related in Inverted Form			
	8/67				—
5/70		11/69		−6	
	12/71		12/71		0
8/73		7/73		−1	
	5/75		6/75		+1
		11/76		—	
			1/78		—
Average Timing at:					
P				−4	
T					0
P + T				−2	

goods inventories (Col. 4) lag at both peaks and troughs, with the pattern conforming positively to the growth cycles.

Turning now to inventories in the United Kingdom,[6] we have somewhat fuller information than was the case in the other countries. The survey results from the Confederation of British Industry cover both finished goods inventories and raw materials inventories.[7] We also have a quantitative series in constant prices for the United Kingdom, but we have not broken it into stages of the production process. This breakdown would be of considerable importance because of the critical role that inventories at different stages—both levels and changes—assume in many theoretical explanations of cycles.

We have already seen in the other countries that finished goods inventory levels frequently lag; indeed, they lag by so long that they are best analyzed as inverted series, in which case they often lead the

Figure 5-8. West Germany, Timing at Growth Cycle Turns, Level of
Finished Goods Stocks, (2.1), Survey Net Balance, 1968-79.

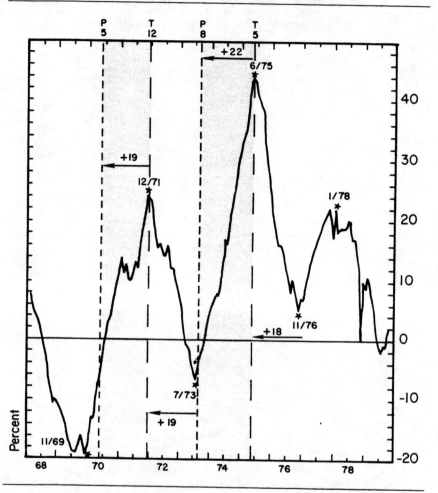

opposite turn. This behavior was quite in line with expectations. Table 5-12 (Cols. 2 and 3) shows that the British finished goods stocks also behave as expected. When viewed as positively conforming to growth cycle turns, the lags average twenty-one months at both peaks and troughs. When considered in inverted form, the timing is reversed, with leads of about three months at both peaks and troughs. On the other hand, raw materials stock levels have customarily been regarded as conforming positively to the cycle, but with a

Table 5-9. West Germany, Timing at Growth Cycle Turns, Change in Finished Goods Inventories, (2.2), First Difference of Survey Net Balance, 1968-79.

Growth Cycle Chronology		Survey		Lead (−) or Lag (+), in Months	
P	T	P	T	P	T
	8/67		9/68		+13
5/70		5/70		0	
	12/71		1/73		+13
8/73		9/74		+13	
	5/75		11/75		+6

Average Timing at:

P	+6	
T		+11
P + T	+9	

Table 5-10. France, Inventory Behavior at Growth Cycle Turns, 1968-79.

Part A. Turning Points

Growth Cycle Chronology (1)		Level of Finished Goods Inventories (2.1), Survey Net Balance				Change in Finished Goods Inventories (2.2), First Difference of Level Series (4)	
		Results Related Positively (2)		Results Related Invertedly (3)			
P	T	P	T	P	T	P	T
	5/68		5/69				6/68
11/69		2/71		3/64		8/70	
	8/71		9/73		2/71		3/73
7/74		4/75		9/72		11/74	
	6/75		6/76		4/75		11/75
		12/77				5/77	

Part B. Lead (−) or Lag (+), in Months

	5/68		+12		—		+1
11/69		+15		−6		+9	
	8/71		+25		−6		+19
7/74		+9		−10		+4	
	6/75		+12		−2		+5

Average Timing at:

P		+12		−8		+6	
T			+16		−4		+8
P + T		+15		−6		+8	

Table 5-11. Italy, Inventory Behavior at Growth Cycle Turns, 1968-79.

Part A. Turning Points

Growth Cycle Chronology (1)		Level of Finished Goods Inventories (2.1), Survey Net Balance				Change in Finished Goods Inventories (2.2), First Difference of Level Series (4)	
		Results Related Positively (2)		Results Related Invertedly (3)			
P	T	P	T	P	T	P	T
2/70		10/71	1/70			6/70	6/69
	9/72		10/73		10/71		1/73
4/74		4/75		10/73		12/74	
	5/75		12/76		4/75		5/76
12/76		10/77		12/76		3/77	
	12/77				10/77		12/78

Part B. Lead (−) or Lag (+), in Months

Growth Cycle Chronology		Positively		Invertedly		Change	
2/70		+20		—		+4	
	9/72		+13		-18		+4
4/74		+12		-6		+8	
	5/75		+19		-1		+12
12/76		+10		0		+3	
	12/77				-2		+12
Average Timing at:							
P		+14		-3		+5	
T			+16		-7		+9
P + T			+15	-4			+7

shorter lag than finished goods. This view is supported by the data in Cols. 8 and 10.

Let us now consider inventory investment, or changes in stocks. We find, as expected, that investment in raw materials stocks as reported in the survey precedes growth cycle turns (Col. 11), while investment in finished goods stocks follows the turns (Col. 12). The quantitative series refers to total inventory investment, not differentiated into production stages. However, it appears that raw materials dominates total inventory investment, so that the timing at growth cycle turns of the total (Col. 13) resembles the survey results for raw materials far more than for finished goods. The fairly short lag in finished goods investment, it may be noted, is in line with the survey results of all three countries previously considered, although the lag is shorter in the United Kingdom than elsewhere.

Table 5-12.   United Kingdom, Inventory Behavior at Growth Cycle Turns, 1968–79.

Part A.   Growth Cycle Turning Points

Cumulated Net Balance (3.2)

	Growth Cycle Chronology (1)		Survey of Finished Goods Stocks — Treated Positively (2)		Treated Invertedly (3)		Survey of Raw Materials Stocks (4)		Survey Net Balance, Raw Materials Stocks (3.1.1) (5)		Survey Net Balance, Finished Goods Stocks (3.1) (6)		Change in Total Stocks [b] (3.1) (7)	
	P	T	P	T	P	T	P	T	P	T	P	T	P	T
		11/58		11/60		9/58		9/59				8/59		11/58
	3/61	2/63	7/63[a]	11/64	11/60	7/63	8/61	11/63	4/60	12/62	12/62	8/63	11/60	2/62
	2/66	8/67	6/67	11/68	11/64	6/67	6/66	4/68	9/64	4/62	4/65	12/67	11/64	2/68
	6/69	2/72	7/71	6/74	11/68	7/71	2/71	9/72	12/68	11/71	8/70	2/72	6/68	5/71
	6/73	8/75	5/75	11/76	6/74	5/75	11/74	5/76	5/73	6/75	8/74	8/75	5/73	2/75
			4/78		11/76	4/78			2/77		5/77		2/77	

(Table 5-12. continued overleaf)

Table 5-12. continued

Part B. Lead (-) or Lag (+), in Months

Date	(2) vs. (1) (8)	(3) vs. (1) (9)	(4) vs. (1) (10)	(5) vs. (1) (11)	(6) vs. (1) (12)	(7) vs. (1) (13)
11/58	+24	-2	+10		+9	0
3/61	a	-5	+5	-11	+9	-4
2/63	+21	+5	+9	-2	+6	-12
2/66	+16	-15	+4	-22	-10	-15
8/67	+15	-2	+8	-4	+4	+6
6/69	+25	-7	+20	-6	+14	-10
2/72	+28	-7	+7	-3	0	-9
6/73	+23	+12	+17	-1	+14	-1
8/75	+15	-3	+9	-2	0	-6

Average Timing at:

	(8)	(9)	(10)	(11)	(12)	(13)
P	+21	-4	+12	-10	+7	-8
T	+21					
P + T	+21	-3	+10	-6	+5	-6

Notes:
a. Crosses opposite turn.
b. In millions of 1975 pounds.

PROFITS

Among the leading indicators for the ten countries considered in earlier chapters, a measure of profits was included for the United States, Canada, Japan, the United Kingdom, and West Germany. Not surprisingly, in all these cases profits led at both peaks and troughs of growth cycles.

Profits have long been recognized as one of the factors likely to presage a change in the direction of cyclical activity.[8] In a free enterprise system, where the quest for profits motivates entrepreneurial activity, it is the decline of profits (actual or prospective) in the later stages of an expansion that leads entrepreneurs to lay off workers and cut back production, thereby engendering a recession. Likewise, it is the improvement in profits, when costs decline relative to prices during a recession, that encourages entrepreneurs to increase production and turn recession into recovery. The role played by widening and narrowing profit margins in the ebb and flow of business cycles was emphasized by Mitchell many years ago when he spoke of the way in which costs "encroached" on prices in late expansion and the reversal of this process in late contraction.[9]

One of the problems in dealing with leading indicators is that, in order to be useful in forecasting, the indicators need to be available sufficiently promptly so that their average lead is not offset by the lag in data availability. In the United States, for example, the comprehensive figures for corporate profits are not available for as much as seven weeks after the end of the quarter to which the data apply. Hence, there is often a gap of four or five months between the latest available figure and the current date. The situation is similar, or worse, in other countries. We have seen in our consideration of orders and stocks that the prompt availability of qualitative indicators enhances their forecasting potential. This can be the case even when survey data exhibit shorter leads at growth cycle turning points than their quantitative equivalents. We are therefore interested in comparing the timing of qualitative measures of profit with their quantitative equivalents where possible, as well as the promptness with which these two types of indicators for profits become available.

In making these assessments we can extend our comparisons by examining the changing relationship between selling prices and labor costs per unit output. Ratios of price to unit labor cost are available for many countries on a monthly basis. We have found that this ratio is a very good proxy for profit margins. In part, this is true because labor costs figure heavily in total costs and their movement over the cycle proves to be typical of the movement of total costs. A related proxy for profit change can be obtained by subtracting changes in unit labor cost from changes in selling price.[10]

We shall now examine the possibility of utilizing qualitative data for getting an early line on the trend of profit margins in market-oriented economies, concentrating on three countries: the United States, United Kingdom, and Japan.[11] Unfortunately, the EEC surveys, which cover many countries, question entrepreneurs on their view of selling-price changes but not on unit labor cost changes. Therefore, the technique for estimating views on implicit profit changes discussed earlier cannot be employed for the EEC surveys. Were a question on cost changes included, the value of the EEC surveys for cyclical analysis would be greatly enhanced.

Let us consider first the comparative behavior of qualitative and quantitative measures of total profits. Dun & Bradstreet, Inc., has for some thirty years conducted a quarterly survey of U.S. manufacturers, wholesalers, and retailers, which includes a question concerning the actual and expected trend of profits as compared to the same date the previous year. The Dun & Bradstreet surveys are available within about two months of the date the survey is conducted. This means that data for past changes from, say, Q_4-1979 to Q_4-1980 (based on a survey conducted in February 1981) are available in April 1981, while expected changes from Q_2-1980 to Q_2-1981 are also available in April 1981. Thus, the reporting lag for actual changes is about four months, while the expected changes are reported about two months before the end of the quarter to which they refer. This reduction in reporting lag might be of considerable assistance when utilizing profit data for forecasting.

Figure 5-9 presents the percent change of the quantitative data on corporate profits after taxes over four quarters, along with two measures of Dun & Bradstreet data similarly calculated. In Table 5-13 the turns in both quantitative and qualitative measures are compared to the U.S. growth chronology. It is clear that the movements of the measures of profit are similar. Moreover, all three measures of profits are quite consistent leaders at both peaks and troughs of growth cycles. Whether one relies on the mean or the median as a measure of the average tendency, it is further clear that the turns in the quantitative figures lead at both peaks and troughs by about as much as the Dun & Bradstreet survey of past profit changes. On the other hand, as is frequently the case, the survey data of expected profits turn with few exceptions after the turns in both the actual profits survey and the quantitative data. Entrepreneurs apparently expect profits to

Figure 5-9. United States, Past and Expected Change in Profits, (3.1.1), Dun & Bradstreet Survey vs. Actual Change in Corporate Profits after Taxes, (3.1), in Current Dollars, Department of Commerce, 1948-81.

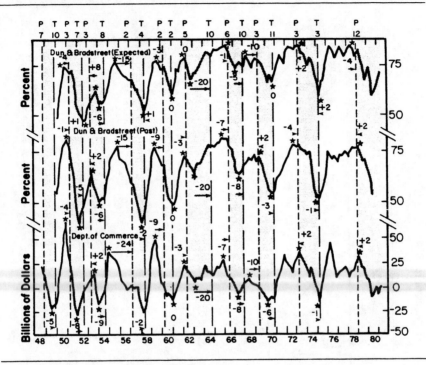

Note:
Shaded areas indicate growth cycles.

rise or fall on the basis of what has most recently been happening to profits. The lag in the behavior of anticipated profits versus the lag in the quantitative data (which averages three or four months) virtually cancels out its lead in availability, which also is about four months. One factor that might favor the use of survey results is the possibility of avoiding false signals. This is particularly valuable when data reflect changes, which are often more volatile in quantitative series than in survey results. In this instance the difference in volatility between the Dun & Bradstreet survey of expected profit changes and the actual changes in profits reported by the Commerce Department is not notable, although the quantitative series exhibits a few more false signals. We conclude that the survey provides useful supplementary information in monitoring profits, but no clear-cut advantage over quantitative measures.

Table 5-13.   United States, Timing of Three Measures of Profits at Growth Cycle Peaks and Troughs, 1949-80.

Part A.   Turning Points

Date of Peak or Trough

Growth Cycle Chronology (1)		Index of Past Change in Profits, Manufacturing, and Trade (3.1), Dun & Bradstreet (2)		Index of Expected Change in Profits, Manufacturing, and Trade (3.1), Dun & Bradstreet (3)		Change in Corporate Profits after Taxes (3.1.1), Department of Commerce (4)	
P	T	P	T	P	T	P	T
3/51	10/49	2/51	2/52	11/50	8/52	11/50	5/49
3/53	7/52	5/53	2/54	11/53	2/54	5/53	11/51
2/57	8/54	11/55	2/58	11/55	5/58	2/55	11/53
2/60	4/58	5/59	2/61	11/59	2/61	5/59	2/58
5/62	2/61	2/62	2/63	5/62	2/63	2/62	2/61
6/66	10/64	11/65	2/67	5/66	5/67	11/65	2/63
3/69	10/67	5/69	8/70	5/68	11/70	5/68	2/67
3/73	11/70	11/72	2/75	5/73	6/75	5/73	5/70
12/78	3/75	2/79		8/78		2/79	2/75

Part B. Lead (–) or Lag (+), in Months

Growth Cycle Chronology (1)		Past vs. Growth Cycles, Dun & Bradstreet (4)		Expected vs. Growth Cycles, Dun & Bradstreet (3)		Change in Corporate Profits vs. Growth Cycles (5)	
P	T	P	T	P	T	P	T
3/51	10/49	–1	n.m.ᵃ	–4	n.m.	–4	–5
3/53	7/52	+2	–5	+8	+1	+2	–8
2/57	8/54	–15	–6	–15	–6	–24	–9
2/60	4/58	–9	–2	–3	+1	–9	–2
5/62	2/61	–3	0	0	0	–3	0
6/66	10/64	–7	–20	–1	–20	–7	–20
3/69	10/67	+2	–8	–10	–5	–10	–8
3/73	11/70	–4	–3	+2	0	+2	–6
12/78	3/75	+2	–1	–4	+2	+2	–1

Mean Timing at:

		Past (4)		Expected (3)		Change (5)	
P		–4		–2		–6	
T			–6		–3		–7
P + T		–5		–2		–6	

Median Timing at:

		Past (4)		Expected (3)		Change (5)	
P		–3		–3		–4	
T			–4		0		–6
P + T		–3		–2		–6	

Note:
a. n.m. = No matching turn.

In Japan the two measures of profit changes also lead at growth cycle turning points, and again the lead for the quantitative series exceeds that for the survey, by about four months on average.[12] The volatility of the survey series is marginally smaller than that of actual profit changes. Hence, in Japan, as in the United States, survey results may aid in monitoring profit changes by virtue of their potentially more prompt availability.

As noted earlier, we can also measure quantitative changes in profit margins with reasonable accuracy by calculating price changes minus cost changes. Moreover, this technique for estimating changes in profit margins can be duplicated using qualitative data. We shall illustrate the possibilities with data from the United Kingdom.

Evidence from Great Britain is particularly effective in illustrating this technique because the survey data can be considered in both a retrospective fashion (the net balance of average cost change during the past four months) and a prospective fashion (considering the next four months). Figure 5-10 and Table 5-14 set forth the U.K. results.

If we first compare the quantitative indicator (Table 5-14, Col. 2) with the survey results based on the retrospective view of price/cost changes (Col. 3), we find that both indicators of profit change lead virtually all U.K. growth cycle turning points. Moreover, the quantitative measure of the price/labor cost differential leads the qualitative measure based on the survey net balances by eight months, on average (see Col. 8). Greater promptness in availability would not offset this discrepancy. There are only four turns, however, and this would not suffice for any firm conclusion. We may note, finally, that the differences in volatility between the two indicators shown in Figure 5-10 are not significant.

Let us now turn to a comparison of the quantitative indicator with the survey results based on the prospective view of price/cost changes. Oftentimes it is argued that surveys of expected changes are of greater use in forecasting than are surveys of past changes. In the United Kingdom the average leads at growth cycle turns of the two survey series are about the same. One leads by an average of seven months, the other by nine months at all turns (Cols. 6 and 7). However, at most of the individual turns the expected changes lag behind the past changes by about four months. Clearly, entrepreneurs' views of what will happen are largely conditioned by what has just happened—a conclusion often reached in similar examinations of retrospective and prospective net balances of survey results. Unfortunately, there are few turns in common (Table 5-14, Part A) between the quantitative and qualitative indicators, but the scant evidence

Figure 5-10. United Kingdom, Price/Labor Cost Differential, Net Balances (Prices less costs), Trend in the Past Four Months and Expected Trend in the Next Four Months, (3.1), 1958-81.

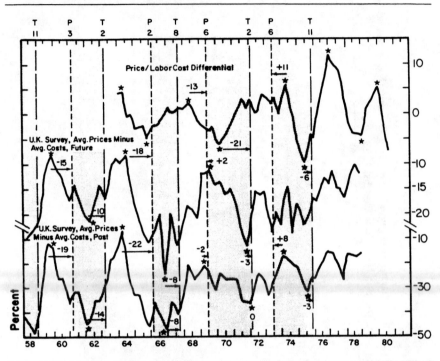

Note:
Shaded areas indicate growth cycles.

available would suggest that the lag in survey turns in retrospective form over the lag in the quantitative indicator will certainly not be eliminated by substituting prospective survey results. Although the prospective results for a given four-month period are available about four months before the retrospective results for the same period, there is no gain from using the prospective series. Its irregular behavior during the 1974-75 recession, where it deviates sharply from the quantitative series, raises a question as to its dependability as an indicator of profit changes.

In sum, profits, whether measured as totals or as margins, lead at growth cycle turns in all the countries for which any information exists. Changes in profits, therefore, lead by even longer intervals. Surveys of profit changes in the form of net balances tend to lead as well, but customarily by shorter intervals than the quantitative data.

Table 5-14. United Kingdom, Timing of Price/Cost Changes at Growth Cycle Turns, Quantitative Series and Survey Results, Trend in Past Four Months and Expected Trend in Next Four Months, 1958-75.

Part A. Turning Points

Growth Cycle Chronology (1)		Change in Price/Labor Cost Differential (3.1.1) (2)		U.K. Survey, Net Balance of Average Price Less Average Cost, Trend in Past Four Months (3.1) (3)		U.K. Survey, Net Balance of Average Price Less Average Cost, Expected Trend in Next Four Months (3.1) (4)	
P	T	P	T	P	T	P	T
	11/58				—		
3/61	2/63	5/64	11/65	8/59	12/61	12/59	4/62
2/66	8/67	n.m.[a]	n.m.	4/64	12/66	8/64	12/66
6/69	2/72	5/68	5/70	4/69	2/72	8/69	11/71
6/73	8/75	5/74	5/75	2/74	8/75	n.m.	n.m.

Part B. Lead (–) or Lag (+), in Months

Growth Cycle Chronology (1)		Change in Price/Labor Cost Differential vs. U.K. Cycles (3.1.1) (2) vs. (1) (5)		Survey Net Balance, Price Less Cost (3.1) (Past) vs. U.K. Cycles (3) vs. (1) (6)		Survey Net Balance, Price Less Cost (3.1) (Expected) vs. U.K. Cycles (4) vs. (1) (7)		Survey (Past) vs. Differential (3) vs. (2) (8)		Survey (Expected) vs. Differential (4) vs. (2) (9)	
P	T	P	T	P	T	P	T	P	T	P	T
	11/58				-14		-10				
3/61				-19		-15					
	2/63				-8		-8				
8/67		-13		-22		-18		+11		+15	
	6/69		-21		0		-3		+21		+18
2/72		+11		-2		+2		-3		n.m.	
	6/73		-3		0		n.m.		+3		n.m.
8/75				+8		n.m.					
Average Timing at:											
P		-1		-15		-10		+8		+15	
T		-12		-6		-7		+12		+18	
P + T		-6		-7		-9		+8		+16	

Note:
a. n.m. = No matching turn.

The timing of prospective profit changes usually lags somewhat behind that of survey reports on recently experienced profit changes, but the fact that prospective data for a given period are available earlier than quantitative data for the same period means that the former can be usefully employed in the forecasting of growth cycle changes. One frequent advantage of survey data that we have not found in the case of profits involves the greater smoothness in the survey data. The volatility in the survey data on profits is as great, or nearly so, as in the quantitative data, despite the limited evidence.

We have noted that the trend in profits can be approximated by subtracting a measure of costs from a measure of prices. Both in qualitative and quantitative terms, these calculations produce series that conform moderately well to the behavior of actual profit changes (where such evidence was available). And the relative behavior of the quantitative and qualitative indicators of profits has been very consistent from country to country whenever comparisons could be made. We conclude that monitoring both quantitative and qualitative indicators of profit changes will enhance our understanding of business cycles and our ability to predict their future course.

PRODUCTION EXPECTATIONS

Before embarking on an analysis of production expectations as recorded by the EEC surveys, the reader should recall our simple convention of assuming that a January survey asking about "the months ahead" is referring to a four-month interval and is, therefore, placed in the middle month—in this case March—which is where the survey net balance would be centered for purposes of comparison with production changes or selling price changes. In addition to comparing expected changes with actual changes in production over four-month intervals, we compare expected levels of production at the end of the interval with the corresponding actual levels. Cumulative net balances at the end of the four-month interval (May, in this case) will then be compared to the index of industrial production.

Figures 5–11 and 5–12 show the net balances of production expectations reported in the West German surveys for each month and the corresponding actual changes in the index of industrial production. As is always the case, series of changes are more volatile than series that reflect levels, and the possibility of false signals is increased. The comparisons are summarized in Table 5–15 (Cols. 9 and 10). While the leads are substantial, as we have come to expect in series reflecting first differences, the relationship of survey results to actual production is similar to what we have found before: the turns in the rate

Figure 5-11.   West Germany, Timing at Growth Cycle Turns, Expected
Change in Production, (3.1), Survey Net Balance, 1968-79.

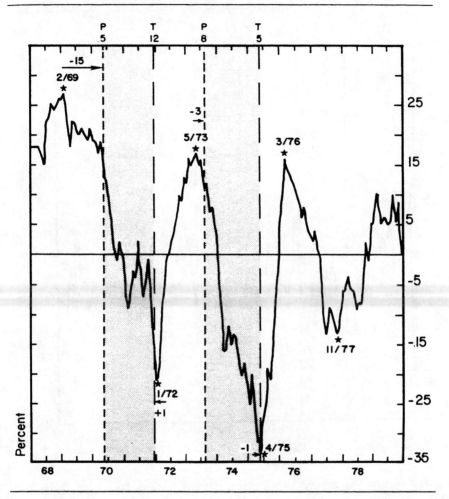

of change in the production index tend to precede expected changes
reported in the survey.

In order to make comparisons with the level of industrial production, it is necessary to cumulate the survey net balances, even though
the procedure we use is not strictly appropriate.[13] The results are
shown in Figures 5-13 and 5-14, and summarized in Table 5-15.
The German evidence suggests that entrepreneurs expect production
levels to be in line with those they are currently experiencing. Thus,

Figure 5–12. West Germany, Timing at Growth Cycle Turns, Percent
Change in the Index of Industrial Production, (3.1), 1968–79.

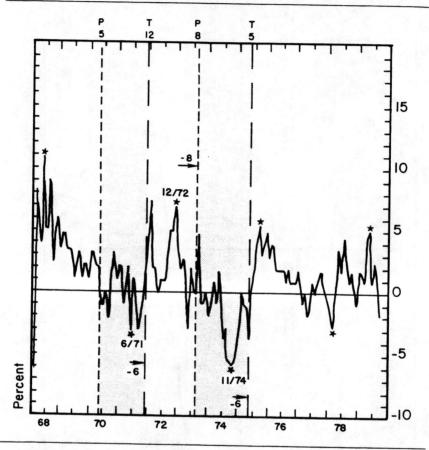

survey results lag actual production turns by some months, although
there are few comparisons possible in West Germany.

Comparison of Figures 5–11 through 5–14 suggests that the survey net balances are much smoother than the actual changes in the
index of industrial production. There are fewer "false signals." Moreover, the survey results are available sooner. The EEC surveys are
available about six weeks after the questionnaires are circulated so
expected levels pertain to a date about two months ahead. In the
case of West German industrial production, data are available about
two months after the month to which they apply. If one takes the
greater smoothness of the survey results into account (along with
their relatively prompt availability), the seven-month lag of the sur-

Table 5-15. West Germany, Behavior of Production and Production Expectations at Growth Cycle Turns, 1968–79.

Part A. Turning Points

Growth Cycle Chronology (1)		Cumulated Survey Net Balance, Expected (3.2) (2)		Industrial Production Index (3)		Survey Net Balance, Expected (3.1) (4)		Change in Production Index (3.1.1) (5)	
P	T	P	T	P	T	P	T	P	T
5/70		1/71				2/69		6/68	
	12/71		8/72				1/72		6/71
8/73		3/74		8/73		5/73		12/72	
	5/75		2/76		7/75		4/75		11/74
		6/77	11/78						

Part B. Lead (−) or Lag (+), in Months

Growth Cycle Chronology (1)		Cumulated Net Balance vs. Chronology (2) vs. (1) (6)		Production Index vs. Chronology (3) vs. (1) (7)		Cumulated Net Balance vs. Production Index (2) vs. (3) (8)		Survey Net Balance vs. Chronology (4) vs. (1) (9)		Change in Production Index vs. Chronology (5) vs. (1) (10)		Survey Net Balance vs. Change in Production Index (4) vs. (5) (11)	
P	T	P	T	P	T	P	T	P	T	P	T	P	T
5/70		+8						-15		-23		+8	
	12/71		+8						+1		-6		+7
8/73		+7		0		+7		-3		-8		+5	
	5/75		+9		+2		+7		-1		-6		+5

Average Timing at:

	(6)	(7)	(8)	(9)	(10)	(11)
P	+8	0	+7	-9	-16	+6
T	+8	+2	+7	0	-6	+6
P + T	+8	+1	+7	-4	-11	+6

Figure 5-13. West Germany, Timing at Growth Cycle Turns, Level of
Production Expectations, Cumulated Survey Net Balance, (3.2), 1968-79.

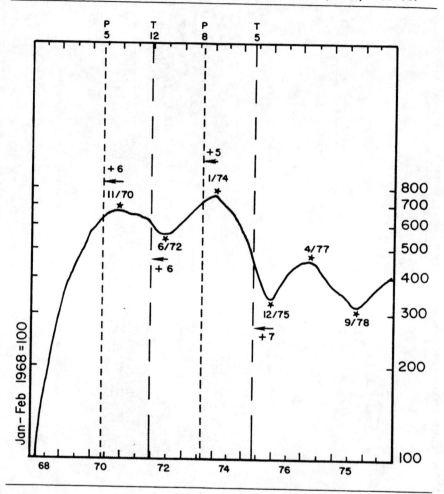

veys behind the turns in actual production is substantially offset.
Hence utilizing both sorts of indicators may give more reliable results
than relying on either alone.

In short, having established the possibilities of the surveys in the
case of Germany, we confine ourselves to what appears to be the
most meaningful comparison for France and Italy, namely the relationship between the cumulated net balances in survey replies and
the production index levels. In Table 5-16 there is a lag in Italian

Figure 5-14. West Germany, Timing at Growth Cycle Turns, Level of Industrial Production, (3.2.1), 1968-79.

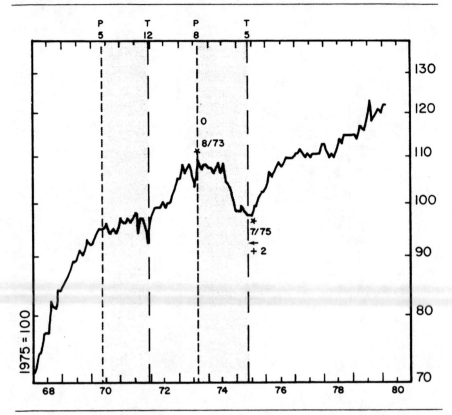

survey result turns relative to both the growth cycle turns and to the actual production turns. While few comparisons are available for France (Table 5-17), the lagging pattern of survey results behind production turns is clearly evident. Nevertheless, the cumulated survey results are far smoother than the actual production index in both France and Italy, a characteristic they share with the German data.

SELLING PRICES

If we now consider how entrepreneurs report their expectation of changes in selling prices, again we find similar results in West Germany, Italy, and France. Figures 5-15 and 5-16 pertain to West Germany as an example, and Tables 5-18 through 5-20 provide a

Table 5-16. Italy, Timing at Growth Cycle Turns, Actual and Expected Level of Production, 1970-78.

Growth Cycle Chronology (1)		Cumulated Survey Net Balance, Expected (3.2) (2)		Industrial Production Index (3.2.1) (3)		Leads or Lags					
						Survey vs. Chronology (4)		Production Index vs. Chronology (5)		Survey vs. Production Index (6)	
P	T	P	T	P	T	P	T	P	T	P	T
2/70	9/72	3/71	7/72	9/70	7/71	+13	-2	+7	-14	+4	+10
4/74	5/75	11/74	10/76	4/74	5/75	+7	+17	0	0	+5	+15
12/76	12/77	6/77	11/78	12/76	12/77	+6	+11	0	0	+4	+9
Average Timing at:											
P						+9		+2		+6	
T							+9		-5		+13
P + T						+9		-1		+10	

Table 5-17. France, Timing at Growth Cycle Turns, Level of Industrial Production, (3.2), Survey Cumulated Net Balance, 1974-79.

| | | | | | | Leads or Lags | | | | | |
| Growth Cycle Chronology (1) | | Cumulated Survey Net Balance, Expected (3.2) (2) | | Industrial Production Index (3.2.1) (3) | | Survey vs. Chronology (4) | | Production Index vs. Chronology (5) | | Survey vs. Production Index (6) | |
P	T	P	T	P	T	P	T	P	T	P	T
7/74	6/75	12/74	2/76	8/74	5/75	+5	+8	+1	-1	+4	+9
		7/77	6/78	6/77	12/77					+1	+6
				8/79							

Average Timing at:

	P	T	P	T	P	T
P	+5		+1		+2	
T		+8		-1		+8
P + T	+6		0		+5	

Figure 5-15. West Germany, Timing at Growth Cycle Turns, Expected Changes in Selling Price (3.1), Survey Net Balance, 1968-79.

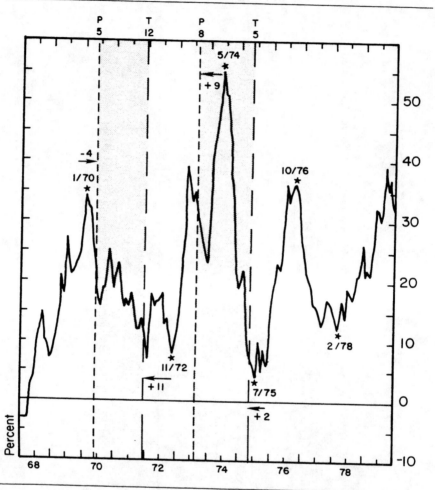

summary for the three countries. We have in each case associated the survey net balances with the rate of change in the most appropriate price index available—the wholesale price index. The evidence of the graphs suggests a major difference between these survey results and those previously covered: Selling-price expectations are no less volatile than the actual changes in equivalent price indexes. With respect to timing we find that in all three countries the survey results lag the growth cycle, whereas the actual turns in the rate of price changes

Figure 5-16. West Germany, Timing at Growth Cycle Turns, Percent
Change in Producer Price Index, (3.1.1), 1968-80.

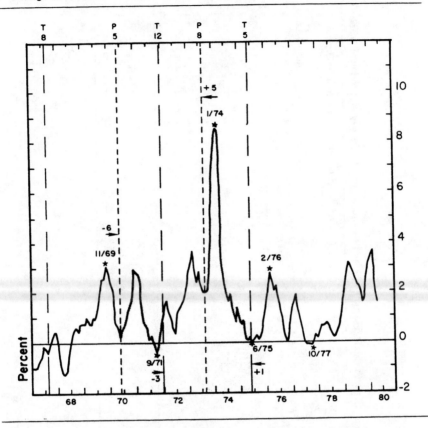

lead the growth cycle (although by an extremely short period in West Germany). In addition, the selling-price expectations lag turns in actual prices. This suggests perhaps that entrepreneurs look to the past in considering price changes and that they continue to maintain their old expectations for some months after there has been a change. (We are examining rates of change in prices. Absolute declines in prices in the recent past have neither been expected nor recorded.)

BUSINESS CONFIDENCE

The notion that tracking the ebb and flow of business confidence can augment one's insight into business cycle developments is not new. Pigou's theory of "errors of judgment" leading alternatively to ex-

Table 5-18.   West Germany, Timing at Growth Cycle Turns, Expected Change in Prices, Survey Net Balance, 1968–79.

| | | Part A. Turning Points | | | | | Part B. Lead (−) or Lag (+), in Months | | | | |
| Growth Cycle Chronology (1) | | Survey Net Balance, Expected Change in Selling Prices (3.1) (2) | | Percentage Change in Wholesale Price Index (3.1.1) (3) | | Survey vs. Chronology (4) | | Price Index vs. Chronology (5) | | Survey vs. Price Index (6) | |
P	T	P	T	P	T	P	T	P	T	P	T
	8/67										
5/70	12/71	1/70	11/72	11/59	9/71	−4	+11	−6	−3	+2	+14
8/73	5/75	5/74	7/75	1/74	6/75	+9	+2	+5	+1	+4	+1
		10/76	2/78	2/76	10/77					+8	+4

Average Timing at:

	P	T	P+T
(4)	+2		+4
(5)	0	−1	−1
(6)	+5	+6	+6

Table 5-19. Italy, Timing at Growth Cycle Turns, Expected Change in Prices, Survey Net Balance, 1968-79.

| | Part A. Turning Points | | | | | | Part B. Lead (−) or Lag (+), in Months | | | | | |
| Growth Cycle Chronology (1) | | Survey Net Balance, Expected Change in Selling Prices (3.1) (2) | | Percentage Change in Wholesale Price Index (3.1.1) (3) | | | Survey vs. Chronology (4) | | Price Index vs. Chronology (5) | | Survey vs. Price Index (6) | |
P	T	P	T	P	T		P	T	P	T	P	T
				9/67	5/68							
2/70	9/72	3/70	8/71	1/70	5/71		+1	−13	−1	−16	+2	+3
4/74	5/75	5/74	9/75	1/74	4/75		+1	+4	−3	−1	+4	+5
12/76	12/77	11/76	2/78	3/76	6/77		−1	+2	−9	−6	+8	+8

Average Timing at:

	(4)	(5)	(6)
P	0	−4	+5
T	−2	−8	+5
P + T	−1	−6	+5

Table 5-20.   France, Timing at Growth Cycle Turns, Expected Change in Prices, Survey Net Balance, 1968–79.

		Part A. Turning Points				Part B. Lead (–) or Lag (+), in Months					
Growth Cycle Chronology (1)		Survey Net Balance, Expected Change in Selling Prices (3.1) (2)		Percentage Change in Wholesale Price Index (3.1.1) (3)		Survey vs. Chronology (4)		Price Index vs. Chronology (5)		Survey vs. Price Index (6)	
P	T	P	T	P	T	P	T	P	T	P	T
	5/68		—	9/67	2/68				–3		
11/69		3/70		9/69		+4		–2		+6	
	8/71		11/70		6/70		–9		–14		+5
7/74		9/74		2/74		+2		–5		+7	
	6/75		9/75		12/74		+3		–6		+9
		11/76		5/76						+6	
			11/77		6/77						+5
				1/79							

Average Timing at:

	Survey vs. Chronology (4)	Price Index vs. Chronology (5)	Survey vs. Price Index (6)
P	+3	–4	+6
T	–3	–8	+6
P+T	+3	–6	+6

cesses of optimism or pessimism is an early example of such thinking. More recently, and in connection with the IFO-Institute's development of qualitative indicators, much attention has been paid to what is called the "business climate indicator." This indicator is based on both retrospective and prospective survey results pertaining to the following replies: "We currently evaluate our business situation for X (the product) as good, substantially unchanged, or poor," and "Our business situation for X (the product) in the next six months in the cyclical respect (that is, excluding seasonal factors) will tend to be more favorable, the same, or less favorable." Net balances based upon these replies make up the "business climate," and it is not surprising that the indicator tracks growth cycle turns with considerable fidelity. The IFO-Institute averages these responses geometrically and has found that the resulting series is relatively smooth (MCD = 1). The Institute's business climate indicator led their production index at the seven cyclical turns for which data were available in the late 1970s, and by an average of six months. This is a significant lead, by comparative standards, and they concluded that in the business climate indicator " . . . a sensitive and early responding indicator has probably been found, which appears to be quite suitable for an early recording of change in the cyclical forces of the macroeconomy."[14] Because the climate indicator is, in effect, a measure of the rate of change, while the production index reflects a level, this result is not surprising.

A similar measure of business confidence in the United Kingdom is available from the Confederation of British Industry in London. The CBI question is retrospective rather than prospective and asks, "Are you more, or less, optimistic than you were four months ago about the general business situation in your industry?" The respondents reply "more," "same," or "less." Both the IFO and CBI survey net balances are analogous to rates of change, and if one wishes them to reflect the *level* of confidence rather than the *rate of change* in confidence the net balances must be cumulated. We have earlier in this chapter suggested that the survey net balances may be useful for a variety of purposes, including—in this case—finding out how business confidence is changing. But if the objective is to compare the *level* of confidence to the growth cycle turns, which reflect the *level* of activity (after allowing for long-run trend), then the net balances must be cumulated. Accordingly, we have cumulated the survey net balances for the United Kingdom, and the resulting series on business confidence is presented in Figure 5-17. Cumulating the results does not obscure the clear cyclical behavior of the series: it is highly conforming and quite smooth. But the leads are short. On balance the

Figure 5-17. United Kingdom, CBI Business Confidence Index, Cumulated Net Balance, (3.2.1), 1958-78.

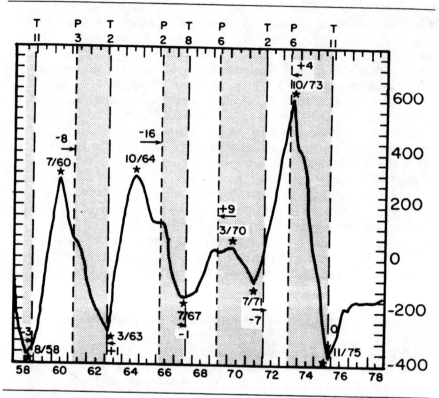

business confidence indicator has a mean lead of three months at peaks, and one month at troughs, with two months reflecting best the lead at all turns. This is well within the parameters traditionally set for roughly coincident indicators—that is, plus or minus three months of the cyclical turn.[15]

CONCLUSIONS

In this chapter we have examined the cyclical behavior of qualitative indicators based on survey responses covering orders or order books, inventories, production expectations, profits, selling prices, and business confidence. We have been at pains to distinguish between measures of level and measures of change in each variable. The difference is crucial in evaluating the net balance for analytical or forecasting purposes. The graphic evidence presented throughout Chapter 5 suggests that survey data can provide indicators that match growth cycles with notable fidelity and give relatively few false signals.

The major findings concerning cyclical timing are summarized in Table 5-21. When analyzed in terms of levels, the qualitative indicators exhibit few systematic and substantial leads vis-à-vis growth cycles. An exception is the level of finished goods inventories when treated invertedly. When analyzed as changes, more and longer leads emerge, both in the survey data and in their quantitative equivalents. In most instances the survey changes lag behind the quantitative changes.

This does not, of course, mean that the qualitative indicators are not useful for forecasting purposes. They are often available more promptly than the quantitative indicators. Hence, qualitative indicators may be needed to get an early notion of what is likely to happen to quantitative indicators for which information is not yet available. If the evidence in this chapter explains a tendency among researchers to overlook this source of information in the United States (where the quantitative data are reported relatively promptly), it is nevertheless true that all market-oriented economies interested in developing early-warning systems for cyclical developments would do well to consider both types of indicators.

Clearly, entrepreneurs' views of the future are profoundly conditioned by the immediate past. Hence, the prospective form of many survey questions yields responses that are either coincident with or lag behind the retrospective form. Nonetheless, the results of this chapter suggest that indicator systems can be enriched by efforts to utilize both types of indicator.

Table 5-21. Summary of Cyclical Timing of Qualitative Indicators and Quantitative Equivalents, Market-Oriented Economies.

Comparisons	West Germany	France	Italy	United Kingdom	United States	Japan
	Average Lead (−) or Lag (+), in Months, at Peaks and Troughs					
Analyzed as Levels (1.1, 2.1, 3.2)						
Order Books, Total (1.1)						
Survey vs. Chronology	−1	−4	−3	—	—	—
Quantitative Measure vs. Chronology	—	—	—	—	—	—
Survey vs. Quantitative Measure	—	—	—	—	—	—
Order Books, Export (1.1)						
Survey vs. Chronology	—	+1	−3	—	—	—
Finished Goods Inventories (2.1) and (3.2)						
Survey vs. Chronology	+21	+15	+15	+21	—	—
Survey (Inverted) vs. Chronology	−2	−6	−4	−3	—	—
Raw Materials Inventories (3.2)						
Survey vs. Chronology	—	—	—	+10	—	—
Production Expectations (3.2)						
Survey vs. Chronology	+8	+6	+9	—	—	—
Quantitative Measure vs. Chronology	+1	0	−1	—	—	—
Survey vs. Quantitative Measure	+7	+5	+10	—	—	—
Business Confidence (3.2)						
Survey vs. Chronology	—	—	—	−2	—	—
Analyzed as Changes (1.2, 2.2, 3.1)						
Order Books, Total (1.2, 3.2)						
Survey vs. Chronology	−8	−13	−13	+2	—	—
Quantitative Measure vs. Chronology	−2	—	—	−6	—	—
Survey vs. Quantitative Measure	−8	—	—	+9	—	—
Order Books, Export (1.2)						
Survey vs. Chronology	−6	−11	−12	—	—	—

Finished Goods Inventories (2.2) and (3.1)						
Survey vs. Chronology	+8	+8	+7	+5	—	—
Raw Materials Inventories (3.1)						
Survey vs. Chronology	—	—	—	-6	—	—
Profits (3.1)						
Survey vs. Chronology	—	—	—	—	-3	-5
Quantitative Measure vs. Chronology	—	—	—	—	-6	-8
Survey vs. Quantitative Measure	—	—	—	—	+1	+4
Price Less Cost (3.1)						
Survey vs. Chronology	—	—	—	-7	—	—
Quantitative Measure vs. Chronology	—	—	—	-6	—	—
Survey vs. Quantitative Measure	—	—	—	+3	—	—
Production Expectations (3.1)						
Survey vs. Chronology	-4	—	—	-8	—	—
Quantitative Measure vs. Chronology	-11	—	—	-7	—	—
Survey vs. Quantitative Measure	+6	—	—	+3	—	—
Selling Price Expectations (3.1)						
Survey vs. Chronology	+4	+3	-1	—	—	—
Quantitative Measure vs. Chronology	-1	-6	-6	—	—	—
Survey vs. Quantitative Measure	+6	+6	+5	—	—	—

Source: Tables 5–2 through 5–20.

NOTES TO CHAPTER 5

1. J.-D. Lindlebauer, "The Business Climate as Leading-Indicator" (*Lecture Notes in Economics and Mathematical Systems*, No. 146), in W. H. Strigel, ed., *In Search of Economic Indicators, Essays on Business Surveys* (Berlin: Springer-Verlag, 1977), p. 62.

2. The results were published in 1960 as a Universities-NBER Conference report, *The Quality and Economic Significance of Anticipations Data* (Princeton, N.J.: Princeton University Press, 1960).

3. Recently, the CBI has introduced a question regarding order books, which is in the same form as the EEC question. But this question is too new to have produced a series long enough to accommodate cyclical analysis.

4. These results were originally presented at the fourteenth CIRET Conference held in Lisbon in September 1979 and were subsequently published in Philip A. Klein and Geoffrey H. Moore, "Industrial Surveys in the United Kingdom, Part I, New Orders," *Applied Economics* 13 (June): 315-17.

5. The averages in Table 5-7 are a bit misleading because of the failure of one pair of turns in the actual series to match growth cycle turns. The average lag of the survey, relative to the quantitative series, is six months, but the difference in the averages for both peaks and troughs, between the survey results and the actual series, is only one month. Closer inspection shows the expected difference between the two at troughs, but not at peaks. The set of turns, which can be compared to the survey results but not to the growth turns (turns are not compared where they cross an opposite turn), occurred in the mid-1960s. The trough in the quantitative series can be compared with the cycle trough in 1967 only by crossing the intervening peak. This anomaly causes the difference in the averages we are comparing.

6. The material in this section, as well as in the subsequent sections on profits and business confidence, pertaining to the United Kingdom was originally published in Philip A. Klein and Geoffrey H. Moore, "Industrial Surveys in the United Kingdom, Part II, Stocks, Profits and Business Confidence Over the Business Cycle," *Applied Economics* 13 (December 1981): 465-80.

7. As was the case with orders, the EEC question asks how stocks are related to "normal" levels (2.1 in Table 5-1), while the CBI asks whether the trend for the past four months has been "up" or "down" (2.1 in Table 5-1). By taking the first difference of the EEC net balances (2.2 in Table 5-1), we can obtain a net balance equivalent to the change in inventories, and by cumulating the CBI net balances (3.2) we can obtain the level equivalent. We can then consider the relationships of levels and changes in inventories to the growth cycle. While the procedures are reversed analytically, both surveys produce information that can be manipulated to relate it to quantitative data for inventory changes and levels.

8. Our discussion of profits draws heavily on Philip A. Klein and Geoffrey H. Moore, "Monitoring Profits During Business Cycles" (Paper presented at the 15th CIRET Conference held in Athens in October 1981, and published in Helmut Laumer and Maria Ziegler, eds., *International Research on Business*

Cycle Surveys [Aldershot, England: Gower Publishing Co., Ltd., 1982], pp. 55-92).

9. Wesley C. Mitchell, *Business Cycles and Their Causes* (Berkeley: University of California Press, 1941), p. 61. Reprinted from Mitchell's 1913 volume, *Business Cycles.*

10. At U.S. growth cycle turns, 1948 to 1978, these measures behaved as follows:

	Mean Lead (-) or Lag (+), in Months		
	Peaks	Troughs	Peaks and Troughs
Corporate Profits	-3	-2	-3
Corporate Profit Margins	-5	0	-3
Ratio, Price to Unit Labor Cost	-11	-5	-8
Price Change Less Unit Labor Cost Change	-6	-6	-5
Profit Margin Change	-7	-5	-6

Source: P. A. Klein and G. H. Moore, "Monitoring Profits During Business Cycles," Tables 1 and 3.

11. We have obtained and analyzed comparable qualitative data for Australia and the results are similar to those summarized here. See Klein and Moore, "Monitoring Profits During Business Cycles."

12. The findings for Japan, based on analysis of the relevant figures (not shown) are as follows: The survey of trade profitability leads the growth cycle chronology by nine months at peaks, by one month at troughs, and by five months at both (there is, however, only one comparison for each turn). Actual operating profits lead by an average of nine months at peaks, eight months at troughs, and eight months at both peaks and troughs. The survey lags actual profits by eight months at peaks, two months at troughs, and four months at both.

13. The expected changes should be cumulated with the previously reported cumulated *actual* changes in order to derive the expected level four months ahead, since respondents presumably know the actual level of production at the time they report prospective changes. Our procedure does not take this into account.

14. Werner H. Strigel, "The 'Business Climate' as Leading Indicator" in W. H. Strigel, ed., *In Search of Economic Indicators*, p. 76.

15. The CBI also includes a question in which replies are not in net-balance form. This question asks what factors are most likely to limit output in the next four months. One possible constraint, the availability of skilled labor, could in principle be a reliable leader by anticipating changes in production. However, the turns in the series are virtually coincident (plus two months at peaks, minus one month at troughs, or zero overall timing). In effect, then, the replies reinforce the conclusion just reached concerning the coincident character of business confidence—by the time entrepreneurs regard skilled labor as the most (or least) likely constraint on production in the immediate future, the peak (or trough) in the cycle has been reached as well.

PART III

APPLYING THE INDICATOR SYSTEM
SYSTEM
World Cycles, International Trade, and Inflation

Chapter 6

IS THERE A WORLD CYCLE?

INTRODUCTION

In 1959 Oskar Morgenstern examined how business cycles spread from country to country, concentrating his attention on the role of financial markets in major industrialized economies (the United States, Great Britain, Germany, and France), during the gold-standard era of 1870–1949 and the interwar period, 1925–38.[1] These countries and periods had been the basis of previous NBER studies.

Later, in the course of an analysis of foreign trade, Mintz developed the concept of a "world cycle" and attempted to quantify it. Her research included consideration of diffusion indexes of business cycles (three countries, 1879–1938; fifteen countries, 1890–1931); diffusion indexes of imports (thirty-four to forty-one countries, 1947–53; twenty countries, 1954–61); and indexes of world imports (1880–1965) and of world manufacturing production (1879–1938).[2] From these data she developed a chronology of world import cycles from 1881 to 1959 and applied it to the analysis of U.S. and British exports and trade balances (see also Chapter 8).

Arthur B. Laffer summarized the results of a number of efforts to derive a world cycle chronology or to measure the correlation among fluctuations in different countries. These efforts included an annual chronology (1890–1932) devised by Moses Abramovitz (who based his work on Willard Thorp's *Business Annals* for eighteen countries), which was updated by Laffer to 1949–1960. He also reviewed studies of the intercountry correlation of unemployment rates, stock prices, interest rates, and wholesale prices.[3] To varying degrees, these researchers discovered evidence of synchronized economic movements among developed countries. More recently, Bert Hickman and Stefan Schleicher found evidence of the synchronization of growth rates in industrial production and real GNP in sixteen countries, but observed less synchronization in rates of change in consumer prices, wage rates, or the monetary base.[4]

At this point, the line of reasoning taken by W. C. Mitchell in 1927 to explain the tendency toward international synchronism should be recalled:

> The basis of this trend toward unity of economic fortunes among communities organized on the European model is that each phase in a business cycle, as it develops in any area, tends to produce the same phase in all the areas with which the first has dealings. Prosperity in one country stimulates demand for the products of other countries, and so quickens the activities in the latter regions. . . . Further, prosperity, with its sanguine temper and its liberal profits, encourages investments abroad as well as at home, and the export of capital to other countries gives an impetus to their trade. A recession checks all these stimuli. A severe crisis in any important center produces quicker and graver results. Demands for financial assistance raise interest rates and reduce domestic lending power in other centers; apprehensions regarding the solvency of international houses may start demands for liquidation in many places; the losses which bankruptcies bring are likely to be felt by business enterprises the world over.[5]

Mitchell's comments, which suggested that instability would tend toward international synchronism, raises significant questions. To what extent have the major industrial market-oriented economies, in fact, moved in synchronous cycle phases during the postwar period? Can one locate a country (or countries) from which prosperity spread to other countries? If so, is it customarily the same country? Whether or not the expansions and contractions are stimulated by changes originating in one country, do these fluctuations spread rapidly enough to other countries to give the appearance of synchronous movements, or do they spread more slowly and possibly with differential lags so that the synchronous movement Mitchell hypothesized fails to materialize?

Most of the earlier work on these questions, by Mitchell, Morgenstern, Mintz, and others, tested whether or not one could establish evidence of international *classical* cycles. Morgenstern, for example, focused on Britain, France, Germany, and the United States and concluded that the four were in the same phase (classical expansion or contraction) about half the time during 1879–1932.[6] For the postwar period we shall search for evidence of synchronous periods or phases of *growth* cycle expansion and contraction on an international scale.

ALTERNATIVE INTERNATIONAL GROWTH CYCLE CHRONOLOGIES

In attempting to develop an index that represents fluctuations in the market-oriented world, we have experimented with a number of possibilities. An obvious measure, from the vantage point taken in this book, would be the composite index we have developed for ten industrialized countries. The primary drawback to such an index is that, as the reader can appreciate, some countries have provided data for a far shorter period of time than the thirty-plus years covered by the economic record for the major countries.

Accordingly, we have settled on a seven-country composite index, combining the roughly coincident indexes for the United States, Canada, the United Kingdom, France, Italy, West Germany, and Japan. These countries represent more than half of the noncommunist world's trade, and their combined GNP is a considerable portion of the total GNP of the market-oriented world as well.

A chronology based upon the trend-adjusted, coincident index for these seven countries is presented in Figure 6-1 and Table 6-1. It is useful to compare the seven-country index to chronologies comprised of a selection of these countries. The six-country index, for example, may be used to examine how growth recessions in the United States are reflected in other countries. The four-country index enables us to consider the relations between European and non–European nations. In addition to these indexes we shall use data prepared by the Federal Reserve Bank of St. Louis on the growth rates in eight industrial economies, which revealed four international growth recessions in the period 1955-73.[7] The peaks occurred in 1955, 1960, 1964, 1969, and 1973; the troughs in 1958, 1961, 1967, and 1971. The chronology represents years in which there is an international consensus of high growth rates or low growth rates in real GNP, industrial production, imports, and exports.[8]

This chronology has the obvious disadvantage of being based on annual data. One would expect peak growth rates to precede the peaks in trend-adjusted indexes, since the indexes do not reach their peaks until the *growth rate* has fallen below the *trend rate*. Barring a sudden, sharp drop the growth rate begins to decline before that. Similarly, the troughs in the growth rate may precede the troughs in trend-adjusted indexes, since the trough in the indexes is not reached

Figure 6-1. International Composite Indexes, by Timing.

Part A. Seven-Country Indexes (United States, Canada, United Kingdom, West Germany, France, Italy, and Japan)

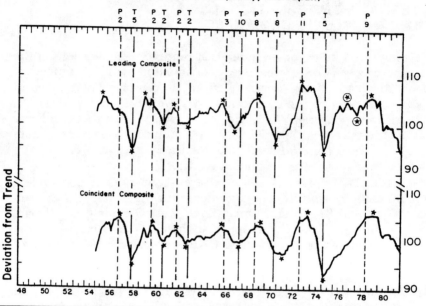

until the growth rate has risen above the trend rate. Table 6-1 bears out these expectations, despite the differences in the countries covered and in the economic data employed. The monthly composite index of all the roughly coincident indicators for the seven countries shows clear cyclical movements, corresponding to similar movements in the annual data for the eight countries in the Federal Reserve report.

We turn now to how the international chronology, based on the seven-country composite index, differs from the individual chronologies of each country. The seven-country index produces a chronology of cycles that matches on a one-to-one basis those in the United States, Belgium (despite its brief length), and Sweden. Three countries reflect the index on a one-to-one basis except for the absence of a recession in 1960–61 in the United Kingdom, West Germany, and France. Canada reflects the international index perfectly except for an extra cycle in 1976–77, a cycle one finds in the Netherlands as well (the latter also skips the 1960–61 recession). The Japanese chronology is similar to the seven-country chronology, but its 1964–66 recession does not match the 1966–67 recession in the other

Figure 6-1. continued

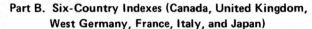

Part B. Six-Country Indexes (Canada, United Kingdom, West Germany, France, Italy, and Japan)

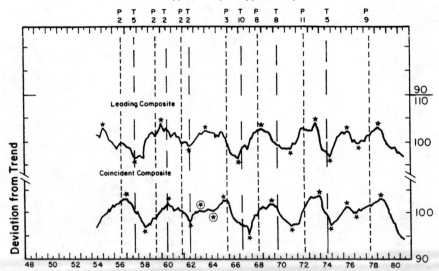

Part C. Four-Country Indexes (United Kingdom, West Germany, France, and Italy)

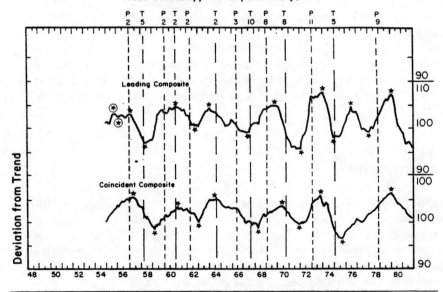

Note:
Vertical P and T lines based on coincident index, seven countries.

Table 6-1.   Three International Growth Cycle Chronologies, 1954–80.

Peaks Trend-Adjusted Index, Monthly			Troughs Trend-Adjusted Index, Monthly		
Seven-Country[a]	Six-Country	Four-Country	Seven-Country	Six-Country	Four-Country
2/57	2/57	5/57			
2/60	3/62	3/61	5/58	2/59	2/59
2/62			2/61		
3/66	7/64	3/66	2/63	2/63	2/63
8/69	6/70	5/70	10/67	5/68	5/68
11/73	11/73	7/74	8/71	2/72	2/72
9/79	2/80	12/76	5/75	9/75	8/75
		11/79			10/77

Note:

a. Chronologies are based on composite indexes of trend-adjusted, roughly coincident indicators. The seven-country index includes the United States, Canada, West Germany, the United Kingdom, France, Italy, and Japan; the six-country index excludes the United States. The four-country index includes the United Kingdom, West Germany, France, and Italy.

countries. Italy is the most divergent, skipping the 1960–61, 1962–63, and 1966–67 recessions and exhibiting extra recessions in 1963–65 and 1976–77.

Despite its limited geographic range, we believe that the seven-country, composite coincident index provides the best currently available chronology of world growth cycles. We will make further use of it, therefore, in the next two sections to make various comparative analyses.

UTILIZING WORLD CYCLE CHRONOLOGIES

It is, of course, possible to consider the behavior of a number of different kinds of economic activity, within individual economies or among several economies via trade and financial flows, during international recessions and the intervening expansions. Such analyses permit detection of systematic differences in the operation of economic variables with respect to these presumed international cycle phases. It should be underscored, however, that here, as with indica-

Table 6-2. Consilience of Cycle Phases in Ten Market-Oriented Economies with Cycle Phases in the International Chronology.

Country	In Phase		Out of Phase	
	Number of Months	*Percent*	*Number of Months*	*Percent*
United States	202	77	60	23
Canada	254	86	42	14
United Kingdom	194	78	53	22
West Germany	178	71	72	29
France	200	83	40	17
Belgium	120	68	56	32
Italy	168	61	108	39
Netherlands	215	77	63	23
Sweden	78	48	83	52
Japan	235	86	38	14
All Countries	1,844	75	615	25

Time Periods Covered:	*Number of Months*	*Dates*
International Composite Index[a]	281	Feb. 1957—Sept. 1979
United States	262	Feb. 1957—Dec. 1978
Canada	296	Nov. 1956—June 1980
United Kingdom	247	Nov. 1958—June 1979
West Germany	250	April 1959—Feb. 1980
France	240	Aug. 1957—Aug. 1979
Belgium	176	Oct. 1964—June 1979
Italy	279	Nov. 1956—Feb. 1980
Netherlands	278	Oct. 1956—Dec. 1979
Sweden	161	Feb. 1965—July 1978
Japan	273	May 1957—Feb. 1980

a. Includes seven countries. See Table 6-1.
Source: Figure 6-1.

tors of cyclical changes, accurate analysis depends on the selection of valid turning points. In any attempt to date an international growth cycle the customary difficulties are compounded. Nevertheless, our international cycle is a fairly general one in the sense that nearly every turn in the international cycle is matched by a turn in each of the countries. In addition, very few countries exhibit extra cycles, or do so infrequently.

This finding suggests that Mitchell was essentially correct in 1927 when he pointed out the trend "toward unity of economic fortunes." Table 6-2 illustrates in somewhat simplified form, the degree of consilience between the ten countries in our sample and the international composite index. In general, the degree of consilience for all these countries over the available period is remarkably high. In only one country, Sweden, were cycles out of phase as much as half the time. As regards consilience, then, the postwar experience with

Table 6-3. Leads and Lags of Growth Cycle Turns in Ten Market-Oriented Economies at International Growth Cycle Turning Points, 1954-73.

	Number of Leads	Number of Coincidences		Number of Lags	Total Number of Timing Comparisons	Average Lead (−) or Lag (+), in Months	
		Rough	Exact			Median	Mean
At Peaks							
United States	3	4	2	2	7	0	−2
Canada	3	5	2	2	7	0	−1
United Kingdom	6	3	0	0	6	−4	−6
West Germany	4	1	0	2	6	−6	−4
France	1	3	0	4	5	+3	+3
Italy	1	1	1	2	4	+2	+2
Belgium	2	1	0	2	4	0	0
Netherlands	3	1	0	3	6	0	+2
Sweden	1	0	0	2	3	+7	+2
Japan	1	2	1	3	5	0	+3
All Countries	25	21	6	22	53	+2	−3
At Troughs							
United States	3	4	2	1	6	0	+1
Canada	1	3	0	5	6	+3	+1
United Kingdom	1	3	1	3	5	+3	+3
West Germany	1	3	2	2	5	0	+3
France	0	2	0	4	4	+5	+5
Italy	0	1	1	2	3	+5	+9
Belgium	1	1	0	2	3	+13	+4
Netherlands	1	4	2	2	5	0	+3
Sweden	1	1	0	2	3	+11	+15
Japan	2	2	0	2	4	+2	+2
All Countries	11	24	8	25	44	+3	+5

At Peaks and Troughs

United States	6	8	4	3	13	0	−1
Canada	4	8	2	7	13	+1	0
United Kingdom	7	6	1	3	11	−2	−2
West Germany	5	4	2	4	11	0	−1
France	1	5	0	8	9	+3	+4
Italy	1	2	2	4	7	+5	+5
Belgium	3	2	0	4	7	+5	+4
Netherlands	4	5	2	5	11	0	+2
Sweden	2	1	0	4	6	+9	+8
Japan	3	4	1	5	9	+5	+3
All Countries	35	45	14	47	97	+2	+2

Source: Figure 6–1.

growth cycles resembles the prewar experience with classical cycles quite closely.

Another point, though, can be raised concerning the validity of a world growth cycle. Our attention has so far focused on whether growth swings are widespread and synchronous among industrial countries. If that tendency were weak, as it no doubt is in the case of crop yields per acre in different countries, we should not be inclined to say there is a world cycle at all, even though there might be fluctuations. On the other hand, we might still legitimately ask whether these general movements are in the nature of random fluctuations over the years. Growth rates might be synchronous across countries but random through time. In the case of crop yields, which are strongly influenced by vagaries in the weather, the movements through time are virtually random.[9] A 1974 study of annual growth rates in sixteen countries during 1950-69, applied to GNP, exports, imports, and output of agriculture, manufacturing, and construction, found that "fluctuations are in most cases not statistically distinguishable from those generated by a random process."[10] The length of runs up or down in the rates of growth was tested for each fluctuation. In a random series of such rates, runs of one year are expected to be most frequent, two-year runs less frequent, and so on (see the first reference cited in Note 9). The authors noted that similar tests applied to quarterly or monthly data might yield a different result, but this would not necessarily reduce the significance of the fact that, *when aggregated into annual time units*, growth rates in many economic series in many countries have the characteristics of random series over time.[11] They remain, however, related from one country to another as we have shown.

We turn now to the question of whether or not many cyclical episodes are triggered by the same country. We should like to examine this question at some future point by analyzing the interrelationships between leading indicators of various sorts of activities and the subsequent impact of the indicators on aggregate economic activity, and we will undertake some initial steps along this line in the following section. Here, we consider simply the timing relationships among the growth cycle chronologies for the ten countries under review.

According to Table 6-3 at peaks there was a clear tendency for the United Kingdom and West Germany to lead and for France, Italy, Sweden, and Japan to lag. Belgium and the Netherlands were as likely to lead as to lag. The United States led at only three of the seven recessions, although the earlier period shows close coincidence, while the later peaks show leads. At troughs the dispersion is slightly smaller, although the United States has led the world index up from

Table 6-4. Sequence of Turns at International Growth Cycle Turning Points, Ten Countries, 1954-79.

Country	Rank Order of Turns at Peaks[a]							Average Rank, Seven Peaks
	2/57	2/60	2/62	3/66	8/69	11/73	9/79	
United States	6.0	2.0	6.0	7.5	2.0	1.0	1.0	3.6
Canada	5.0	1.0	5.0	6.0	1.0	5.0	5.0	4.0
United Kingdom	2.0	n.a.[b]	2.5	5.0	3.0	2.0	2.5	2.8
West Germany	1.0	n.a.	1.0	3.0	6.0	3.0	8.0	3.7
France	7.5	n.a.	n.a.	7.5	5.0	7.0	4.0	6.2
Italy	3.5	n.a.	n.a.	n.a.	4.0	6.0	8.0	5.4
Belgium	n.a.	n.a.	n.a.	1.0	9.0	9.0	2.5	5.4
Netherlands	3.5	n.a.	2.5	4.0	10.0	10.0	6.0	6.0
Sweden	n.a.	n.a.	n.a.	2.0	8.0	8.0	n.a.	6.0
Japan	7.5	n.a.	4.0	n.a.	7.0	4.0	8.0	6.1

Country	Rank Order of Turns at Troughs						Average Rank, Six Troughs
	5/58	2/61	2/63	10/67	8/71	5/75	
United States	1.0	1.0	5.0	5.0	1.5	1.5	2.5
Canada	3.0	2.0	4.0	6.0	1.5	8.5	4.2
United Kingdom	4.0	n.a.	3.0	3.0	7.0	7.0	4.8
West Germany	7.0	n.a.	3.0	3.0	5.0	3.5	4.3
France	6.0	n.a.	n.a.	7.0	4.0	5.0	5.5
Italy	8.0	n.a.	n.a.	n.a.	10.0	3.5	7.2
Belgium	n.a.	n.a.	n.a.	8.0	3.0	8.5	6.5
Netherlands	2.0	n.a.	3.0	3.0	9.0	6.0	4.6
Sweden	n.a.	n.a.	n.a.	1.0	8.0	10.0	6.3
Japan	5.0	n.a.	1.0	n.a.	6.0	1.5	3.4

Notes:
a. Turns are ranked from longest lead (1) to shortest lead or longest lag (5).
b. n.a. = Not available, either because index does not cover the period or does not show a corresponding turn.
Source: Figure 6-1.

Table 6-5. Leads and Lags of International Composite Indexes at their Respective Growth Cycle Turning Points.

	Lead (–) or Lag (+), in Months, of Leading vs. Coincident Index at Growth Cycle Peaks and Troughs							

	P 5/57	T 2/59	P 3/61	T 2/63	P 2/64	T 3/65	P 3/66	T 5/68
Four-Country[a] Indexes	– 21	– 9	– 7	0	+ 8	n.m.[d]	n.m.	– 9

	P 2/57	T 2/59	P 3/61	T 2/63	P 7/64	T 5/68	P 6/70	T 2/72
Six-Country[b] Indexes	0	– 8	– 1	– 4	– 6	– 11	– 7	0

	P 2/57	T 5/58	P 2/60	T 2/61	P 2/62	T 2/63	P 3/66	T 10/67
Seven-Country[c] Indexes	– 17	– 3	– 9	– 2	– 3	– 12	0	– 6

Notes:
a. United Kingdom, West Germany, France, and Italy.
b. Canada, United Kingdom, West Germany, France, Italy, and Japan.
c. United States, Canada, United Kingdom, West Germany, France, Italy, and Japan.
d. n.m. = No matching turn.

recession more often (three times) than any other country. Japan led twice. No other country led the world index up more than once. Taking peaks and troughs together, we find that the individual country turns, based on the medians, occurred within three months of the international turn for every country except France, Italy, Belgium, and Sweden, all of which lag.[12]

Another way of looking at the evidence is shown in Table 6-4, which records the sequence in which the matching peaks and troughs in the ten countries occurred. The first country to turn is given a rank of one, the last a rank of ten. When a country is not available at a given turn (designated by n.a.), the highest possible rank is reduced by one. When two or more countries turn in the same month, a tie is indicated by averaging the two rankings. Since no country attains a rank of one at more than two of the seven peaks, it is clear that no country can be said to lead invariably the other countries into recession. On the other hand, the United States has a rank of one at two of the troughs, and is tied for first at two more, so that at four of the six troughs the United States was one of the first countries to turn. It is not unreasonable, therefore, to conclude that, according to

Table 6-5. continued

Lead (–) or Lag (+), in Months, of Leading vs. Coincident Index at Growth Cycle Peaks and Troughs (continued)							Average Lead (–) or Lag (+), in Months					
							Median			Mean		
P 5/70	T 2/72	P 7/74	T 8/75	P 12/76	T 10/77	P 11/79	P	T	P&T	P	T	P&T
–9	0	–2	–1	+1	+4	–2	–2	0	–2	–5	–2	–4

P 11/73	T 9/75	P 2/80										
+3	–7	0					0	–7	–4	–2	–6	–4

P 8/69	T 8/71	P 11/73	T 5/75	P 9/79								
–4	–9	–9	–2	–6			–6	–4	–6	–7	–6	–6

the above data, the United States tends to lead other countries out of recession. At peaks, however, the role of initiator shifts from country to country, seemingly at random. This point has not generally been recognized.[13]

LEADING AND LAGGING INDICATORS OF INTERNATIONAL CYCLE TURNS

The previous section described the validity and usefulness of an international growth cycle chronology (based on summary measures of cyclical activity) and the construction of a composite index (based on the roughly coincident indicators for each country). An alternative approach is to relate turns in national leading or lagging indicators to the international cycle chronology.

A comparison based on international composite indexes of all leading and coincident indicators is given in Figure 6-1 and Table 6-5. The indexes in the table have been computed three ways: the first including all seven countries in our "world composite indexes," the second excluding the United States, and the third limited to four European countries. By omitting the U.S. data, the results are independent of any of the U.S. information that was used to classify the indicators as leading or lagging. As Figure 6-1 shows, the leading indexes trace out each of the cycles identified by the coincident indexes, thus helping to confirm their validity. The table records the timing of the cycles in the leading indexes vis-à-vis the coincident indexes. As a rule, at each of the international growth cycle turns, the leading index turns before the coincident index. There are very few exceptions to this expected order—in the seven-country index, the 1966 peak is the sole exception. For the six-country index, there are four exceptions—three exact coincidences for the leading index and one three-month lag. For the four-country index, there are five exceptions—two are exact coincidences and three are lags. Thus, by the strictest standards of expected behavior even the four-country leading index leads the coincident index at two-thirds of the individual turns.

When we examine whether one country seems to trigger the spread of economic instability internationally, the behavior of the leading indicators at international turns is clearly of considerable importance. Careful inspection of the leads shown in Table 6-6 for peaks reveals a variety of outcomes. Not only is there diversity in the length of the lead among countries at individual peaks, there is also diversity within individual countries at different peaks. Moreover, the length of the lead at peaks varies from peak to peak. There does not seem to be any firm rule, therefore, for the leading, coincident, or lagging indicators of any country to lead the other countries into recession. The situation is similar at troughs. No single country seems regularly to act as bellwether in leading the industrial economies into or out of recession.

The ordering of turns in the entire sequence from leading to lagging indicators at the international cycle turning points does not significantly alter our previous conclusion that instability is not customarily set off by one particular country. The United States, Canada, and the United Kingdom have usually been among the first, while France, Italy, Belgium, and Sweden have usually been among the last to participate in changes in the international cycle, both at peaks and troughs, and for all three categories of indicators. In order to understand which country will lead other countries into recession or into recovery at any particular point in time, it is clearly essential to examine specific economic developments for each nation. However, neither the economic situation in a particular country nor the particular set of economic policies developed in any country has, based on our evidence, resulted in its consistently turning first. The picture is more complete if we include the timing of leaders and laggers because our perspective on instability recognizes that one cyclical phase tends to merge into the next. Our emphasis on growth cycles rather than classical cycles has not produced any evidence suggesting that this perspective should be changed.

Table 6-6. Timing at International Growth Cycle Turning Points, Composite Indexes of Leading, Roughly Coincident, and Lagging Indicators, Ten Countries.

Leading	Lead (-) or Lag (+) at Peaks, in Months							Leading	
	2/57	2/60	2/62	3/66	8/69	11/73	9/79	Median	Mean
United States	-17	-9	n.m.ᵃ	0	-6	-9	-6	-8	-7.8
Canada	-11	-6	-3	-2	-5	+4	+4	-3	-2.7
United Kingdom	n.m.	+1	n.m.	-16	-12	-8	+2	-8	-6.6
West Germany	-18	+6	n.m.	-13	0	-10	-7	-9	-7.0
France	+6	n.m.	-9	+3	+6	+6	0	+5	+2.0
Italy	n.a.ᵇ	+8	n.m.	n.m.	0	-4	n.a.	0	+1.3
Belgium	n.a.	n.a.	n.a.	n.a.	-1	+2	+1	+1	0
Netherlands	-21	n.m.	-12	+2	+12	+5	+5	+4	0
Sweden	n.a.	n.a.	n.a.	-4	+3	+6	n.m.	+3	+1.7
Japan	-1	n.m.	-6	n.m.	+6	+3	+5	+3	+1.4

Roughly Coincident	Lead (-) or Lag (+) at Peaks, in Months							Coincident	
	2/57	2/60	2/62	3/66	8/69	11/73	9/79	Median	Mean
United States	+1	0	+2	0	-5	0	-9	0	-1.6
Canada	-4	-4	+1	0	-6	+3	0	0	-1.4
United Kingdom	-14	n.m.	-11	-1	-3	+9	-3	-3	-3.8
West Germany	-16	n.m.	-12	-11	+11	-9	+5	-10	-5.3
France	+9	n.m.	n.m.	+4	+5	+8	+5	+5	+6.2
Italy	n.a.	n.a.	n.m.	n.m.	+7	+5	n.a.	+6	+6.0
Belgium	+3	n.m.	n.m.	-24	+16	+2	+4	+3	+1.8
Netherlands	-5	n.m.	-11	-4	+17	+9	+5	0	+2.0
Sweden	n.a.	n.a.	n.a.	-10	+9	+6	+3	+5	+2.0
Japan	0	n.m.	-6	-20	+3	-1	+5	-1	-3.8

(*Table 6-6. continued overleaf*)

Table 6-6.   continued

Lagging	Lead (−) or Lag (+) at Peaks, in Months							Lagging	
	2/57	2/60	2/62	3/66	8/69	11/73	9/79	Median	Mean
United States	+7	+3	+6	+8	+2	+8	+7	+7	+5.9
Canada	−1	+1	+7	+4	+3	+8	+7	+4	+4.1
United Kingdom	−11	n.m.	−11	+4	+11	+3	+7	+3	+1.6
West Germany	n.a.	n.a.	n.a.	−2	+13	0	n.a.	+6	+5.5
France	n.a.	n.a.	n.a.	n.a.	+2	+12	n.a.	+7	+7.0
Italy	n.a.	n.a.	n.a.	n.a.	+13	+13	n.a.	+13	+13.0
Belgium	n.a.	n.a.	n.a.	+10	+12	+14	+8	+11	+11.0
Netherlands	n.a.	n.a.	−9	+4	+12	+9	+5	+5	+4.2
Sweden	n.a.	n.a.	n.a.	+6	−3	n.m.	n.a.	+2	+1.5
Japan	+6	n.m.	+3	−16	+15	+8	+11	+7	+4.5

Leading	Lead (−) or Lag (+) at Troughs, in Months						Leading	
	5/58	2/61	2/63	10/67	8/71	5/75	Median	Mean
United States	−3	−2	n.m.	−6	−9	−2	−3	−4.4
Canada	−6	−3	−3	+1	−7	+16	−3	−0.3
United Kingdom	+1	n.m.	−11	−11	−5	+2	−5	−4.8
West Germany	+9	n.m.	+3	−8	0	−6	0	−0.4
France	+6	n.m.	−7	+8	+6	+4	+6	+3.4
Italy	+2	n.m.	+23	n.m.	+3	+37	+13	+16.25
Belgium	n.a.	n.a.	n.a.	+4	−4	+5	+4	+1.7
Netherlands	−6	n.m.	0	−11	+3	+5	0	−1.8
Sweden	n.a.	n.a.	−1	+6	+11	+33	+8	+12.3
Japan	+3	n.m.	−4	n.m.	+6	−3	0	+0.5

| | Lead (−) or Lag (+) at Troughs, in Months | | | | | | Coincident | |
Roughly Coincident	5/58	2/61	2/63	10/67	8/71	5/75	Median	Mean
United States	−1	0	+9	0	−9	+2	0	0
Canada	+3	0	+5	+4	−9	+5	+4	+1.3
United Kingdom	+6	n.m.	0	+1	+6	+6	+6	+3.8
West Germany	+9	n.m.	0	−2	+11	+3	+3	+4.2
France	+15	n.m.	n.m.	+7	−3	+4	+6	+5.8
Italy	n.a.	n.a.	n.m.	n.m.	+19	0	+10	+9.5
Belgium	+9	n.m.	n.m.	+7	+11	+6	+8	+8.3
Netherlands	0	n.m.	0	+1	+15	+2	+1	+4.5
Sweden	n.a.	n.a.	n.a.	−3	+9	+37	+9	+14.3
Japan	+8	n.m.	−1	−19	+8	−3	−1	−1.4

| | Lead (−) or Lag (+) at Troughs, in Months | | | | | | Lagging | |
Lagging	5/58	2/61	2/63	10/67	8/71	5/75	Median	Mean
United States	+3	+5	+21	+5	+7	+7	+6	+8.0
Canada	+7	+4	+1	+13	+15	+33	+10	+12.2
United Kingdom	+10	n.m.	+9	+8	+8	+11	+9	+9.2
West Germany	n.a.	n.a.	n.a.	+2	+12	+9	+9	+7.7
France	n.a.	n.a.	n.a.	+8	+12	+6	+8	+8.7
Italy	n.a.	n.a.	n.a.	+17	+17	+6	+17	+13.3
Belgium	n.a.	n.a.	n.a.	+12	+13	+9	+12	+11.3
Netherlands	+3	n.m.	0	+4	+12	+9	+4	+5.4
Sweden	n.a.	n.a.	n.a.	−2	n.m.	−15	−8	−8.5
Japan	+15	n.m.	+4	−13	+13	−45	+4	−5.2

Notes:
a. n.m. = No matching turn.
b. n.a. = No indicator available.

NOTES TO CHAPTER 6

1. Oskar Morgenstern, *International Financial Transactions and Business Cycles* (New York: NBER, 1959), especially pp. 32–73.

2. Ilse Mintz, *Trade Balance during Business Cycles: United States and Britain since 1880*, Occasional Paper No. 67 (New York: NBER, 1959; and *Cyclical Fluctuations in the Exports of the United States since 1879*, Studies in Business Cycles No. 15 (New York: NBER, 1967).

3. Arthur B. Laffer, "The Phenomenon of Worldwide Inflation: A Study in International Market Integration," June 1974. (Unpublished.)

4. Bert Hickman and Stefan Schleicher, "The Interdependence of National Economies: Evidence from the Link Project," *Weltwirtschaftsliches Archiv* 114, Heft 4 (1978): 642–708.

5. W. C. Mitchell, *Business Cycles, The Problem and Its Setting* (New York: NBER, 1927), p. 446.

6. Morgenstern, *International Financial Transactions*, p. 45.

7. Geoffrey H. Moore, "The State of the International Business Cycle," *Business Economics* (September 1974).

8. An alternative that we have not explored, which would provide wider geographic coverage, would be to trend-adjust the United Nations quarterly index of industrial production.

9. See W. Allen Wallis and Geoffrey H. Moore, *A Significance Test for Time Series and Other Ordered Observations*, Technical Paper No. 1 (New York: NBER, 1941), pp. 36–42; Geoffrey H. Moore, "Harvest Cycles" (Ph.D. dissertation, Harvard University, 1947).

10. Joseph A. Licari and Mark Gilbert, "Is There a Postwar Growth Cycle?" *Kyklos* 27, no. 3 (1974).

11. A different kind of test was applied to the duration of business cycle expansions and contractions measured in months. The distribution of durations was not significantly different from what would be expected in a series whose first differences were randomly ordered in time (J. Huston McCulloch, "The Monte Carlo Cycle in Business Activity," *Journal of Economic Inquiry* 13 (September 1975): 303–20). Tests were applied to the NBER business cycle chronologies for the United States (1854–1970), France (1865–1938), Germany (1879–1932), and Great Britain (1854–1938). A similar result for U.S. expansions and contractions (1854–1957) was obtained by Arthur M. Okun, "On the Appraisal of Cyclical Turning Point Predictors," *Journal of Business of the University of Chicago* 33, no. 2 (April 1960): 101–20. These results are not inconsistent with those for annual growth rates cited in the text, since growth rates are obtained by differencing. The practical implication of these tests is that knowledge of how long an expansion or contraction has already lasted is of little use in predicting when it will end. See E. E. Anderson, "Further Evidence on the Monte Carlo Cycle in Business Activity," *Journal of Economic Inquiry* 15, no. 2 (April 1977): 269–76.

12. In a recent study of U.S. growth cycle timing compared to the timing of a number of Pacific Basin countries, we found that the United States generally led at growth cycle turns for all the countries surveyed except Taiwan. See Philip A. Klein, "Forecasting Growth Cycles with Indicators in Pacific Basin Countries," *Columbia Journal of World Business* (Fall 1983): 3–19. Another recent study of synchronization in international business cycles is Colin Lawrence, "The Role of Information and the International Business Cycle," *Journal of International Economics* 17 (1984): 101–120.

13. In this connection, P. A. Klein has compared matched turns of classical cycle turning points for the United States and the United Kingdom for the periods available (1854–1938) and concluded that U.S. turns were apt to lag British turns (at both peaks and troughs) prior to World War II. For a comparable period (1879–1932), the average suggested a small lag for United States turns behind German turns, both at peaks and troughs. However, this was the result of a fairly long lag at both peaks and troughs in the earlier period (1879–1914) and a fairly long lead in the period covering the interwar years. See Klein, *Business Cycles in the Postwar World: Some Reflections on Recent Research* (Washington, D.C.: American Enterprise Institute, 1976), Table 7, p. 30.

Chapter 7

MONITORING INTERNATIONAL TRADE FLOWS WITH LEADING INDICATORS

Several books produced at the National Bureau of Economic Research in the 1950s explored the application of the Mitchellian perspective in studies of international trade. In 1959, for example, Oskar Morgenstern published *International Financial Transactions During Business Cycles.*[1] Ilse Mintz's trade studies examined the potential impact of external trade on U.S. domestic cycles, which led to her seminal works on growth cycle measurement. In several papers prepared for the NBER and published between 1959 and 1967, Mintz noted that there were good reasons to believe that fluctuations in world imports would be closely related to fluctuations in U.S. exports.[2] Although domestic supply and demand affect the volume of U.S. exports, world demand, as represented by world imports exclusive of U.S. imports, was expected to have a significant influence on export volume and export prices. Mintz proceeded to test this hypothesis with data on U.S. export quantities, unit values, and total values from 1881 to 1961, examining total exports and exports of finished manufactures, semi-manufactured goods, crude materials, and foods.

For each of these groups Mintz found a consistent, positive relationship with world imports. During expansions in world imports, U.S. export quantities, prices, and values rose; during contractions in world imports, they fell (or rose at a slower rate). And the relationship persisted—it applied to the period 1881–1913 and to the period 1921–61. For the value of total U.S. exports, it applied to every single cycle in world imports during both these periods. For prices and quantities of total exports, it applied to every cycle in world imports after 1921, and to a clear majority of cycles before then. The relationship was somewhat weaker for prices than for quantities, and somewhat weaker for food than for the other products. But in general the relationship held.

In considering ways in which we could test and possibly elaborate upon Mintz's findings, we began by examining patterns emerging from trade between the United States and several of the larger market-oriented economies for which an indicator system had been developed.

We discovered that spurts and recessions in growth have had a marked effect on the volume of both exports and imports. U.S. exports to Canada, the United Kingdom, West Germany, and Japan, for example, grew almost six times as fast when those countries were in an expansion phase of their growth cycle than when they were in a contraction phase. Similarly, exports out of these countries and into the United States (our imports from them) grew more than three times as fast during upswings in the U.S. growth cycle as during its downswings. As a result, movement in our trade balance has been profoundly affected by whatever differences may occur in the timing and severity of recessions and recoveries here and abroad.[3]

As shown in Part A of Table 7-1, during three recent upswings in Japan (1959-61, 1962-64, and 1966-70), our exports to Japan grew at an average rate of $2.7 million a month. But, during the three Japanese downswings (1961-62, 1964-66, and 1970-72), they actually declined slightly, by an average of $0.3 million a month. U.S. exports to the four countries combined grew at an average rate of over $11 million per month during growth cycle upswings, as compared with U.S. export growth averaging only $1.9 million per month during growth cycle downswings. Overall, U.S. export growth during upswings in foreign growth cycles exceeded export growth during adjacent downswings in eighteen out of the twenty possible comparisons. In contrast, and as expected, the relationship of U.S. exports to U.S. growth cycles is not as systematic.[4]

U.S. imports from all four countries combined grew at an average rate of nearly $18 million per month during the five U.S. growth cycle upswings, but at less than a third that rate, $5½ million per month, during the four downswings between 1958 and 1973 (Part B, Table 7-1). The average rise in U.S. imports from Japan, for example, was $5.4 million per month during U.S. upswings, but only $1.5 million per month during U.S. downswings. The fluctuations in our economic growth rate are as important to Japan as their fluctua-

Table 7-1.   Changes in U.S. Exports and Imports During Growth Cycles: Monthly Data.

Part A.   Changes in Exports during Foreign Growth Cycles

U.S. Exports to:	Average Number of Months in Foreign Growth Cycle		Average Change per Month in U.S. Exports during Foreign Growth Cycle[a] (millions $)			Conformity Index[b]
	Upswings	Downswings	Upswings	Downswings	Ratio Upswing/Downswing	
Japan, 1959–72	34	18	+2.7	−0.3	—[c]	+100
United Kingdom, 1958–72	28	25	+1.4	+0.2	7.0	+100
West Germany, 1959–73	25	22	+3.0	+0.3	10.0	+67
Canada, 1958–70	18	19	+4.0	+1.7	2.4	+71
Total			+11.1	+1.9	5.8	

Part B.   Changes in Imports during U.S. Growth Cycles

U.S. Imports from:	Average Number of Months in U.S. Growth Cycle		Average Change per Month in U.S. Imports during U.S. Growth Cycle[a] (millions $)			Conformity Index[b]
	Upswings	Downswings	Upswings	Downswings	Ratio Upswing/Downswing	
Japan, 1958–73	24	14	+5.4	+1.5	3.6	+100
United Kingdom, 1958–73	14	14	+2.1	−0.5	—[c]	+100
West Germany, 1958–73	24	14	+2.3	+1.0	2.3	+50
Canada, 1958–73	24	14	+7.8	+3.6	2.2	+75
Total			+17.6	+5.6	3.1	

Notes:
a. Changes during upswings and downswings are measured from three-month averages of seasonally adjusted data centered on growth cycle peaks and troughs.
b. A slower rate of growth during a growth cycle downswing than in an adjacent upswing is counted as an instance of positive conformity, the opposite as negative conformity. The number of positive instances minus the number of negative instances, divided by the total number, times 100, is the conformity index. It can range from +100 to −100.
c. Denominator of ratio is negative.

Table 7-2.   Changes in U.S. Exports and Imports during Growth Cycles: Annual Data (Annual changes in millions of dollars).

	Changes during Importing Country's Growth Cycle				Changes during Exporting Country's Growth Cycle			
	Period Covered	Upswings	Downswings	Conformity Index[b]	Period Covered	Upswings	Downswings	Conformity Index[b]
U.S. Exports to:								
Japan	1954–72	+393	–87	+100	1952–73	+285	+304	0
United Kingdom	1951–72	+176	+4	+100	1952–73	+184	–5	+67
West Germany	1952–73	+355	+38	+56	1951–73	+172	+67	+33
Canada	1950–70	+555	+86	+82	1951–73	+622	+10	+85
Total[a]		+386	+25	+83		+316	+91	+47
U.S. Imports from:								
Japan	1952–73	+485	+184	+83	1954–72	+258	+579	–75
United Kingdom	1952–73	+191	+1	+83	1951–72	+176	+90	0
West Germany	1951–73	+249	+118	+83	1952–73	+378	+179	+11
Canada	1951–73	+642	+287	+69	1950–70	+524	+376	+64
Total[a]		+392	+153	+80		+356	+252	+6

Notes:
a. Based on all available annual changes for the four countries.
b. See note (b) to Table 7-1.

tions are to the United States. Similar comments can be made about the three other countries covered in the table.

Annual export and import data, which extend further back than the monthly data used in Table 7-1, confirm and extend these findings (Table 7-2). The left-hand section of the table shows that U.S. trade with each of the four countries and with the four combined is greatly influenced by the state of the growth cycle in the importing country. The right-hand section, on the other hand, shows that conformity to the growth cycle in the exporting country is decidedly mixed. Where relations between growth cycles in the two trading countries are close, as in the case of the United States and Canada, good conformity of exports to the exporter's growth cycle may simply reflect the fact that the importer's and exporter's cycles are very similar.

In contrast, U.S. exports to Japan are unrelated to the U.S. growth cycle, whereas Japan's exports to the United States are inversely related to Japan's growth cycle. When the Japanese economy is growing rapidly, Japan imports more from the United States and exports less to the United States. During downswings in the Japanese growth rate, Japan imports less from the United States and exports more.

In short, we find that the volume of exports is clearly influenced by the state of the growth cycle in the *importing* country, but not consistently related to the state of the growth cycle in the *exporting* country. This no doubt reflects the complexity of the relationship between exports and the exporting country's business cycles: some countries, for example, are more dependent upon foreign trade than others. However, Table 7-2 does suggest that trade balances (exports minus imports) conform inversely to growth cycles in each of the four countries, due to the more rapid growth of imports during the upswing phase of the importing country's growth cycle.

Putting all these results together, it appears that growth cycles exert a powerful influence upon the volume of trade—a useful fact for trade analysis and all the more significant because consideration of trade flows played no part in the identification of growth cycle turning points.

THE USE OF LEADING INDICATORS IN FORECASTING CHANGES IN TRADE FLOWS

One of the implications of the above findings, in conjunction with those reported in earlier chapters, is that we should be able to utilize the leading indicators as an early-warning system to forecast changes in foreign trade flows. A country's demand for imports is likely to closely follow fluctuations in its domestic economic fortunes. Imported materials are used in domestic production, and imported finished goods are sold directly in domestic markets. The leading indicators include a number of factors pertaining to these demands for imports: orders placed for goods in the importing country; the accumulation or liquidation of inventories; marginal adjustments in the utilization of labor (e.g., by shortening or lengthening the workweek); prices paid for industrial materials; new commitments to invest in plants and equipment; and price/cost relations affecting profit margins. These are not the only elements bearing upon decisions to import, of course, but they are sufficiently important to have a significant relationship to import demand.

The leading indicators can be used either to forecast aggregate demand and the latter used to forecast imports, or they can be used to forecast imports directly. We have chosen the direct route in the experiments described below. The system can be applied to exports as well as to imports, provided the exports go to countries represented in the leading indexes. Hence, it can be used to obtain forecasts of trade balances among these countries.

The forecasts are limited in nature, since the leading indexes do not lead aggregate demand (or imports) by more than four to six months on the average. Nevertheless, the system can be used to forecast next year's trade at the end of the preceding year, and predict the rate of trade growth three or four quarters ahead of the latest available data.

Methodology

The variable we have chosen to illustrate the forecasting technique is the percentage change in U.S. exports. Forecasting change is more challenging than forecasting levels, because levels are often largely dominated by long-run trends. We have experimented with both annual and quarterly forecasts and report here on our efforts regarding manufactured goods exports as a whole and several commodity groups. Exports can be measured in terms of quantity, unit value, and total value, and we have experimented with forecasting all three. We shall concentrate on quantity forecasts. The forecasts themselves are generated by the percentage change in the leading index for the country (or countries) to which U.S. exports are going. The index is assumed to lead the flow of exports into the area under review by six months.

The percentage change in the leading index is the independent variable. For annual (calendar-year) forecasts, the six-month lead implies that changes in the leading index between fiscal years (years ending June 30, overlapping the calendar years by six months) are required. In order to make forecasts before the calendar year has begun (or rather, before data for any part of the calendar year are available), we assume that the fiscal year overlapping the calendar year to be forecast can be approximately represented by the December figure for the leading index. This is (approximately) the central month of the fiscal year. Thus, to forecast the percentage change in exports from year (1) to year (2) we may use the percentage change between the average value of the leading index for the fiscal year average ending June 30 of year (1) and its value in December of year (1). This measure is the twelve-month change, smoothed. An alternative, which we have come to employ more frequently, is the six-month change, smoothed. It consists of the percentage change in the index from an average of the twelve months immediately prior to the current month and hence is more up-to-date than the smoothed twelve-month change. No data for year (2) are employed in the forecast. We further assume a linear relationship between the percentage changes in exports and in the leading index. Our regressions are of the form:

$$\Delta Q_t = a + b \Delta LD_{-1}$$

where ΔQ_t is the percentage change in export quantity from year $(t-1)$ to year (t), and ΔLD_{-1} is the percentage change in the leading index between the fiscal-year average and December of year $(t-1)$. A simple adaptation of this scheme enables us to apply it to quarterly data.

Wherever we use composite leading indexes for several countries the indexes are usually weighted by the country's GNP in 1970, expressed in U.S. dollars. The broadest group includes the six largest countries considered in this book: Canada, the United Kingdom, West Germany, France, Italy, and Japan. These countries collectively took 51 percent of total U.S. exports in 1970, and 47 percent of U.S. manufactured goods exports. Another group includes only the four European countries in the above list. At various times we have employed export weights rather than GNP weights, but the difference in results is usually not substantial.

By means of this method we obtain an independent variable based on percentage changes in the leading indexes of U.S. trading partners and use it to forecast subsequent percentage changes in U.S. exports to these countries. The size and significance of the correlation coefficients and mean errors thereby constitute a measure of the success obtained by this simple forecasting technique.

We have not been able in all instances to match the geographic coverage of the export data with that of the leading indexes. Thus, we have used the composite leading index for four Western European countries to forecast exports to all Western European countries. Also, we have used the six-country composite index to forecast total U.S. exports to all countries. We experiment briefly as well with the reverse—forecasting the exports from several other countries. There is a possible source of error in these experiments, though the possibility is somewhat mitigated by the likelihood that some of the countries not covered by our leading indexes may experience cyclical movements similar to those that are covered.

In the remainder of this chapter we shall first examine the use of world imports as a way to forecast U.S. exports. Then we will show how leading indicators can be used to forecast (1) annual U.S. export quantities, (2) annual exports from other major market-oriented economies, (3) annual exports of selected U.S. manufacturing and commodity groups, (4) annual exports of developing countries to all countries, and (5) quarterly U.S. imports, exports, and trade balances.

USING WORLD IMPORTS TO FORECAST U.S. EXPORTS

One of the implications of Mintz's research was that if a way could be found to forecast world imports, it should provide useful forecasts of U.S. exports. To this end we have examined the relationship of world imports to U.S. exports in recent years to test Mintz's theory and the relationship between our leading index for six major industrial countries and world imports (excluding U.S. imports) to see whether, despite the limited geographic coverage of the leading index, it has some ability to forecast world imports.

Figure 7–1 (bottom panel) reveals that the close relation between changes in world imports and U.S. exports that Mintz found for 1881–1913 and for 1921–61 has persisted. The correlation (r^2) is 0.92 for 1955–75.[5] The middle panel of the figure shows that the prior changes in the six-country leading index are moderately related to world imports. The correlation (r^2) is 0.32 for 1957–75 and is statistically significant. Since 1962, however, the rate of change in world imports has always exceeded the rate of change in the leading index. One important reason for this is that the world import data are in current prices while the leading index is in physical units or constant prices. World inflation has increased the value of world imports since the 1960s. A rough allowance for this can be made by

Figure 7-1. Annual Percentage Changes in World Imports, U.S. Exports, and Six-Country Leading Index.

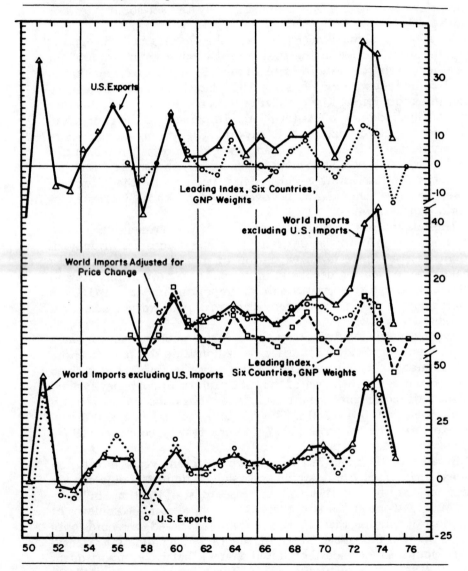

adjusting world imports for price changes, as shown by the dotted line in the middle panel.[6] With this adjustment, correlation with the prior changes in the leading index is increased (to 0.52), implying that about half the variance in the year-to-year changes in the volume of world imports is accounted for by the six-country leading index.

In the upper graph of Figure 7-1, the changes in U.S. exports and the prior change in the six-country leading index are brought together. Again, the rate of increase in U.S. exports exceeds that in the leading index every year since 1962, largely because of the inflation in export prices. The correlation (r^2) is 0.69, which means that the leading index accounts for nearly 70 percent of the variance in the year-to-year changes in U.S. exports. The leading index is more closely related to U.S. exports than to world imports.[7] Hence, in this section we shall use the leading index directly rather than as an instrument for forecasting world imports. Its value for the latter purpose, however, should not be overlooked by those interested in world trade as a whole.

The relation of the leading index to world trade can also be shown in another way. Mintz demonstrated that at certain times virtually all countries participate in an expansion of imports; at other times a majority experience a decline in imports. These proportions rise and fall in waves and these waves have an important impact on U.S. exports since they reflect a widening or narrowing of world demand for U.S. products.

Mintz constructed diffusion indexes, based on changes in the value of imports by individual countries, to demonstrate this phenomenon. The number of countries experiencing a rise in imports at a given time, taken as a percentage of the total number of countries covered by the data, constitutes the diffusion index. Her index covered thirty-four countries (1881-1939, 1949-53) using annual data; and thirty-five to forty-one countries (1947-53) and twenty countries (1954-61) using quarterly data.[8]

Because of the rapid rate of inflation in recent years, a diffusion index constructed from data on the value of imports would show a large majority of countries with increases most of the time. In bringing Mintz's work up to date, therefore, we have compiled indexes of the quantity, rather than the value, of imports based on records published by the Statistical Office of the United Nations for twenty-three countries (outside the United States) that issue import quantity indexes on a quarterly basis.[9] These countries imported 92 percent of the total imports of all countries outside the United States (and outside the centrally planned economies). Since the indexes are

Figure 7-2. Import Diffusion and Rates of Change in U.S. Exports and in Six-Country Leading Index.

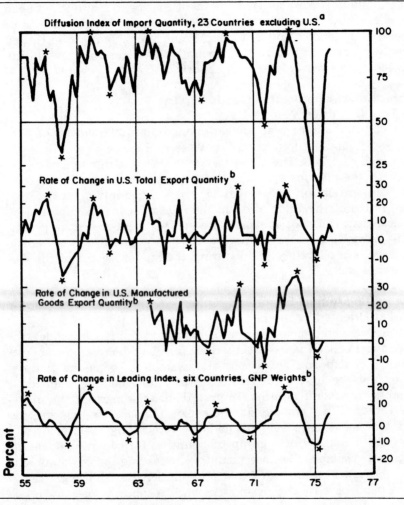

Notes:
a. Percentage of countries with rising import quantity over same quarter one year ago.
b. Percentage change from same quarter one year ago.

not adjusted for seasonal variations, we have measured changes over the same quarter a year ago. Figure 7-2 shows the diffusion index for import quantities from 1955 to 1976.

The rate of change in the U.S. export quantity over the same quarter a year ago is also shown in the figure. A high percentage of countries with rising imports is clearly good for U.S. exports, while a low percentage is associated with poor U.S. export performance. This is what the Mintz record showed for the earlier period, and it has been just as true since then. The figure's bottom graph shows the rate of change in the leading index for six countries excluding the United States, with clear cycles related to both the diffusion of world imports and the growth rate in U.S. exports.

Forecasting Manufactured Goods Exports to Four Countries: Annual Data

Forecast and actual year-to-year changes in total quantity of U.S. exports of manufactured goods to Western Europe as a whole are shown in Figure 7-3. The major swings in the rates of change in U.S. exports of these goods appear to be fairly well reflected in the forecasts. The correlation coefficient (r^2) is 0.73, implying that about three-fourths of the fluctuation in the rates of change is captured by the forecasts. The root mean square error is 5.6 percentage points. The fit seems to be best during the 1973-75 period, but the correspondence is moderately good during the milder swings of the earlier years as well.

Forecasting Annual Exports for Other Market-Oriented Economies

Earlier we noted that the rate of change in the leading index for six countries other than the United States could be related to cycles in total U.S. exports. This is but one example of a general finding: Leading indexes in general anticipate the movement in coincident indicators by several months. Import demand is part of the movement captured by coincident indicators. Hence, leading indexes ought to constitute a valuable aid for forecasting exports of any country to a country or a group of countries for which such leading indexes are available. Because a composite leading index comprising six of the larger countries of the ten considered in this book represents a good part of the developed world economy we have previously noted it can be utilized to forecast total exports of any country to the "world." Figures 7-4, 7-5 and 7-6, dealing with the exports of manufactured goods of the United Kingdom, West Germany, and Japan respectively, show that the technique works quite well in all these cases to forecast their exports. The lowest correlation coefficient is .69 (for Japan) indicating that no less than two-thirds of the fluctuations in exports can be captured in the fluctuations in the leading composite index for six major countries. That the method has limitations is clear. It does not include tariff changes, supply

Figure 7-3. Forecast and Actual Percent Changes in U.S. Exports of Manufactured Goods to Western Europe, Quantity, Using Leading Index for Four Countries,[a] 1964-76.

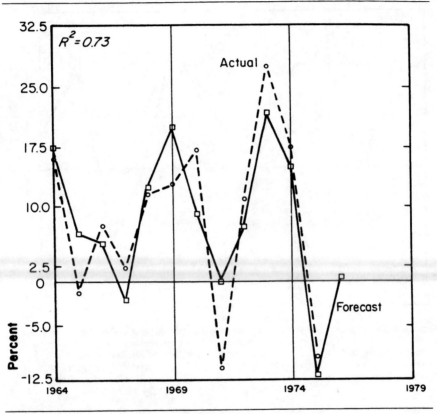

Note:
a. United Kingdom, West Germany, France, and Italy. GNP weights employed in composite leading index.

conditions, or pricing policy changes, for example. But it is useful, nonetheless.

Forecasting Exports from Developing Countries: Annual Data

A subject receiving increasing attention involves trade between developing and older industrialized market-oriented economies. Figure 7-7 illustrates that the forecasting technique under review can assist developing countries in assessing future trade with any

Figure 7-4. Forecast and Actual Percentage Changes in Quantity of United Kingdom Exports of Manufactured Goods to Six Countries, 1965-77.

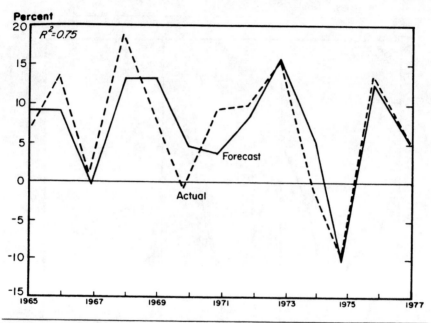

Note:
Forecasts are based on the percentage change in the leading index for six countries, weighted by U.K. exports, over the six months preceding the forecast year. The six countries and the U.K. export weights (1970) are: United States (.378), Canada (.117), West Germany (.205), France (.141), Italy (.098), Japan (.061). The regression equation (and t statistics) is: $\Delta E = 2.6 + 2.4 \ \Delta Ld$, fitted to 1965-76.   (1.7) (5.5)

country for which leading indicators have been constructed. Using the six major market-oriented economies to approximate the world trade of the developing economies, we can account for over 60 percent of the changes in the export trade of developing countries during the period 1964-77. The fit is better in the 1960s than in the 1970s, although the forecast clearly reflected the actual changes associated with the 1973-75 recession.

Forecasting U.S. Manufactured Goods Exports: Quarterly Data

We have utilized the general method illustrated above in a variety of tests. In one group we attempted to forecast the change in U.S. exports of several products to the world. The results are summarized

Figure 7-5. Forecast and Actual Percentage Changes in Quantity of West German Exports of Manufactured Goods to All Countries, 1965–77.

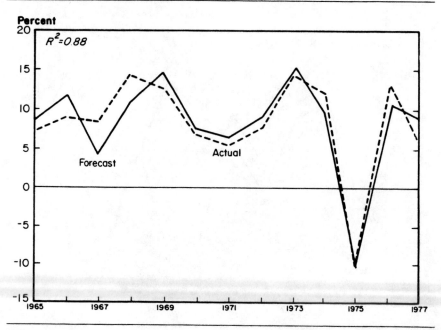

Note:

Forecasts are based on the percentage change in the leading index for six countries, weighted by West German exports, over the six months preceding the forecast year. The six countries and the West German export weights (1970) are: United States (.250), Canada (.026), United Kingdom (.098), France (.339), Italy (.244), Japan (.043). The regression equation (and t statistics) is: $\Delta E =$ 4.6 + 2.4 ΔLd, fitted to 1965–76.
(5.0) (8.6)

in Table 7-3 and suggest that the leading indexes can indeed be applied to forecasting trade in specific products six months ahead. Not only can the method be applied on an annual basis to individual commodities, it can also be adapted, as suggested earlier, to forecasting with greater continuity by using quarterly data. Figure 7–8 depicts the quantity of U.S. manufactured goods being exported. Recall that the change in the leading index between its average for a fiscal year and the figure for the following December is used to forecast calendar-year changes in exports, which are equivalent to changes in four-quarter averages four quarters apart. Where quarterly data are available these averages can be moved forward one quarter at a time, thereby bringing them more nearly up to date. Similarly, the changes

Figure 7-6.   Forecast and Actual Percentage Changes in Quantity of
Japanese Exports of Manufactured Goods to All Countries, 1965-77.

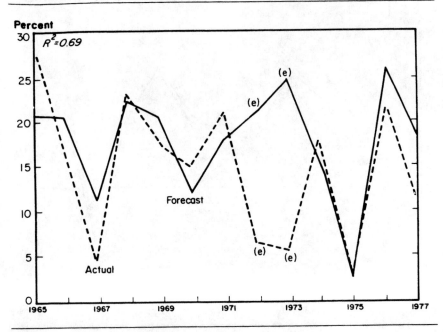

Note:
Forecasts are based on the percentage change in the leading index for six countries, weighted by Japanese exports, over the six months preceding the forecast
year. The six countries and the Japanese export weights (1970) are: United
States (.769), Canada (.071), United Kingdom (.061), West Germany (.069),
France (.016), Italy (.024). The regression omits 1972 and 1973 (marked e),
which were seriously affected by the dollar devaluation. The regression equation
(and t statistics) is: $\Delta E = 15.4 + 1.8 \, \Delta Ld$, fitted to 1965-76.
$$(9.7) \ (4.3)$$

Table 7-3.   Correlation of Forecast and Actual Changes in U.S. Exports
of Individual Commodities to All Countries, Using Leading Index for Six
Countries, GNP Weights.[a]

Product	r^2
Chemicals (SITC 5)	0.76
Textiles (SITC 6)	0.81
Machinery and Transportation Equipment (SITC 7)	0.53
Miscellaneous Manufactures (SITC 8)	0.68

Note:
a. Canada, United Kingdom, West Germany, France, Italy, and Japan.

Figure 7-7. Forecast and Actual Percent Changes in Quantity of Exports of Developing Market Economies to All Countries, 1964–77.

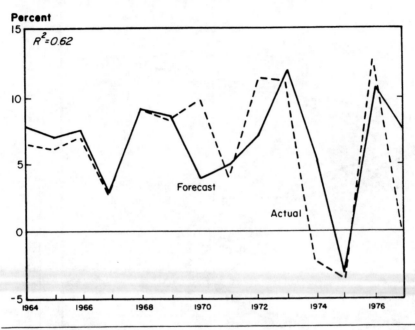

Note:
Forecasts are based on the percentage change in the leading index for seven countries, weighted by GNP weights, over the six months preceding the forecast year. The seven countries are: United States, Canada, United Kingdom, West Germany, France, Italy, Japan. The regression equation (and t statistics) is:
$\Delta E = 4.2 + 0.6\, \Delta Ld$, fitted to 1964–76.
  (3.9) (4.1)

in the leading index can be moved forward three months at a time so the forecasts are more up to date as well.[10]

All the data shown in Figure 7-8 are rates of change over four-quarter intervals. The dotted line is the usual four-quarter change (i.e., change from same quarter a year ago), plotted in the terminal quarter of the span. These rates exhibit considerable erratic movement, since the end points are only one quarter long. When the end points are four quarters long, as in the scheme described, the rates of change are much smoother. This is shown by the solid line. Here the rates are plotted in the second quarter of the second of the two four-quarter periods compared. For example, the change from calendar-year 1963 to calendar-year 1964 is plotted in 1964.2. This is the

Figure 7–8. Quarterly Forecast and Actual Percent Changes, U.S. Exports of Manufactured Goods, Quantity.

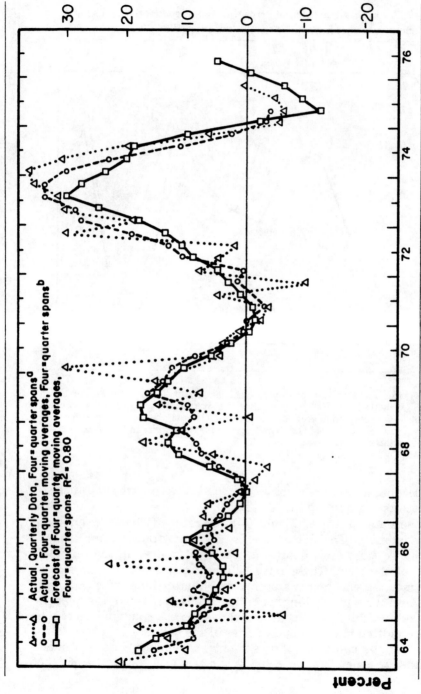

△⋯⋯△ Actual, Quarterly Data, Four-quarter spans[a]
○—○ Actual, Four-quarter moving averages, Four-quarter spans[b]
□ Forecast of Four-quarter moving averages,
Four-quarter spans R[2] = 0.80

Notes: Forecasts are based on six-country leading index, GNP weights.
a. Plotted in terminal quarter.
b. Plotted in second quarter of terminal year.

same point at which the change from 1963.2 to 1964.2 (dotted line) is plotted.

The dash line in the figure is what we attempt to forecast. The line with hollow, square points is the forecast, based on the leading index for six countries. It traces the major swings in the rate of growth of manufactured goods export quantities with considerable fidelity and identifies the cyclical peaks and troughs in these rates at about the time they occurred. The value of r^2 is 0.80 and the root mean square error is 4.3 percent.[11]

We have not carried the experiments with quarterly forecasts any further, but it is clear that forecasting exports by means of a leading index for one's export partners is eminently feasible and can be carried out both annually and with quarterly data. Much testing remains to be done.

Applications of the technique can be extended in several ways. One of the ultimate objectives of our research is to use the leading indexes to forecast trade flows in both directions and, hence, to forecast the trade balance. This can be done on a bilateral or multilateral basis. The former has the advantage in that pairs of countries can be chosen for both of which leading indexes are available. The latter has the advantage of comprehensiveness and broader interest. For the present we have chosen the multilateral approach, and have used the export and import data from the U.S. national accounts. These are available quarterly, seasonally adjusted, in constant (1972) dollars. To forecast the rate of change in import quantity we use the U.S. leading index. To forecast the rate of change in export quantity we use the leading index for six countries (excluding the United States).

Treating these data in the manner described above, we find that for the period 1968–76 the percentage change in exports is forecast with an r^2 of 0.72; the corresponding r^2 for imports is 0.59. Figures 7–9 and 7–10 show the actual and forecast rates of change during the sample period as well as before (1956–68) and after (1976–79). The cyclical swings are fairly well represented outside the sample period, but the errors of estimate are clearly much greater.

The forecast percentage changes can readily be translated into changes in billions of 1972 dollars by multiplying by the actual levels for the preceding year. Subtracting the forecast change in imports from the forecast change in exports yields the forecast change in net exports (Figure 7–11). Again, the cyclical swings are moderately well represented, both within and outside the sample period, but the r^2 is only 0.47 for the sample period and 0.31 for the entire period 1958–78.

Figure 7-9. Actual and Forecast Rates of Change in U.S. Exports of Goods and Services (in 1972 $), 1956-78.

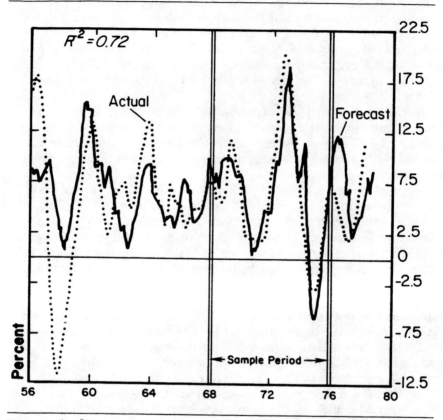

Note:
Percent change in exports is computed from four-quarter moving averages one year apart, placed in the 5th month of the second year. Forecasts are based upon percent change in leading index for six countries (Canada, United Kingdom, West Germany, France, Italy, Japan), during last six months prior to year being forecast (smoothed). Regression fitted to 1968-76.
Source: Center for International Business Cycle Research, July 1979.

We can use the forecast changes to estimate the *level* of net exports in the year ahead. As in most regressions, the closeness of fit to the levels is markedly better than to the changes, with an r^2 of 0.81 over the sample period and 0.67 over the entire period (Figure 7-12). Since the cyclical movements in the level of net exports are large, this result is rather impressive, although there is some tendency for the forecasts to lag behind the actual data.

Figure 7-10. Actual and Forecast Rates of Change in U.S. Imports of Goods and Services (in 1972 $), 1956-78.

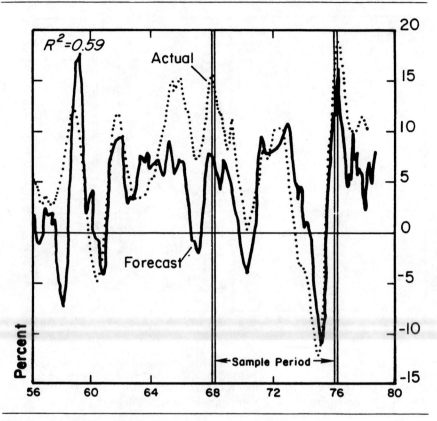

Note:

Percent change in imports is computed from four-quarter moving averages one year apart, placed in the 5th month of the second year. Forecasts are based upon percent change in U.S. leading index during the last six months prior to year being forecast (smoothed). Regression fitted to 1968-76.

Source: Center for International Business Cycle Research, July 1979.

CONCLUSIONS

Although modern market-oriented economies are clearly interrelated by much more than their trade relations, the possibility that instability can be transmitted from one economy to another via trade has long been recognized. Our consideration of this idea in the light of the growth cycle chronologies suggests that while trade is clearly a major link among market-oriented economies, no single factor can

Figure 7-11.   Actual and Forecast Changes in U.S. Net Exports of Goods and Services (in 1972 $), 1957-78.

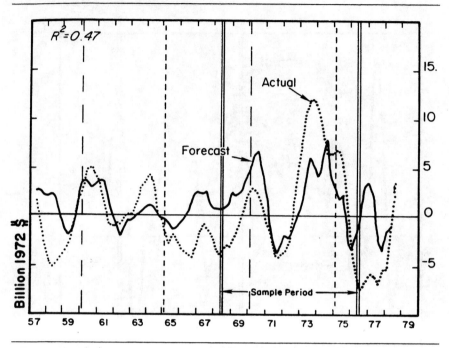

Note:
Actual change in net exports is computed from four-quarter moving totals one year apart, placed in 5th month of second year. Forecast change is derived from forecast change in exports minus forecast change in imports.
Source: Center for International Business Cycle Research, July 1979.

serve adequately to explain the international path of instability. While during much of the postwar period growth cycles have been relatively synchronous (an observation made in Chapter 6), no country in our survey consistently turns down or up first. We have concluded, therefore, that the notion that cyclical disturbances invariably begin in the United States and subsequently spread to other economies, often in exacerbated form, is not borne out by the evidence. There have, of course, been peaks in U.S. growth cycles that preceded those in other economies, but there have also been times when this was not the case. We earlier established the fact that the United States has traditionally experienced more recessions than most other economies, and this alone would suggest that there must be factors that enable other economies to continue to expand, or at least to maintain previous levels during U.S. contractions. We have

Figure 7–12. Actual and Forecast Levels of U.S. Net Exports of Goods and Services (in 1972 $), 1957–78.

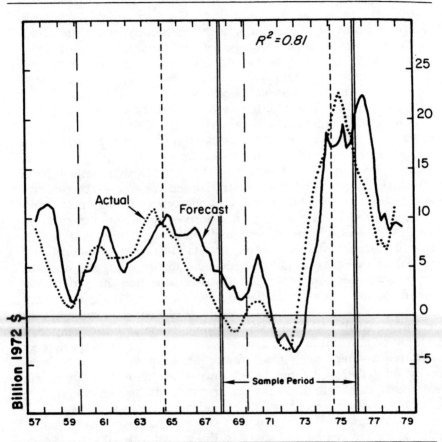

Note:
Actual levels of net exports are four-quarter moving averages, placed in the 5th month of the year. Forecast levels are derived from forecast changes.
Source: Center for International Business Cycle Research, July 1979.

seen as well that there are instances where other economies turned down first (frequently West Germany) or produced cycles not clearly related to U.S. cycles (in Japan, for example).

If the relationships are not simple, or exclusively determined by trade, it is nevertheless true that trade is very much affected by the state of growth cycles, and that both growth cycles and trade flows can be forecast by leading indicators.

The tests described in the preceding sections of this chapter suggest that annual forecasts of exports, imports, and the trade balance using leading indexes can account for about half the variance in the year-to-year changes in these variables. When we employ quarterly data, we find that we can account for as much or slightly more of the variance, but when we subtract the forecast changes in imports from the forecast changes in exports to obtain the trade balance the percentage of variance explained falls to well below one-half, although the cycles still show up reasonably clearly.

Much of the investigation reported here has been limited to simple, two-variable regressions between the physical volume of trade flowing to a country and a composite leading index pertaining to economic activity in one or more countries as it impinges on that country. The independent variable often used in this connection is the income or output of the country, which is supposed to generate demand for imports. Our view is that the types of economic activities represented by the leading indicators—capital investment commitments, inventory investment and purchasing, marginal adjustments in the demand for labor, profitability, and monetary and financial flows—likewise generate demand for imports, and do so at a prior date. New orders for goods usually antedate the production of goods or the income that the production generates. The accumulation of goods in inventories often precedes their sale or use in production, especially when prices are rising. These activities may lead to an increase in imports. A favorable environment for imports may also develop when the outlook for profits improves, when credit is readily available, and when confidence that these conditions will continue is high. All these factors are included among the leading indicators from which our composite indexes are constructed.

It is therefore not surprising that the regressions perform moderately well in forecasting changes in the growth rate of trade flows, both during the period to which they are fitted and outside that period. Obviously, we have not developed a complete forecasting model. The regressions take no direct account of the influence of other factors on the physical volume of trade, such as the prices of imported or exported goods and exchange rates. The unexplained portion of the variance in the growth of trade is not negligible. On the other hand, the forecasts developed in this chapter obviously are superior to a naive "no change" forecast, and the fact that they correlate significantly with the actual changes shows that they are also superior to a naive forecast based on a constant rate of growth (which would *not* be correlated with the actual changes). Forecasts made by practitioners in this field do not always fare well against such standards. As an *Economic Report of the President* (January 1976) stated, the U.S. trade balance has "proved extremely difficult to forecast," and this has increased the difficulty of forecasting gross national product, since net exports are a highly variable constituent thereof. An appraisal of trade balance forecasts over semi-annual intervals during the period 1967–73 concluded that for most countries the forecasts were no better than those generated by a naive "no change" model.[12]

Although we have explored a number of possibilities for forecasting changes in trade flow using leading indexes, we have by no means exhausted the field. For example, focusing attention on the United States, one could attempt to forecast imports in as much detail, by country of origin, or type of commodity, as has been attempted here for exports. The forecasting errors involved in both exports and imports could be carefully examined to see whether they are related to other factors such as the competitive position of the United States vis-à-vis other economies, changes in exchange rates, and so forth.[13] Comparisons with other forecasting models could be extended in order to determine more precisely why the leading indicators technique sometimes works well and why at other times it does not. The focus could obviously be switched from the United States to any one of the other countries involved in the trade forecasts of this chapter. Indeed, since the exports of many of the developing countries are destined for one or another of the major industrial countries for which we have leading indicators, the latter's capacity to forecast the demand for the developing countries' exports could be explored further. Another area for study is the use of particular leading indicators instead of composite indexes as the forecasting instrument. Finally, the work on quarterly forecasting introduced in this discussion could be extended in many directions.

These various lines of research would require far more resources than we have been able to devote to this subject. What has already been done, however, seems sufficient to substantiate the conclusion that the use of composite leading indexes in forecasting changes in a country's trade position offers a useful new adjunct to currently available ways of forecasting changes in international trade relations. It is illustrative of the variety of uses that, we trust, will be found for the emerging system of international economic indicators.

NOTES TO CHAPTER 7

1. Princeton University Press for the National Bureau of Economic Research.

2. Ilse Mintz, *Trade Balances during Business Cycles: U.S. and Britain since 1880*, Occasional Paper No. 67 (New York: NBER, 1959); *American Exports during Business Cycles, 1879-1958*, Occasional Paper No. 76 (New York: NBER, 1961); *Cyclical Fluctuations in the Exports of the United States since 1879* (New York: NBER, 1967). Note especially the justification for using world imports rather than world income, and for excluding U.S. imports but not U.S. exports from the world total in these works.

3. These findings are in general conformity with Mintz's studies cited in note 2. They are also consistent with results reported by Arthur B. Laffer, "The Trade Balance and Economic Activity," October 28, 1974. (Unpublished.)

4. Conformity indexes relating U.S. exports to foreign growth cycles (see last column of Part A, Table 7-1) are all positive and high. Indexes relating U.S. exports to U.S. growth cycles range from negative to positive: Japan, -50; United Kingdom, +50; West Germany, -25; and Canada, +100. The high positive index for Canada no doubt reflects the close relationship between U.S. and Canadian growth cycles. Cf. also Table 7-2. The evidence on which these findings are based, presented country by country and cycle by cycle, is in Philip A. Klein, *Business Cycles in the Postwar World: Some Reflections on Recent Research* (Washington, D.C.: American Enterprise Institute, 1976) Sec. 3, pp. 37-39.

5. For U.S. exports of manufactured goods, 1957-75, the correlation with total world imports is about the same, 0.87.

6. The allowance is approximate, because we use the unit value of total world imports to adjust the value of world imports excluding U.S. imports.

7. The six countries took 51 percent of U.S. exports in 1970, and accounted for 47 percent of world imports (excluding U.S. imports) in the same year. The difference does not seem to be large enough to explain the better correlation with U.S. exports.

8. Ilse Mintz, *Trade Balances during Business Cycles: U.S. and Britain since 1880*, Occasional Paper No. 67 (New York: NBER, 1969), pp. 68-69; *Tested Knowledge of Business Cycles*, 42nd Annual Report of the National Bureau of Economic Research (June 1962), p. 8.

.9. All countries with quarterly indexes of import quantities were included provided they imported at least 0.5 percent of total world imports (excluding the United States) in 1972.

10. The method has several virtues. It makes the rate of change in the exports relatively smooth, and the four-quarter moving-average technique tends to accentuate cyclical rather than irregular movements. It is also possible to vary the assumed lag between the leading index and the trade variable being forecast. While we have assumed a six-month lag in the examples in this chapter because it is reasonably satisfactory, it may very well be more appropriate in specific cases to assume other lags.

11. This is approximately the same result as for the annual (calendar-year) forecasts (r^2 = 0.81), as indeed it should be, since the data for every fourth observation are the same as those used in the calendar-year forecasts.

12. D. J. Smyth and J. C. K. Ash, "Forecasting GNP, Rate of Inflation, and Balance of Trade: OECD Performance," *The Economic Journal* 85, no. 338 (June 1975): 361-64.

13. In a recent study prior movements in both the leading indexes and exchange rates were found to be important. See "Forecasting Export Markets for U.S. Manufactured Goods," Center for International Business Cycle Research, Columbia University, January 1984, unpublished.

Chapter 8

MONITORING INFLATION RATES
DURING GROWTH CYCLES

There is no economic problem more widely discussed and more perplexing for policymakers in modern market-oriented economies than
bringing down inflation rates. For many years and in many countries
inflation rates have appeared to be impervious to efforts aimed at
reducing them. Some indication of the variety of experience in different countries is provided by Table 8–1. The first two columns
show the long-run tendency, while the third column shows the rate
of inflation in a short period in the recent past.

Economists have speculated at length over the differences in inflation rates of modern economies. Here we are concerned with the relation between inflation and growth cycle experience. Inflation rates

Table 8–1. Inflation Rates in Seven Market-Oriented Economies.

| Country | *Consumer Price Index* | | |
	Index, *December 1982* *(1967 = 100)*	*Annual Rate,* *1967 to* *December 1982*	*Change Over* *12 Months,* *December 1982*
United States	292.4	7.2	3.9
Japan	306.0	7.5	2.1
West Germany	199.4	4.6	4.6
United Kingdom	522.9	11.3	5.4
France	386.4	9.1	9.7
Italy	594.4	12.1	16.3
Canada	313.4	7.6	9.3

Source: *Business Conditions Digest*, Dept. of Commerce (May 1983): 95–96.

Table 8-2. Inflation Rate Cycles in Seven Market-Oriented Economies vs. the United States, 1949-80.

Part A. Inflation Rate Cycles[a]

United States		West Germany		Italy		France		United Kingdom		Japan		Canada	
P	T	P	T	P	T	P	T	P	T	P	T	P	T
2/51	7/49	6/51	3/50	4/51	3/50	6/51	8/49	8/51	n.m.[b]	3/51	4/50		2/50
10/53	3/53	n.m.	11/53	7/54	9/53	n.m.	n.m.	n.m.	n.m.	10/53	10/52	8/54	10/52
8/57	10/54	3/56	n.m.	5/58	5/57	3/58	11/53	11/55	1/54	7/57	12/54	12/56	7/55
10/59	3/59	n.m.	5/59	n.m.	4/59	n.m.	n.m.	n.m.	7/59	2/60	3/58	n.m.	n.m.
10/66	6/61	10/65	n.m.	2/63	n.m.	6/62	6/61	4/65	n.m.	4/65	11/60	n.m.	10/61
2/70	5/67	n.m.	12/67	n.m.	9/68	3/69	7/67	6/71	10/67	7/69	7/67	6/69	n.m.
10/74	6/72	12/73	n.m.	10/74	n.m.	7/74	1/71	6/75	4/72	2/74	4/72	12/74	12/70
3/80	6/76	5/80	9/78	2/80	9/75	3/80	1/78	4/80	5/78	6/80	8/75	6/81	8/76

Part B.   Lead (–) or Lag (+), in Months, at U.S. Inflation Rate Turns

United States Inflation Rate Chronology		West Germany		Italy		France		United Kingdom		Japan		Canada	
P	T	P	T	P	T	P	T	P	T	P	T	P	T
	7/49	+4	+8	+2	+11	+4	+1	+6	n.m.	+1	+9	+1	+7
2/51	3/53	n.m.	n.m.	+9	+6	n.m.	n.m.	n.m.	n.m.	0	-5	+10	-5
10/54	8/57	-17	-11	+9	+31	+7	-9	-21	-9	-1	+2	-8	+9
3/59	10/59	n.m.	+2	n.m.	+1	n.m.	n.m.	n.m.	+4	+4	-12	n.m.	n.m.
6/61	5/67	-12	n.m.	-41	n.m.	-52	0	-18	n.m.	-18	-7	n.m.	+4
2/70	6/72	n.m.	+7	n.m.	+16	n.m.	+2	-11	+5	+16	+2	-8	n.m.
10/74	6/76	-10	n.m.	0	n.m.	-3	-17	-8	-2	-8	-2	+2	-18
3/80		+2	+27	-1	-9	0	+19	+1	+23	+3	-10	+15	+2
Mean at:													
P		-7		-4		-9		-8		0		+2	
T			+7		+9		-1		+4		-3		0
P + T		0		+3		-4		-3		-2		+1	
Median at:													
P		-10		+1		0		-10		0		+2	
T			+7		+9		+1		+4		-4		+3
P + T		+2		+4		0		-2		0		+2	

Notes:
a. Based on turning points in the rate of change in the consumer price index.
b. n.m. = No matching turn.

may be analyzed for evidence of cyclical behavior, which can be related to growth cycle turns, in precisely the same way that the other variables we have considered can be studied. We have chosen to measure inflation rates by examining the movements in the consumer price index for seven countries, and the results of this analysis are summarized in Table 8-2.

We shall turn our attention to the relationship between real growth cycles and inflation rate cycles in each country shortly, but before doing so it is useful to compare the timing of turns in the inflation rates for other countries to turns in the U.S. inflation rate cycles, just as we did with respect to growth cycles in Chapter 6. The evidence is shown in Part B of Table 8-2. If it is difficult to argue convincingly that any one country consistently leads other countries into or out of real growth cycles, it is equally difficult to prove that inflation rates move earlier in one country than in another. One might expect the Common Market countries to influence one another's inflation rates more strongly than any influence from the United States. But the evidence in the table does not support this notion very strongly.

Indeed, the table suggests that no particular country invariably initiates inflationary outbursts or retreats from such outbursts. If we compare the turning points in inflation rate cycles for any particular country with those of the United States, we find great variation in the timing of both peaks and troughs.

In the general frustration over unacceptably high inflation rates in recent years, it is easy to overlook the fact that inflation rates themselves are cyclical. It is possible to examine these cycles in inflation rates in much the same way we considered cycles in indicators of instability. In Figure 8-1 and Tables 8-3 to 8-9 we compare inflation rate cycles with the growth cycle chronologies developed in earlier chapters. The evidence shows that reductions in inflation rates have continued to occur in the 1970s, and that these reductions have almost always been associated with growth recessions.

Taking the seven countries as a group, there have been a total of forty-six growth recessions since 1950, and there have been thirty-six periods during which inflation rates fell. Only two reductions in inflation rates were not accompanied by growth recessions. Inflation rates usually began falling after the onset of recession.

In the United States there have been nine declines in the inflation rate since 1948 and each has been accompanied by a growth recession (Table 8-3). Only twice during this period did the decline in inflation rate precede the onset of recession. During the 1962-64 growth recession there was no decline in inflation. The actual infla-

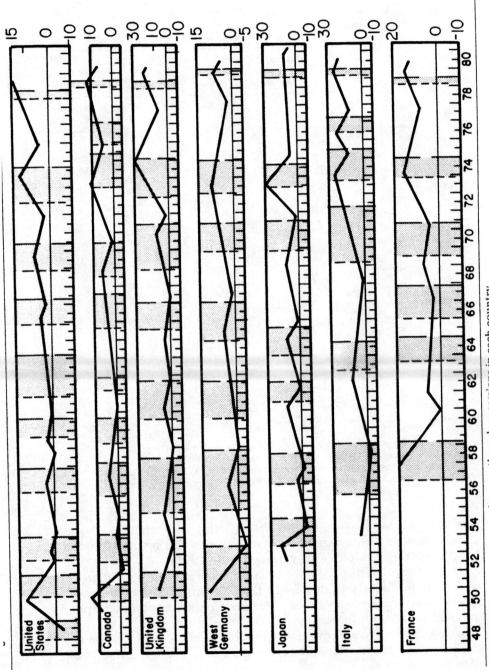

Note: Shaded areas represent the growth cycle recessions in each country.

Table 8-3. United States, Behavior of Inflation at Growth Cycle Turns.

Date of Growth Cycle[a]		Rate of Change in Consumer Price Index[b]			
		Date of Turn and Lead (−) or Lag (+), in Months		Percentage Rate at Inflation	
Peak (1)	Trough	Peak (2)	Trough	Peak (3)	Trough
7/48					
	10/49		7/49 (−3)		−3.1
3/51		2/51 (−1)		12.8	
	7/52		3/53 (+8)		0.2
3/53		10/53 (+7)		1.7	
	8/54		10/54 (+2)		−1.2
2/57		8/57 (+7)		3.7	
	4/58		3/59 (+11)		0.2
2/60		10/59 (−4)		1.9	
	2/61		6/61 (+4)		0.6
5/62		n.m.[c]		—	
	10/64		n.m.		—
6/66		10/66 (+4)		4.0	
	10/67		5/67 (−5)		2.1
3/69		2/70 (+11)		6.3	
	11/70		6/72 (+19)		2.9
3/73		9/74 (+18)		12.4	
	3/75		6/76 (+15)		4.9
12/78		3/80 (+15)		15.2	

Average Timing at:

P		+7 mos.		+7.2%	
T			+5 mos.		+0.8%
P + T			+6 mos.	+4.0%	

Notes:
a. Based on the consensus of turning points in trend-adjusted data for selected measures of aggregate output, income, sales, and employment.
b. Change over six months, smoothed (not centered). Centering the rates would increase the leads by three months and reduce the lags by three months.
c. n.m. = No matching turn.

tion rate was negative at two of the inflation rate troughs. The top U.S. inflation rates remained relatively modest during the 1950s and 1960s but attained double-digit levels in the 1970s.

There is greater disparity between inflation rate cycles and growth recessions in Canada (Table 8-4) than for any other country considered here. A number of recessions occurred without a corresponding decline in the inflation rate. Nevertheless, the average lag of the inflation rate at growth cycle turns is about the same in Canada as in the United States, and the average size of the swings in inflation also have been about the same.

Table 8-4. Canada, Behavior of Inflation at Growth Cycle Turns.

Date of Growth Cycle[a]		Rate of Change in Consumer Price Index[b]			
		Date of Turn and Lead (−) or Lag (+), in Months		Percentage Rate at Inflation	
Peak	Trough	Peak	Trough	Peak	Trough
(1)		(2)		(3)	
4/51		4/51 (0)		13.3	
	12/51		12/52 (+12)		−1.9
3/53		8/54 (+17)		1.3	
	10/54		7/55 (+9)		0.0
11/56		11/56 (0)		3.9	
	8/58		n.m.		—
10/59		n.m.[c]		—	
	3/61		10/61 (+8)		0.0
3/62		n.m.		—	
	5/63		n.m.		—
3/66		n.m.		—	
	2/68		n.m.		—
2/69		6/69 (+4)		5.8	
	12/70		12/70 (0)		0.9
2/74		12/74 (+10)		12.3	
	10/75		n.m.		—
5/76		n.m.		—	
	7/77		8/76 (−11)		5.5
9/79		n.m.		—	
	6/80		n.m.		—

Average Timing at:
P		+6 mos.		+7.3%	
T			+4 mos.		+0.9%
P + T		+5 mos.		+4.1%	

Notes:
a. Based on the consensus of turning points in trend-adjusted data for selected measures of aggregate output, income, sales, and employment.
b. Change over six months, smoothed (not centered). Centering the rates would increase the leads by three months and reduce the lags by three months.
c. n.m. = No matching turn.

In the United Kingdom (Table 8-5), as in the United States, inflation rate declines normally follow growth recessions, although there was a decline in inflation in 1976 (see Figure 8-1) unaccompanied by recession. There were also two inflation rate declines that preceded the onset of recession, although in general recessions preceded inflation rate declines. Inflation rates, moreover, continued to decline for more than a year after an upturn in the growth cycle. The inflation rates themselves are highly cyclical, rising to far higher levels at peaks than in the United States.

Table 8-5.   United Kingdom, Behavior of Inflation at Growth Cycle Turns.

Date of Growth Cycle[a]		Rate of Change in Consumer Price Index[b]			
		Date of Turn and Lead (−) or Lag (+), in Months		Percentage Rate at Inflation	
Peak (1)	Trough	Peak (2)	Trough	Peak (3)	Trough
3/51		8/51 (+6)		13.8	
	8/52		1/54 (+17)		0.3
12/55		11/55 (−1)		7.6	
	11/58		7/59 (+8)		0.0
3/61		8/61 (+6)		6.3	
	2/63		7/63 (+5)		0.6
2/66		4/65 (−10)		5.6	
	8/67		10/67 (+2)		0.7
6/69		6/71 (+24)		10.6	
	2/72		4/72 (+2)		4.7
6/73		6/75 (+24)		30.1	
	8/75		5/78 (+33)		7.0
6/79		4/80 (+10)		20.8	

Average Timing at:
P		+8 mos		+13.5%	
T			+11 mos.		+2.2%
P + T		+10 mos.		+8.3%	

Notes:
a. Based on the consensus of turning points in trend-adjusted data for selected measures of aggregate output, income, sales, and employment.
b. Change over six months, smoothed (not centered). Centering the rates would increase the leads by three months and reduce the lags by three months.

In West Germany (Table 8-6), where perhaps the memory of the staggering inflation levels of the 1920s has been instrumental in motivating policies to keep inflation down, a reduction in inflation accompanied five of the seven recessions. Recoveries from recessions were also usually accompanied within a short time by a renewed rise in inflation. The peak inflation rates were modest compared to the other countries considered here, with the trough rates either negative or very low.

In Japan (Table 8-7) all the reductions in the inflation rate were accompanied by growth recessions. Here, however, we note that peaks of the inflation rate cycles often preceded the onset of growth recessions, and in half of the recoveries the inflation rate began to rise before the growth cycle turned around. The Japanese inflation rates at cyclical peaks were high in comparison to other countries, but the declines from peak to trough were large.

Table 8-6. West Germany, Behavior of Inflation at Growth Cycle Turns.

Date of Growth Cycle[a]		Rate of Change in Consumer Price Index[b]			
		Date of Turn and Lead (−) or Lag (+) in Months		Percentage Rate at Inflation	
Peak (1)	Trough	Peak (2)	Trough	Peak (3)	Trough
2/51		6/51 (+4)		12.4	
	2/54		11/53 (−3)		−3.2
10/55		4/56 (+6)		3.7	
	4/59		5/59 (+1)		−0.2
2/61		n.m.[c]		—	
	2/63		n.m.		—
5/65		10/65 (+5)		4.6	
	8/67		12/67 (+4)		0.6
5/70		n.m.		—	
	12/71		n.m.		—
8/73		12/73 (+4)		8.5	
	5/75		10/78 (+41)		2.1
2/80		5/80		6.0	

Average Timing at:

P		+5 mos.		+7.0%	
T			+11 mos.		−0.2%
P + T		+8 mos.		4.3%	

Notes:
a. Based on the consensus of turning points in trend-adjusted data for selected measures of aggregate output, income, sales, and employment.
b. Change over six months, smoothed (not centered). Centering the rates would increase the leads by three months and reduce the lags by three months.
c. n.m. = No matching turn.

In Italy (Table 8-8) the inflation rate/growth cycle relationship is similar to the pattern found in other countries except that there was one recession—the rather lengthy one from late 1969 to September 1972—during which the inflation rate continued to rise. There were no declines in inflation rate unaccompanied by a growth recession. A decline in inflation either coincided with or preceded a growth recession in every case but one. The tenacity of Italian inflation rate difficulties can be seen in the high rates attained at peaks and the high (if somewhat lower) rates at inflation cycle troughs since the mid-1970s.

France, like Canada, provides an example in 1965-66 of a growth cycle expansion without a matching rise in the inflation rate (Table 8-9). On the whole, however, the correspondence between growth cycles and inflation in France resembles experience elsewhere. Growth recessions and declines in inflation match. At turning points leads have occurred about as frequently as lags.

Table 8-7. Japan, Behavior of Inflation at Growth Cycle Turns.

Date of Growth Cycle [a]		Rate of Change in Consumer Price Index [b]			
		Date of Turn and Lead (–) or Lag (+), in Months		Percentage Rate at Inflation	
Peak (1)	Trough	Peak	Trough (2)	Peak	Trough (3)
12/53		10/53 (–2)		18.1	
	6/55		12/54 (–6)		–3.2
5/57		7/57 (–2)		5.4	
	1/59		3/58 (–10)		–1.2
1/62		11/61 (–2)		10.2	
	1/63		9/62 (–4)		2.7
7/64		4/65 (+9)		10.0	
	2/66		6/67 (+17)		1.5
6/70		7/69 (–11)		9.8	
	1/72		4/72 (+3)		3.5
11/73		2/74 (+3)		30.0	
	3/75		8/75 (+5)		7.9
2/80		6/80 (+4)		9.2	

Average Timing at:

P		0 mos.		+13.2%	
T			+1 mo.		+1.9%
P + T			0 mos.		+8.0%

Notes:

a. Based on the consensus of turning points in trend-adjusted data for selected measures of aggregate output, income, sales, and employment.

b. Change over six months, smoothed (not centered). Centering the rates would increase the leads by three months and reduce the lags by three months.

The record for the seven countries as a group, therefore, establishes a close association between growth cycles and inflation (see Figure 8-1). Altogether 98 growth cycle peaks and troughs occurred in the seven countries, and at 78 of these, or 80 percent, there was a matching turn in the inflation rate. In 51 instances the inflation turn occurred after the growth cycle turn. In 5 instances the turns coincided, while in 22 the inflation turn occurred first. Inflation lagged the growth cycle more than twice as often as it led. Slow growth has been conducive to slower inflation, rapid growth to faster inflation.

This relationship is well founded in the theory underlying business cycle indicators reviewed in Chapter 1. Periods of rapid growth produce conditions that lead to rising rates of inflation, while periods of slow growth have the opposite effect. When ordering is brisk and order backlogs accumulate, sellers have more opportunities and incentives to raise prices, and buyers are less adverse to paying them.

Table 8-8. Italy, Behavior of Inflation at Growth Cycle Turns.

Date of Growth Cycle[a]		Rate of Change in Consumer Price Index[b]			
		Date of Turn and Lead (−) or Lag (+), in Months		Percentage Rate at Inflation	
Peak	Trough	Peak	Trough	Peak	Trough
(1)		(2)		(3)	
10/56		7/54 (−27)		5.8	
	7/59		4/59 (−3)		−2.5
9/63		2/63 (−7)		9.4	
	3/65		9/68 (+42)		0.5
8/69		n.m.[c]		—	
	9/72		n.m.		—
4/74		9/74 (+5)		26.0	
	5/75		10/75 (+5)		10.4
12/76		12/76 (0)		22.2	
	10/77		4/78 (+6)		11.3
2/80		2/80 (0)		22.3	
Average Timing at:					
P		−6 mos.		+17.1%	
T			+12 mos.		+4.9%
P + T		+2 mos.		+11.7%	

Notes:
a. Based on the consensus of turning points in trend-adjusted data for selected measures of aggregate output, income, sales, and employment.
b. Change over six months, smoothed (not centered). Centering the rates would increase the leads by three months and reduce the lags by three months.
c. n.m. = No matching turn.

Costs of production tend to creep up, labor turnover increases, control over efficiency and waste tends to decline. New commitments for investment are made in an optimistic environment, building up the demand for limited supplies of skilled labor and construction equipment. Credit to increase inventories is more readily available and is also in greater demand, even if higher interest rates must be paid for it, thus raising costs. Labor unions see better opportunities to obtain favorable contract settlements, and their members are more willing to strike to get them. These conditions apply to more and more firms and industries and produce upward pressure on more and more prices. Indeed, one of the principal factors underlying a rising rate of inflation in the general price level is not just that some prices rise in big jumps but that more prices rise at more frequent intervals.

During periods of slow growth or actual decline in aggregate economic activity, the opposite conditions prevail. Firms and industries cut back their output, reduce or eliminate overtime, shave costs, give

Table 8-9.   France, Behavior of Inflation at Growth Cycle Turns.

		Rate of Change in Consumer Price Index[b]			
Date of Growth Cycle[a]		Date of Turn and Lead (−) or Lag (+), in Months		Percentage Rate at Inflation	
Peak (1)	Trough	Peak (2)	Trough	Peak (3)	Trough
8/57		3/58 (+7)		20.5	
	8/59		6/61 (+22)		0.8
2/64		5/62 (−21)		6.2	
	6/65		n.m.		—
6/66		n.m.[c]		—	
	5/68		7/67 (−10)		2.2
11/69		5/69 (−5)		6.5	
	11/71		1/71 (−10)		4.4
5/74		7/74 (+2)		15.3	
	6/75		1/78 (+33)		8.0
8/79		3/80 (+7)		14.2	

Average Timing at:
P		−5 mos.		+12.5%	
T			+9 mos.		+3.8%
P + T		+2 mos.		+9.0%	

Notes:
a. Based on the consensus of turning points in trend-adjusted data for selected measures of aggregate output, income, sales, and employment.
b. Change over six months, smoothed (not centered). Centering the rates would increase the leads by three months and reduce the lags by three months.
c. n.m. = No matching turn.

bigger discounts off list prices, reduce inventories, repay bank debt, and postpone new investment projects or stretch out existing ones. Quit rates decline and labor demands for pay raises become more conservative. Interest rates drop. As price increases become less widespread and less frequent, and as more price cutting occurs, the rate of inflation declines.

Price pressures are, therefore, part of the overall set of interrelationships that make up the aggregate economic activity under study. The cyclical variation in rates of inflation is clearly part of the process indicators attempt to monitor. As such, the conclusions based on Figure 8-1 are to be expected. But they do not address the efficacy (or futility) of any of the policies pursued in any of the countries under review to moderate inflation. We find inflation rate fluctuations occurring among the seven countries during periods of governmental intervention as well as during periods of governmental inaction; inflation rates fluctuate in countries pursuing monetarist policies, incomes policies, or traditional monetary-fiscal counter-cyclical policies. The cycles appear in countries with a relatively large public sector and in those with relatively small public sectors. They occur when governmental deficits are large relative to GNP and when they are small (or even replaced by a surplus). Under all these diverse circumstances the link between inflation rate reduction and recessions appears to be strong.

Careful analysis of the pattern reflected in movements in leading, roughly coincident, and lagging indicators can find quite as legitimate a place in the study of inflation rates as it does in the study of fluctuations in real aggregate economic activity. The conclusion to be drawn from the evidence in this chapter is mainly that fluctuations in both real and price phenomena are distinctly part of the same process, and we might expect, therefore, that a system of indicators that proves helpful in monitoring fluctuations in real activity can readily be adapted to monitoring fluctuations in inflation rates. Research in this area ought, therefore, to have a high priority.

Chapter 9

TOWARD AN IMPROVED INTERNATIONAL SYSTEM OF BUSINESS CYCLE INDICATORS

Wesley Clair Mitchell published his first major work on business cycles in 1913 and he founded the National Bureau of Economic Research in 1920. For more than fifty years the bureau was the focus of research in the Mitchellian tradition, beginning with the publication of Willard Thorp's *Annals* in 1926 and continuing through a long list of major contributions to the measurement and analysis of economic instability. A significant step toward wide public use of these results was taken in 1961 when the Department of Commerce began publishing monthly a collection of the leading, coincident and lagging indicators selected by the National Bureau. The initiation of *Business Conditions Digest* (called *Business Cycle Developments* for the first seven years of its life) represented official recognition that whatever other techniques may be used in analyzing instability, the notion of reliable leading, coincident, and lagging indicators had been widely accepted as a diagnostic tool.

The initiation of the International Economic Indicators (IEI) project at the National Bureau in 1973 by Moore and Klein was in one sense an explicit extension of the Mitchellian indicator approach to the international economic scene and in another sense a return to the international perspective with which Mitchell began. The IEI project rested on two basic questions:

1. Is the notion of a growth cycle a useful approach to the study of cyclical instability in a number of market-oriented economies?

That is, can growth cycle chronologies be established for them in a comparable manner?

2. Can rough equivalents for the U.S. leading and lagging indicators of classical cycles be found for other countries, and, if so, do they exhibit comparable tendencies to lead or lag at growth cycle turning points in those countries?

The overriding conclusion of the present study is that both of these questions can be answered in the affirmative. We began by adapting the National Bureau's computer program, which had been designed to date classical cycle turning points, to date the growth cycle turning points. Briefly, this adaptation involved taking deviations from a flexible (yet smooth) long-term trend in order to isolate short-run movements in the data. A list of computer-selected cyclical turning points in the principal measures of aggregate economic activity was then derived for each of the countries under study. After reviewing and occasionally modifying the results, we devised a growth cycle chronology for each country based on the consensus among these turning points. Just as the selection of business cycle reference dates has always been a crucial analytical step in the work on classical cycles, so, too, is the selection of appropriate growth cycle chronologies in growth cycle analysis.

One major decision we made in our work with indicators was to recognize explicitly the impact of generally higher inflation rates. Accordingly, all indicators that are measured in terms of value are deflated by a price index. This was not a common practice among business cycle analysts prior to the 1970s. Today we know of no growth cycle studies that do not work with series expressed in constant prices or in physical units so as to separate real from price phenomena.

We have thus far produced growth cycle chronologies for more than a dozen countries in the research program that is now conducted at the Center for International Business Cycle Research at Columbia University. In this book we have concentrated attention on the ten major industrialized market-oriented economies.[1] Some of the more interesting implications should now be summarized. In the United States, from 1948 to 1980, there have been ten growth cycles. Seven of them correspond to the seven classical cycles dated by the NBER (although the precise dates of peaks and troughs differ, as would be expected in series in which turning points are selected from trend-adjusted data). One of the additional three growth cycle episodes occurs at the time of the Korean War, and two in the 1960s. While the data are not adequate for a comparable period in all the other countries studied, it would appear that the United States has continued to manifest a greater number of cyclical episodes (with correspondingly shorter duration) than most other countries.

Ten Canadian growth cycles can also be discerned in the period 1949-80; six U.K. growth cycles, 1950-75; six West German growth cycles, 1950-75; six Japanese growth cycles, 1953-80; four Belgian growth cycles, 1955-80; five French growth cycles, 1955-80; and five Italian growth cycles, 1955-81. The appearance of a classical cycle in all seven of these countries in 1973-75 and again in 1980-82 argues strongly for the continued monitoring of both classical and growth cycles despite the greater complexity that such a course will initially engender in research activities. Clearly, constructing growth cycle chronologies for countries other than the United States by adapting the Mitchell technique to growth cycle research can be regarded as eminently feasible.

An independent check on the usefulness of the growth cycle turning points can be performed by associating them with the leading and lagging indicators classified by their typical behavior at classical turning points in the United States. Admittedly, utilizing the short list of classical cycle indicators established for the U.S. in 1966 was an expedient, but it has proved to be an efficient way to test the feasibility of developing leading and lagging indicators of growth cycle turning points, in the United States as well as elsewhere.

Our findings with respect to these indicators may be summarized very simply. When the twenty-four U.S. indicators were recast in growth cycle terms they all retained their original timing classification. The leading indicators were as successful in anticipating growth cycles (including the three growth cycles that had no classical cycle counterpart) as they had been in anticipating classical cycles. There were occasional instances of both skipped and extra cycles, but certainly no more than has been the case in using these series as indicators of classical cycles.

With few exceptions the classification of indicators taken over from U.S. classical cycles is as valid for foreign growth cycles as it is for U.S. growth cycles. While some individual indicators are inappropriately related to individual growth turns (as has always been the case at classical cycle turns in the United States as well), in general, the exceptions are only slightly more frequent at foreign growth turns than they are at U.S. growth turns, and both are acceptably consistent with the U.S. classical cycle record. It is fair to add, however, that instances when the indicator system fails to produce the expected temporal pattern are more numerous for the smaller foreign countries included in the study (e.g., Belgium, the Netherlands, and Sweden). Whether this suggests that the indicator system is basically less appropriate for smaller economies, or for economies more dependent on foreign trade, is difficult to say. Certainly, much remains to be done to improve the reliability of the indicator systems in all countries. While the overall performance rate of the indicator system in foreign economies is remarkably high, the areas where indicators have not performed well constitute a major item for future research. In addition, the lack of comparable data for particular indicators is especially pronounced as soon as one moves beyond the five or six largest and most industrialized economies. By demonstrating that indicator systems are useful diagnostic additions to other techniques of forecasting and cyclical analysis, we hope to spur the improvement and availability of data in all economies where business cycles continue to manifest themselves.

One searches with scant success for evidence that particular indicators are consistently less reliable in one country than another. The exceptions to expected patterns appear to be distributed more or less randomly among indicators and across countries. The major exceptions among the leading indicators are as follows. In Italy, the typical timing for the average workweek is a lag. Building permits lag in West Germany and do not match growth cycles in Sweden. In the United Kingdom and the Netherlands industrial materials prices lag, and in Sweden the change in consumer credit lags. Among the roughly coincident indicators, the poorest performer is retail sales, which leads by more than three months in Japan, Italy, and Belgium, but lags by more than three months in West Germany and Sweden. Employment exhibits a clear-cut tendency to lag in France and to a lesser extent in Italy, Sweden, and the United Kingdom. In sum, the behavior of the six roughly coincident indicators is strongly supportive overall of their U.S. classification. Among the lagging indicators, business loans exhibit a median lead in West Germany, while short-term interest rates show a short lead in the Netherlands.

This completes the list of indicators diverging from the expected pattern. The average timing for each indicator, for all countries taken together, shows the expected median timing, except in the case of employment, which shows a two-month lag. In no case is the number of countries in which an indicator fails to produce the expected average timing greater than three. Six of the twelve leaders, four of six roughly coincident indicators, and three of the six laggers show no countries diverging from the timing classification of these indicators at U.S. classical cycles.

In short, one can locate examples of anomalous behavior, but such behavior is no more prevalent among foreign countries than it has typically been in the United States at classical cycle turns. Moreover, these anomalies in indicator behavior appear to be randomly scattered. It is, of course, important to continue monitoring the record of growth cycle indicators both here and abroad, as indeed we have done for many years with indicators of classical turning points in the United States. We fully anticipate that the lists of indicators will be revised from time to time and that there will continue to be additions to and deletions from the list of "most reliable indicators." But there is no reason now to suppose that the basic classification of indicators is any less permanent or more ephemeral for foreign countries. In the United States structural changes and data improvements have accounted for substitutions in the list of indicators of classical turns far more often than changes in classification (which have, in fact, been extremely rare historically). Moreover, a major question that will need to be resolved in the future concerns the conflict between the virtues of maintaining a common list for all countries and the usefulness of obtaining the most sensitive and reliable list for forecasting in each country.

One of the more encouraging signs for the future analysis of international economic indicators has been the general acceptance among OECD countries of the feasibility of developing growth-cycle chronologies and indicator systems. The OECD has agreed to measure growth cycles in terms of "output—broadly defined" and to construct corresponding lists of indicators classified by timing. This effort has resulted in a good many national chronologies covering the postwar years. Indeed, the Secretariat has even attempted chronologies for those few OECD countries that have not produced a chronology of their own, with the result that—as we have already noted—growth cycle chronologies have proliferated in recent years.

The indicator system that we have developed is based primarily on "quantitative indicators." While "qualitative indicators" based on opinion surveys are not unknown in the United States, reliance has never been placed heavily on them because of the wealth of quantitative statistics. Nevertheless, qualitative measures often have considerable utility because of the greater promptness with which they become available and the greater smoothness survey net balances often exhibit in comparison to the equivalent quantitative series. One of our concerns in this book has centered on the usefulness of these qualitative indicators in cyclical analysis. We find that when the survey net balances are appropriately treated, the actual lead at turns is not as long, in many cases, as is the case with the comparable quantitative series. Augmenting the forecasting potential of quantitative indicators is not the only—or perhaps even the primary—function of qualitative indicators. In many situations one is interested in entrepreneurial attitudes in and of themselves. This is surely a major purpose behind the harmonized surveys carried out by the European Economic Commission. We have concluded that while qualitative indicators can sometimes provide valuable evidence with which to diagnose cyclical developments, their advantages lie primarily in terms of the up-to-date information they contain.

In addition to constructing growth cycle chronologies and indicator systems, we have considered several possible extensions, and new applications of these indicators, for example, in the development of the concept of a world cycle. We found that from a composite index of all the roughly coincident indicators for all the countries under review we could identify a chronology of peaks and troughs that represented generally consilient cycles in all the countries. We also found that a composite of the leading indicators for all countries anticipated the turns in this world growth cycle chronology. Furthermore, the data suggest that no country can be termed a consistent initiator of world upswings or downswings.

If it is difficult to conclude that the sequence of cyclical changes runs invariably from any one or two countries to the other countries, it is still pertinent to inquire whether overall changes in international economic instability can be forecast by individual countries so as to predict changes in their imports or exports. We have tested this notion and conclude that cyclically sensitive trade flows can be forecast with the help of leading indicators. One test was based on U.S. trade with six other countries. We showed that exports are conditioned primarily by the stage of the growth cycle in the importing country or countries, with the result that any exporting nation can forecast its exports to any other country or group of countries for which a leading index is available.

We considered the implications of this finding not only for U.S. exports but for imports as well. And we examined the possibilities of forecasting total manufacturing exports by the United States to the other countries and summarized the results for a number of individual commodities as well. Because the countries we examined comprised nearly half of total U.S. export demand, the results were moderately encouraging regarding the use of leading indexes to forecast total U.S. exports.

We then reversed the process and found that British exports of manufactured goods, as well as those of West Germany, Japan, and all the less-developed countries could be reasonably well forecast with changes in the leading index for the six major countries, which together absorb a large percentage of the world's imports. Increased availability of leading indexes for other countries will likely yield significant dividends in the form of greater accuracy in forecasting trade flows. The method can be adapted to take account of changes in exchange rates and to forecast changes in trade balances.

Finally, we explored very briefly the possibilities of forecasting changes in inflation rates by means of leading indicators. This exercise provided a cogent example of the critical relationships among business cycle theory, measurement, and analysis. Because inflation has become a problem endemic to many market-oriented economies, it was necessary for us to deflate price-denominated indicators so as to separate real from inflation rate fluctuations. But it is nevertheless true that both kinds of fluctuations emerge from the interaction of supply and demand pressures. It is the sequential logic of these interrelationships that forms the rationale for the leading, roughly coincident, and lagging indicators.

This is not to argue in support of the proposition that inflation is a real rather than a monetary phenomenon—it is perhaps more accurate to say that real and monetary phenomena are themselves interrelated and the behavior of the indicators is related to both, even if the effects are best viewed separately. Our examination of the behavior of industrial materials prices (an early indicator of changing inflation rates) and consumer prices (used to measure inflation rates) within the growth cycle chronologies suggested that the view taken here of the relationship between inflation and growth cycle indicators is both reliable and useful. As such, it suggests yet another area in which cycle indicators could contribute to forecasting efforts.

MEASUREMENT AND THEORY: THE APPROPRIATE MIX

Some readers may feel that the evidence we have presented is so convincing, or so close to what they expected, that our findings almost speak for themselves. Nevertheless, to us it has seemed necessary to present all the initial evidence for each of the countries considered. This approach, analyzing each series and each turning point for which evidence can be found, has been the traditional approach taken by Mitchell and his followers.

Other readers may feel that our detailed display of evidence signifies nothing, because it is not placed explicitly in the context of a complete theory or model of the business cycle with all of the international implications spelled out. Without such a theory, some may claim, we do not really know how the system works, how parts fit the whole, or how confident one can be that these relations will persist. This debate was discussed in considerable detail in Chapter 1.

Clearly, there is merit in developing a detailed explanatory system. We take the view, however, that useful results can be achieved without it—useful in the sense that partial results are understandable or explainable and capable of being tested against future data or data for other economies. Moreover, such partial results may have other advantages. They can be reached more quickly and hence provide useful information at an earlier date, and they can be comprehended more readily by a larger group of potential users. The leading indicators we now possess, for example, are easier to understand than some other current approaches to forecasting. The idea that new orders for goods contain useful information about future sales, output, employment, and income is not difficult to comprehend, and not difficult to observe in the data.[2] Consequently, this idea was being used by forecasters for many years before it was incorporated into econometric models. In fact, the development and improvement of new-orders data was one of the recommendations in Burns and Mitchell's original study of 1938.[3]

Although we have not organized our work on indicators around the concept of a large-scale international economic model, this does not mean that partial theories or explanations have not played an important role. Without them one would have little or no confidence that past relationships would persist or be applicable elsewhere. Partial theories have always been a part of Mitchellian business cycle research. For every indicator we have had a hypothesis (or several hypotheses) explaining its behavior. Many reports outlining and testing these hypotheses have been published over the years. Moreover, the tests have frequently been replicated using new data. The successive studies of indicators (Mitchell and Burns in 1938, Moore in 1950 and 1960, Moore and Shiskin in 1967, and Zarnowitz and Boschan in 1975) are such a series of replications. Stanback's work on inventories (1962) replicated that of Abramovitz (1950); Kessel's (1965) and Cagan's (1966) work on interest rates replicated that of Macaulay (1938); Klein's work on consumer credit (1971) replicated that of Haberler (1942); and Hultgren's work on costs and profits (1965) replicated that of Mitchell (1913).[4] Of course, each author added some new hypothesis or revised or expanded an old one, and all had more data against which to test their hypotheses.

CLASSICAL CYCLES AND GROWTH CYCLES

If the publication of *Business Conditions Digest* can be viewed as the official demise of the debate over the appropriateness and usefulness of the NBER technique in studying classical business cycles, it was ironically followed by another debate—premature, as it turned out— concerning the possible obsolescence of the classical business cycle. Some have argued, of course, that growth cycles merely represent a newer form of the classical cycles measured for the United States, Britain, France, and Germany. It is worth remembering, though, how rapidly one's perspective can change, and how dangerous it is to allow a fundamental perspective to be altered by short-lived events. In the 1960s and early '70s, prior to the severe recession of 1973-75, there was not only little real concern about business cycles in foreign countries (let alone the possibility of world cycles), but not much concern with cycles in the United States either. One of those who was concerned was Ilse Mintz, who saw the potential value of a new attempt to measure growth cycles,[5] and she reported her work on this very topic at the Fiftieth Anniversary colloquium held at the National Bureau in 1970. In this connection Paul Samuelson commented:

> Now that the National Bureau is fifty years old, it has worked itself out of one of its first jobs, namely the business cycle. I don't know when the American Cancer Society was founded, but by similar reasoning fifty years after that date some optimist could hope to cross cancer off his list. The Bureau was thus in danger of becoming just a museum of fossils; but nobody likes to work himself out of a job, so you naturally redefined the field to study. I predicted some time ago that this would happen, and Ilse Mintz . . . has confirmed my prediction.[6]

No doubt Samuelson would agree that this view, expressed in 1970, was premature, and that the appearance four years later and again eight years after that of relatively severe, classical recessions might justify continued attention to business cycle research. Today the preoccupation of the National Bureau of Economic Research with both classical cycle and the growth cycle analysis is continued at the Center for International Business Cycle Research at Columbia University.

Erik Lundberg has written:

> History never repeats itself in exactly the same way. There are such important differences between the catastrophic United States depression of 1929-33 and the mild recessions of 1926-27 and 1960-61 that from some points of view they can well be classified in different categories. But if we assume there is empirical evidence to make it sensible to talk about the United States experience with cyclical instability over the period 1919-64 as a tolerably homogeneous set of phenomena, what about, for instance, British, Dutch, or Swedish economic developments during the

same period? Or similar experiences in Japan, Australia, or South American countries? Do we have empirical evidence permitting us to classify the instability experiences of these countries in the same category?[7]

Consideration of the issues raised in this passage by Lundberg is radically different if approached from the context of our work on growth cycle measurement. To begin with, the important differences in various U.S. cycles referred to earlier are now seen as related cyclical episodes even though of varying severity. The reliability of traditional indicators in relation to growth cycles suggests that *all* cycles, whether classical or growth, have much in common. Cycles may then be viewed as occupying a continuum from most to least severe, and that as classical cycles become less pronounced it becomes increasingly necessary to measure them as growth cycles. Their commonality is certainly underscored by the consistency with which indicators of one type of cycle can be fruitfully applied to the analysis of the other.

Concerning the question of whether the "tolerably homogeneous set of phenomena" of U.S. economic experience is or is not the same as that found in foreign countries, we can clearly advance an answer if we utilize the evidence developed in the preceding chapters. The fact that the same methodology can be adapted with considerable success to dating growth cycles in foreign countries and that rough equivalents of U.S. classical cycle indicators bear reasonably consistent temporal relationships to growth cycle turning points both in the United States and in each of the other countries thus far tested is just the sort of evidence that Lundberg called for. Indirectly, too, an answer is suggested by the fact that the methodology is being used by international organizations such as the OECD and EEC as well as by statistical agencies, central banks, and research institutes in different countries on every continent.

Far from becoming fossils, therefore, cycles are simply being viewed as phenomena sufficiently alike to justify isolation for purposes of analysis, but subject nonetheless to an endless series of changes and variations as they appear sequentially through the economic history of each of the economies in which they appear. Moreover, the term "fossil" connotes antiquated persons or things. If antiquated means dead as well as old then it cannot possibly apply to the growth cycle manifestation of the historic instability of market-oriented economies. Cycles are old, but unhappily even classical cycles are far from dead.

AGENDA FOR THE FUTURE

We believe the work reported in this volume can open many doors for those who wish to gain an understanding of economic instability and inflation in the modern world. The potential for further analysis and ongoing research has been increased considerably by the introduction of the growth cycle concept, by the development of a widely applicable methodology for constructing growth cycle chronologies, and by the identification of reasonably consistent leading and lagging indicators of these growth cycle turning points in the major industrialized economies dealt with in this book.

The computer programs developed originally at the National Bureau and later revised at the Center for International Business Cycle Research are available to all who request them. By exporting the methodology we hope to facilitate both the research process and its practical application throughout the industrialized world. Continued research is needed on such questions as how instability is transmitted from one country to another, whether it can be said to find its genesis more often in one country or countries than in others, how and why countries find that their economic fortunes are tied more surely or with greater impact to certain other countries, how these matters affect trade, financial markets, and prices, and how they are affected by economic policies.

A further possible extension of this work—only touched on in our earlier discussion—is to apply the analysis to the exports of developing countries, insofar as their exports flow to the industrialized countries for which we have leading indicators. The countries we have already covered import a substantial share of products from developing nations, and demand for such imports fluctuates with the rise and fall of growth cycles. The leading indicators for the countries analyzed above, to say nothing of those we hope will ultimately be constructed, could be of considerable value to the developing nations in appraising their markets.

There is scarcely an organization engaged in economic research today that is not deeply involved in studying the causes and consequences of inflation. At the Columbia Center, for example, the application of the leading indicator approach to forecasting inflation is being actively extended and has already attracted wide interest. Since there appears to be a clear sequence of changes involving the financial, commodity, and labor markets that are ultimately reflected in the rate of inflation in consumer prices, this sequence has enabled us to construct a leading index of inflation for the United States and to explore its capacity to forecast inflation.[8] In addition, we have studied the possible extension of this method to other countries.[9] We believe that continued work on inflation indicators can, in short, play a role in the worldwide effort to understand the inflation process better and thus control it more effectively.

Another area at the frontier of indicator analysis concerns its application to forecasting employment conditions. At the Columbia Center a new U.S. index has been constructed based on those leading indicators directly pertinent to employment or unemployment (the average workweek in manufacturing, overtime hours in manufacturing, initial claims for unemployment insurance, short-duration unemployment, and a measure of changes in part-time employment due to slack demand for employees). The index appears to yield useful forecasts of changes in unemployment and might well be developed for other countries.

The sequential relationships among groups of indicators is also leading to the development of objective "signals" of forthcoming changes, based upon the composite leading and coincident indexes. These indexes each contain what is called a "target trend," which is the long-run trend in the economy since 1948. The target trend adjustment standardizes the trends so that both indexes have a trend equal to the long-run rate for the economy. Differences among the indexes observable at any particular time must be due to short-run factors. When, therefore, the six-month smoothed rate of change in any given index is less than the target trend rate, it is rising at a rate below its long-run rate of growth, and presages a growth recession. The signals that have been developed so far involve sequential changes in both leading and coincident indexes and provide early warnings and subsequent confirmation. These relationships obviously are derived from typical behavior of the indexes during a number of previous recessions. Though originally devised to improve the efficacy of countercyclical public-works programs, the possibilities in this approach are broad.[10]

In the United States the effort to bring the experience of past growth recessions and recoveries to bear in forecasting future developments has resulted in a periodic report of the Columbia Center called "Recession-Recovery Watch." The publication tracks monthly changes in the composite indexes, as well as in many individual indicators, against their average behavior in previous business cycles over comparable intervals after the last peak or trough. In this way current developments can be assessed in the light of past experience. While this approach appears promising in improving our ability to monitor ongoing growth cycle developments, it has not yet been explored to any great extent for other economies. The thrust of much that has been reported in these pages suggests that this particular line of inquiry might be a promising path to pursue.

In determining whether and to what degree economic fluctuations in industrial market-oriented countries may have widened in scope and become more nearly synchronized, data on new orders for goods, formation of business enterprises, contracts for industrial and commercial construction, housing starts, inventory investment, price/cost ratios, and other domestically sensitive measures of economic change should be particularly instructive, in part because they have seldom, if ever, been examined from this point of view. At the same time, it would be essential to examine the more internationally sensitive measures, such as industrial materials prices, security prices, interest rates, and foreign trade. Conceivably, the internationally sensitive variables may have become less stable at the same time that the domestically oriented variables have become more stable, as indeed Mintz showed for U.S. exports.[11]

Closely related to this type of analysis would be comparative international studies of particular economic processes such as inventory accumulation; credit, the money supply, and interest rates; orders, production, and investment; consumption and income; and so on. The NBER has studied these processes and others for the United States over many years, but only occasionally on an international scale. With new data and new methods these studies could be extended to other countries. One example is provided by Desmond O'Dea's analysis of the behavior of labor market indicators in postwar Britain.[12] Our preliminary work has already suggested that certain economic variables, such as those pertaining to employment, or the housing market, or to foreign trade, may not be related to one another in precisely the same way in every country. For example, it is evident that in many countries housing starts are highly sensitive to cyclical fluctuations, and it is generally believed that monetary policy has a large impact upon this industry. But in Japan housing starts are relatively stable, though still performing as a leading indicator. What is the source of this immunity and what implications does it have for economic policy? In Sweden we saw that the turns in housing starts could not even be related to the growth cycle chronology. The explanation there lay in the highly regulated nature of the housing industry. Whatever the explanations for anomalous behavior may be, the indicator data we have assembled, supplemented by related data, ought to facilitate a number of comparative studies of this type.

One of the products of the IEI project is a methodology for measuring long-run trends. The method is flexible enough to reveal changing long-term rates of growth quite promptly, yet is little affected by the short-run cyclical movements that have been our primary concern. Trend rates of growth are derived for every indicator, and can be brought up to date every few years without extensive revision of results for earlier years. A method of extrapolation to future years has been built into the program, although we have not tested it extensively. If business cycles—whether classical or growth cycles— are part of a long-run process best regarded as growth at irregular rates, it follows that the study of what determines underlying growth rates ought to contribute to the understanding of economic instability and vice versa. In this connection, therefore, the trend measures that we derived as part of our study of growth cycles for every series ought to open up a wealth of material that could be the focus in studies of economic growth, of productivity and costs, of capital investment, of market shares and competitiveness, and of inflationary trends.

In order to make the indicator data promptly and widely available on a current basis, in original as well as trend-adjusted form, together with trend rates of growth, composite indexes, and other analytical measures described and illustrated earlier, an international data bank is essential. Major steps in this direction have already been taken. It is technically feasible for such a data bank to be supplied daily with new data from a network of computers in the countries producing the data and at the same time to make the analytical products of the data bank accessible through computer terminals to users of the data. This is, in fact, the way in which several data banks operate, including what was formerly the National Bureau's data bank of U.S. economic time series. In this instance the indicators are updated each day, and companies, universities, and government agencies obtain the data either through a time-sharing system or by purchasing magnetic tapes updated monthly.

We have earlier indicated that the computer programs developed in the course of the work reported on in this book have been made available to the OECD, the EEC, to a number of government agencies, as well as to private research organizations. The Columbia Center now issues a monthly report on the standing of the indicators in major countries, and the Conference Board circulates a summary report to its member companies. In this effort we have had the cooperation of the OECD, as well as several government agencies both in the U.S. and in other countries. But much needs to be done to improve the timeliness and accuracy of the data transmitted, as well as to expand its coverage internationally. As a reporting system of this kind develops, not only will the countries involved be encouraged to improve the quality, comparability, and timeliness of their statistics, but the resulting international exchange of data and research findings will greatly enhance our understanding of the causes and consequences of international economic fluctuations.

NOTES TO CHAPTER 9

1. At the Center, in addition to the ten countries considered here, visiting scholars have developed growth cycle chronologies for Switzerland, Australia, South Korea, Taiwan, Malaysia, Israel, Venezuela and South Africa. Several of these are shown in Appendix 2B.

2. Compare Victor Zarnowitz, *Orders, Production and Investment: A Cyclical and Structural Analysis*, Studies in Capital Formation No. 22 (New York: NBER, 1973).

3. The wording of their recommendation is of some interest in the present context:

> Perhaps the most promising thing that might be done along these lines is to start with the hypothesis that the new orders placed today will be the output of tomorrow, and that a forecasting index might therefore be made by combining reports on orders in many lines of business, including contracts for construction. In analyzing time series we have found the rough rule to hold, that orders for commodities and construction contracts make cyclical upturns and downturns before corresponding reference dates for revivals and recessions. . . . But it should be noticed that a good index of orders is likely to prove a better forecaster of business cycle recessions than of business cycle revivals (*Statistical Indicators of Cyclical Revivals* [NBER, 1938], pp. 11–12).

The index Burns and Mitchell suggested was compiled by Zarnowitz in 1973 (*Orders, Production and Investment*, p. 629–32) and has been one of the twelve leading indicators in the Commerce Department's list since 1975. The "rough rule" has held consistently at business cycle peaks and troughs ever since 1948, and the leads at peaks have, as anticipated, been consistently longer than at troughs. The "hypothesis" has proved useful, despite its apparent simplicity.

4. Moses Abramowitz, *Inventories and Business Cycles, with Special Reference to Manufacturers* (New York: NBER, 1950); Phillip Cagan, "Changes in the Cyclical Behavior of Interest Rates," *Review of Economics and Statistics* (August 1966), Reprinted as Occasional Paper 100, New York, NBER; Gottfried Haberler, *Consumer Installment Credit and Economic Fluctuations* (New York: NBER, 1942); Thor Hultgren, *Cost, Prices, and Profits; Their Cyclical Relations*, NBER Studies in Business Cycles 14, 1965; Reuben A. Kessel, "The Cyclical Behavior of the Term Structure of Interest Rates," NBER Occasional Paper 91, 1965; Philip A. Klein, *The Cyclical Timing of Consumer Credit, 1920–67* (New York: NBER, 1971); Frederick R. Macaulay, "Some Theoretical Problems Suggested by the Movements of Interest Rates, Bond Yields, and Stock Prices in the United States Since 1856" (New York: NBER, 1938); Wesley C. Mitchell, *Busi-*

ness Cycles (Berkeley: University of California Press, 1913); Wesley C. Mitchell and Arthur F. Burns, *Statistical Indicators of Cyclical Revivals*, Bulletin 69 (New York: NBER, May 28, 1938); Geoffrey H. Moore, "Statistical Indicators of Cyclical Revivals and Recessions," NBER Occasional Paper 31, 1950. Reprinted in *Studies in Business Cycles* 10. Also reprinted in *Business Cycle Indicators*, vol. 1, G.H. Moore, ed. (New York: NBER, 1960); Geoffrey H. Moore, "Leading and Confirming Indicators of General Business Changes," in *Business Cycle Indicators*, vol. 1, G.H. Moore, ed. Princeton University Press for National Bureau of Economic Research, 1961; Geoffrey H. Moore and Julius Shiskin, *Indicators of Business Expansions and Contractions*, NBER Occasional Paper 103, 1967; Thomas M. Stanback, *Postwar Cycles in Manufacturers' Inventories* (New York: NBER, 1962); Victor Zarnowitz and Charlotte Boschan, "Cyclical Indicators: An Evaluation and New Leading Indexes." U.S. Department of Commerce, *Business Conditions Digest* (May 1, 1975). Reprinted in *Handbook of Cyclical Indicators* (BCD, 1977): 170–184; Victor Zarnowitz and Charlotte Boschan, "New Composite Indexes of Coincident and Lagging Indicators" (BCD, November 1975). Reprinted in *Handbook of Cyclical Indicators* (BCD, 1977): 185–199.

5. Another early National Bureau effort in the direction later taken by growth cycle research is Ruth P. Mack's work on "sub-cycles." See, for example, *Consumption and Business Fluctuations, A Case Study of the Shoe, Leather, Hide Sequence* (New York: NBER, 1956).

6. Paul Samuelson, Discussion in Victor Zarnowitz, ed., *The Business Cycle Today*, Fiftieth Anniversary colloquium, I (New York: NBER, 1972), p. 167.

7. Erik Lundberg, *Instability and Economic Growth* (New Haven: Yale University Press, 1968), p. 7.

8. Geoffrey H. Moore and Stanley Kaish, "A New Inflation Barometer," *The Morgan Guaranty Survey* (New York: Morgan Guaranty Trust Company, July 1983, pp. 7-10, and December 1983, pp. 7-10) for the development of the U.S. inflation indicator.

9. A report by Philip A. Klein, prepared for the London Conference of the International Conference of Forecasters in July 1984, extended the Moore-Kaish approach to most of the other major countries covered in this book.

10. See Victor Zarnowitz and Geoffrey H. Moore, "Sequential Signals of Recession and Recovery," *Journal of Business* (January 1982). Reprinted in Geoffrey H. Moore, *Business Cycles, Inflation, and Forecasting*, Ballinger, 1983, Chapter 4.

11. Ilse Mintz, *Cyclical Fluctuations in the Exports of the United States since 1879* (New York: NBER, 1967).

12. Desmond J. O'Dea, "The Cyclical Timing of Labor Market Indicators in Great Britain and the United States," *Explorations in Economic Research* (Winter 1975).

BIBLIOGRAPHY

Note: This bibliography is divided into general references and analytical references by country. It is by no means comprehensive but includes the major general works plus the country studies most germane to our work.

GENERAL STUDIES

Adelman, Irma and Frank L. Adelman. "The Dynamic Properties of the Klein-Goldberger Model." *Econometrica* 27 (October 1959).

Agmon, Tamir. "The Relations Among Equity Markets: A Study of Share Price Co-movements in the United States, United Kingdom, Germany and Japan." *Journal of Finance* (September 1972).

Auerbach, Alan J. "The Index of Leading Indicators: 'Measurement Without Theory' Thirty-five Years Later." *Review of Economics and Statistics* 64 (November 1982): 589–595.

Bronfenbrenner, Martin, ed. *Is the Business Cycle Obsolete?* New York: Wiley Interscience, 1969.

Bry, Gerhard and Charlotte Boschan. *Cyclical Analysis of Time Series: Selected Procedures and Computer Programs.* NBER, Technical Paper 20, 1971.

Burns, Arthur F. *The Business Cycle in a Changing World.* NBER, 1969.

Burns, Arthur F. and Wesley C. Mitchell. *Measuring Business Cycles.* New York: NBER, 1946.

Cagan, Phillip. "The Influence of Interest Rates on the Duration of Businss Cycles." In Jack M. Guttentag and Phillip Cagan, eds., *Essays on Interest Rates*, vol. 1. NBER, 1969.

Chow, Gregory and Geoffrey H. Moore. "An Econometric Model of Business Cycles." *Econometric Models of Cyclical Behavior*, Bert G. Hickman, ed., NBER, Studies in Income and Wealth. 36 (1972).

Conference Board. *International Economic Scoreboard*, New York, monthly.

Gilbert, Milton. "The Post War Business Cycle in Western Europe." *American Economic Review* (May 1962).

Gordon, R. A. and L. R. Klein. *Readings in Business Cycles.* American Economic Association (Richard D. Irwin, Inc., Homewood, Illinois), 1965.

Haberler, Gottfried. *Prosperity and Depression.* New York: League of Nations, 1937.

Granzer, R. "Comparative Evaluation of Business Surveys in OECD Countries." London: 11th CIRET Conference, September 1973. (Mimeo.)

_____ . "Cyclical Indicators for Manufacturing Industries." *OECD Economic Outlook* (December 1973).

Klein, P. A. "Analyzing Growth Cycles and Leading Indicators in Pacific Basin Countries." *Columbia Journal of World Business* (Fall 1983): 3-15.

_____ . *Business Cycles in the Postwar World: Some Reflections on Recent Research.* Washington, D.C.: American Enterprise Institute, Domestic Affairs Study 42, 1976.

_____ . "The Neglected Institutionalism of Wesley Clair Mitchell." *Journal of Economic Issues* (December 1983): 867-899.

_____ . "Recent Work on International Economic Indicators: Problems and Prospects." *Industri-konjunkturen.* Swedish Federation of Industries, 1976, pp. 115-128.

Klein, P. A. and G. H. Moore. "The Leading Indicator Approach to Economic Forecasting—Retrospect and Prospect." *Journal of Forecasting* 2 (April–June 1983): 119-135.

_____ . "Monitoring Profits During Business Cycles." In H. Laumer and M. Ziegler, eds., *International Research on Business Cycle Surveys.* Hampshire, England: Gower, 1982.

_____ . "Industrial Surveys in the U.K.: Part I New Orders." *Applied Economics* 13, no. 2, June 1981, pp. 167-180.

_____ . "Industrial Surveys in the U.K.: Part II Stocks, Profits, and Business Confidence Over the Business Cycle." *Applied Economics* 13, no. 4 (December 1981): 465-480.

Koopmans, Tjalling. "Measurement Without Theory." *Review of Economic Statistics* (August 1947).

Laffer, Arthur B. "International Business Cycles 1954-65." Stanford Business School. (Mimeo.)

_____ . "The Phenomenon of Worldwide Inflation: A Study in International Market Integration," (mimeo), University of Chicago, June 1974.

Licari, Joseph A. and Mark Gilbert. "Is There a Postwar Growth Cycle?" *Kyklos* 27, no. 3 (1974).

Löwenthal, P. "An Updating of the Indicators Approach to Forecasting Turning Points." London: 11th CIRET Conference, September 1973.

Lundberg, Erik. *Instability and Economic Growth.* New Haven, Conn.: Yale University Press, 1968.

Maddison, Angus. "The Postwar Business Cycle in Western Europe." *Banca Nationale del Lavoro Quarterly Review*, June 1960.

Mark, Jerome A. "International Employment Indicators." U.S. Bureau of Labor Statistics, 1972. (Mimeo.)

McCulloch, J. Huston. "The Monte Carlo Cycle in Business Activity." *Economic Inquiry* 13 (September 1975).

Michaely, Michael. *Balance-of-Payments Adjustment Policies: Japan, Germany and the Netherlands.* NBER, Occasional Paper 106, 1968.

Mintz, Ilse. *Cyclical Fluctuations in the Exports of the United States since 1879.* NBER, Studies in Business Cycles 15, 1967.

_____ . *Dating Postwar Business Cycles: Methods and Their Application to Western Germany, 1950–67.* NBER, Occasional Paper 107, 1970.

_____ . *Trade Balances during Business Cycles: U.S. and Britain since 1880.* NBER, Occasional Paper 67, 1959.

Mitchell, Wesley Clair. *Business Cycles and Their Causes.* Berkeley: University of California Press, 1913 (reprinted 1959).

_____ . *Business Cycles: The Problem and Its Setting.* NBER, 1927.

Moore, Geoffrey H. *Business Cycles, Inflation and Forecasting*, 2nd ed. Cambridge, Mass.: Ballinger, 1983.

_____ . *Business Cycle Indicators.* NBER, 1961.

_____ . "Forecasting Foreign Trade with Leading Indicators." In Werner H. Strigel, ed., *Problems and Instruments of Business Cycle Analysis.* Berlin: Springer-Verlag, 1978.

Moore, Geoffrey H. and P.A. Klein. "Further Applications of Leading Indicators to Forecasting Foreign Trade Flows and Balances." In Werner H. Strigel, ed., *Business Cycle Analysis.* Westmead, England: Gower, 1980.

Moore, Geoffrey H. and Melita H. Moore. *International Economic Indicators: A Sourcebook.* Westport, Conn.: Greenwood Press, 1985.

Moore, Geoffrey H. and W.C. Shelton. "International Economic Indicators: A Proposal." *Business Economics* (May 1972).

Moore, Kathleen Harriet. "The Comparative Performance of Economic Indicators for the United States, Canada, and Japan." *Western Economic Journal* (December 1971).

Morgenstern, Oskar. *International Financial Transactions and Business Cycles* (NBER, 1969).

Okun, Arthur M. "On the Appraisal of Cyclical Turning Point Predictors." *Journal of Business.* The University of Chicago, 33, no. 2 (April 1960).

Strigel, Werner H. *Trade Cycle Indicators Derived from Qualitative Indicators.* Munich: CIRET Study No. 19, 1972.

Thorp, Willard. *Business Annals.* NBER, 1926.

Vining, Rutledge. "Koopmans on the Choice of Variables to be Studied and of Methods of Measurement." *Review of Economics and Statistics* 31 (May 1949).

COUNTRY STUDIES

Argentina

Mey, Luis, B. La Preparacion de Indicadores Economicos para Argentina. *Revista de la Universidad Argentina de la Empresa.* Buenos Aires, February 1964.

Australia

Beck, M.T., M.G. Bush, and R.W. Hayes. "The Indicator Approach to the Identification of Business Cycles." Sydney: Reserve Bank of Australia, Occasional Paper 2 (2nd ed.), June 1973.

Boehm, Ernst A. and Geoffrey H. Moore. "New Economic Indicators for Australia, 1949-1984." Parkville, Victoria: University of Melbourne, Department of Economics, Research Paper No. 116, August 1984.

Bush, M.G. and A.M. Cohen. "The Indicator Approach to the Identification of Business Cycles." Sydney: Reserve Bank of Australia, 1968.

Hill, Judith. "Indicator Analysis." *Economic Monograph No. 257.* Economic Society of Australia and New Zealand, Victorian Branch, 1963.

Mallyon, J.S. "Statistical Indicators of the Australian Trade Cycle." *Australian Economic Papers* (June 1966).

Waterman, A.M.C. "The Timing of Economic Fluctuations in Australia: January 1948 to December 1964." *Australian Economic Papers* (June 1967).

Austria

Tichy, Gunther. "Indikatoren der Österreichischen Konjunktur 1950 bis 1970." Österreichisches Institut fur Wirtschaftsforschung, No. 4, 1972.

Belgium

Kredietbank. "A Synthetic Cyclical Indicator for the Belgian Economy." Weekly Bulletin No. 46, December 8, 1972.

"Rajeunissement de la Courbe Synthétique des Principaux Résultats de L'Enquete Mensuelle de la Banque Nationale." *Bulletin de la Banque Nationale de Belgique* 58, Anneé, Tome II, No. 3, September 1983, pp. 3-31.

Canada

Beckett, W.A., Associates Ltd. "Canadian Business Cycle Composite Indicators." *Monthly Business Analysis* (June 1973). (Special report.)

Beckett, W.A. "Indicators of Cyclical Recessions and Revivals in Canada." In G.H. Moore, ed., *Business Cycle Indicators*, vol. I. NBER, 1961.

Brecher, I. and S.S. Reisman. *Canada–United States Economic Relations.* Ottawa: Queen's, 1957.

Bryce, R.B. "The Effects on Canada of Industrial Fluctuations in the United States." *Canadian Journal of Economics and Political Science* (August 1939).

Chambers, E.J. "Late Nineteenth Century Business Cycles in Canada." *Canadian Journal of Economics and Political Science* 30, no. 3 (August 1964).

_____. "Canadian Business Cycles Since 1919." *Canadian Journal of Economics and Political Science* 24, no. 2 (May 1958).

Daly, D.J. "Composite Indexes of Leading Indicators, United States and Canada." York University, May 1973. (Unpublished.)

_____. "The Post-War Persistence of the Business Cycle in Canada." In Martin Bronfenbrenner, ed., *Is the Business Cycle Obsolete?* New York: Wiley Interscience, 1969.

Daly, D. J. and Derek A. White. "Economic Indicators in the 1960s." *Proceedings* of the Business and Economics Statistics Section, American Statistical Association (August 1967).

Hay, K. A. J. "Early Twentieth Century Business Cycles in Canada." *Canadian Journal of Economics and Political Science* 32, no. 3 (August 1966).

Kaish, Stanley. "A Note on Dating Canadian Growth Cycles." *Canadian Journal of Economics* 15, no. 2 (May 1982): 363-68.

Marcus, E. *Canada and the International Business Cycle*. New York: Brokman Associates, 1954.

Poapst, J. V. "The Residential Mortgage Market." Working paper prepared for the Royal Commission on Banking and Finance, November 1962. (Mimeo.)

Rosenbluth, Gideon. "Changes in Canadian Sensitivity to United States Business Fluctuations." *Canadian Journal of Economics and Political Science* (November 1957).

_____. "Changing Structural Factors in Canada's Cyclical Sensitivity." *Canadian Journal of Economic and Political Science* 24, no. 1 (February 1958).

Schwartz, Charles. "The Cyclical Momentum of Economic Activity in Canada, 1953-1973." Working paper, Department of Industry, Trade and Commerce (May 1974).

White, Derek A. *Business Cycles in Canada*. Economic Council of Canada, 1967.

France

Klein, P. A. and G. H. Moore. "Growth Cycles in France." *Revue Economique* 32, no. 3 (May 1981): 468-489.

Italy

Klein, P. A. and G. H. Moore. "Cronologia dei Cicli di Cresita Italiani nel Dopoguerra." *Rassegna della Lettura Sui Cicli Economici*, 1979, 3/4, Istituto Nazionale Per lo Studio della Congiuntura, Rome, pp. 1-30.

Lenti, Libero. "Business Cycles and Price Trends in Italy." Banco di Roma, 28 (May 1973).

Miconi, G. *La méthode du National Bureau of Economic Research a New York et son application au diagnostic sur l'économie italienne*. Rome: Istituto Nazionale per lo Studio della Congiuntura, 1961.

Japan

Baba, M. and I. Sugiura. *Keikihendo no Bunseki to Yosoku* (Measuring Business Cycles and Forecasting), Tokyo, 1961.

Bank of Japan, Statistics Department. "Compilation and Analysis of Indexes of Business Cycles in Japan, 1951-1957."

Fujino, Shozaburo. "Business Cycles in Japan, 1868-1962." *Hitosubashi Journal of Economics* (June 1966).

Shinohara, Miyohei. "Growth and Cycles in the Japanese Economy." *Economic Research Series 5*, Tokyo: The Institute of Economic Research, Hitosubashi University, 1962.

The Netherlands

Post, J.G. "Een Conjunctuurindicator voor de Nederlandse Economie." (A Business Cycle Indicator for the Dutch Economy). Amsterdam National Bank, 1973.

van der Lem, J. T. M. "Conjuncuurindicatoren en conjuncuuronderzoek in Nederland." (Business Cycle Indicators and Business Cycle Research in the Netherlands). *Reply* in October 1973 issue.

New Zealand

Haywood, E. "The Dating of Post-War Business Cycles in New Zealand, 1946-70." Reserve Bank of New Zealand, research paper no. 4, March 1972.

Preston, D. A. "The Three-Year Cycle: An Analysis of Economic Fluctuations in Post-War New Zealand." Master's thesis, University of Wellington, 1964.

Sweden

Klein, P. A. *Growth Cycles in Postwar Sweden.* Stockholm: Swedish Federation of Employers, 1981.

United Kingdom

Drakotos, Constantine. "Leading Indicators for the British Economy." *National Institute Economic Review* (May 1963).

Klein, Philip A. "Postwar Growth Cycles in the United Kingdom: An Interim Report." *Explorations in Economic Research* 3, no. 1 (Winter 1976).

Matthews, R.C.O. "Postwar Business Cycles in the United Kingdom." In Martin Bronfenbrenner, ed., *Is the Business Cycle Obsolete?* New York: Wiley Interscience, 1969.

Mintz, Ilse. *Trade Balances During Business Cycles: U.S. and Britain since 1880.* NBER, Occasional Paper 67, 1959.

O'Dea, Desmond J. *Cyclical Indicators for the Postwar British Economy.* Occasional Paper 28, Cambridge University Press, 1975.

——. "The Cyclical Timing of Labor Market Indicators in Great Britain and the United States." NBER, *Explorations in Economic Research* 2, no. 1 (Winter 1975).

United States

Mintz, Ilse. "Dating United States Growth Cycles." NBER, *Explorations in Economic Research* 1, no. 1 (Summer 1974).

Moore, Geoffrey H. "Economic Indicator Analysis During 1969-1972." In Paul David and Melvin Reder, eds., *Nations and Households in Economic Growth*, 1974.

——. "Forecasting Short-Term Economic Change." *Journal of the American Statistical Association* 64, no. 325 (March 1969).

——. *Business Cycle Indicators.* New York: NBER, 1961.

——. "Price Behavior During Growth Recessions." *Perspectives on Inflation.* The Conference Board of Canada, Canadian Studies No. 36, January 1974.

Moore, Geoffrey H. and Julius Shiskin. *Indicators of Business Expansions and Contractions.* NBER, Occasional Paper 103, 1967.

Moore, Geoffrey H. and Victor Zarnowitz. "Sequential Signals of Recession and Recovery." *Journal of Business.* University of Chicago, January 1982.

Shiskin, Julius. *Signals of Recession and Recovery: An Experiment with Monthly Reporting.* NBER, Occasional Paper 77, 1961.

Zarnowitz, Victor, ed. *The Business Cycle Today.* NBER, 50th Anniversary Colloquim, vol. 1, 1972.

_____ . *Orders, Production, and Investment: A Cyclical and Structural Analysis.* NBER, Studies in Business Cycles No. 22, 1973.

Zarnowitz, Victor and Charlotte Boschan. "Cyclical Indicators: An Evaluation and New Leading Indexes." *Business Conditions Digest* (May 1975).

West Germany

Bry, Gerhard. *Wages in Germany, 1871–1945.* New York: NBER, 1960.

Klein, P. A. "Postwar Growth Cycles in the German Economy." In W. Schröder and R. Spree, eds., *Historische Konjunkturforschung.* Stuttgart: Klett–Cotta, 1980.

Lindbauer, J. D., G. Nerb, and Ch. C. Roberts. *An Indicator System for the West German Economy Employing Tendency Data and Official Statistics.* Munich: IFO Institut, 1971.

Mintz, Ilse. *Dating Postwar Business Cycles: Methods and Their Application to Western Germany, 1950–67.* NBER, Occasional Paper 107, 1970.

Schmidt, Carl T. *German Business Cycles, 1924–1933.* New York: NBER, 1934.

Theiler, Hans. *Nicht-monetare Indikatoren zur Bestimmung von Konjunkturtendenzen* (Dargestellt am Beispiel der BR Deutschland). Zurich, 1971.

INDEX

ABOUT THE AUTHORS

Philip A. Klein has been on the staff of the Department of Economics at The Pennsylvania State University since 1955. He was for many years a member of the Research Staff of the National Bureau of Economic Research and since 1977 has been a Research Associate at the Center for International Business Cycle Research now located at Columbia University. He has been a Consultant to the United Nations, the OECD in Paris, and the Commission of the European Communities in Brussels. He is an Adjunct Scholar at the American Enterprise Institute. He received his B.A. and M.A. from the University of Texas and his Ph.D. from the University of California (Berkeley). He has worked with Geoffrey H. Moore for almost thirty years and has coauthored another book with him previously (*The Quality of Consumer Instalment Credit*) which appeared in 1967. Together they launched the International Economic Indicators Project at the National Bureau in 1973, a project that they subsequently transferred to the Center for International Business Cycle Research. Klein has been associated with the Association for Evolutionary Economics for many years and was President of this organization in 1977. He has written widely for the *Journal of Economic Issues*, and elsewhere in connection with this interest.

Geoffrey H. Moore is Director of the Center for International Business Cycle Research, Graduate School of Business, Columbia University, formerly at Rutgers University, He is Director-at-Large

381

of the National Bureau of Economic Research and was on the staff of the National Bureau from 1939 to 1979. He served as Commissioner of Labor Statistics, U.S. Department of Labor, from 1969 to 1973. In addition, he has taught at New York University and Columbia University, was a Senior Research Fellow at Stanford University's Hoover Institution and an Adjunct Scholar at the American Enterprise Institute, and is the author of *Business Cycles, Inflation and Forecasting* and numerous articles. Dr. Moore received a B.S. and an M.S. from Rutgers University and a Ph.D. from Harvard University.

DATE DUE

DEMCO 38-297